TENNESSEE

Parenting Plans and Child Support Worksheets:

Building a Constructive Future for Your Family

MILES MASON, SR.

MemphisDivorce.com

ISBN: 978-1-59571-984-3

Designed and published by

Word Association Publishers
205 Fifth Avenue
Tarentum, Pennsylvania 15084

www.wordassociation.com
1.800.827.7903

To James C. McWillie and his late wife, Elizabeth.
For everything.

DISCLAIMER

The general information in this book is not, nor is it intended to be, specific legal advice. You should consult an attorney for specific legal advice regarding your individual situation.

This book is provided as a general reference work and is for informational purposes only. You are advised to check for changes to current law and to consult with a qualified attorney on any legal issue. The receipt of or use of this book does not create an attorney-client relationship with the Miles Mason Family Law Group or any of its attorneys.

This book was prepared for a general readership and cannot take into consideration the facts of each particular case, so it is not legal advice. Neither the Miles Mason Family Law Group nor any of its attorneys has an attorney-client relationship with you. The thoughts and commentary about the law in this book are provided merely as a public service and do not constitute solicitation or legal advice.

While we endeavored to provide accurate information in this book, we cannot guarantee that the material provided herein (or linked to herein) is accurate, adequate, or complete. This general legal information is provided on an "as-is" basis. We make no warranties and disclaim liability for damages resulting from its use.

Legal advice must be tailored to the specific circumstances of each case, and laws are constantly changing, so nothing provided in this book should be used as a substitute for the advice of competent counsel. The material in this book may be considered advertising under applicable rules.

CONTENTS

FOREWORD 1

ACKNOWLEDGMENTS 3

SECTION I: Parenting Plans

1. An Action Plan for Parents...7
2. Tennessee's Parenting Plan Law...14
3. What to Tell the Kids 18
4. Coparenting Dos and Don'ts...21
5. Infants and Young Children—Age-Appropriate Plans 25
6. Diffusing Tension in a High-Conflict Divorce 28
7. What to Do with a Child Reluctant to Visit 31
8. Teens and Divorce 33
9. Special-Needs Children 35
10. Advice for the Very Angry Parent 37
11. Tips for the Stepparent 40
12. Using Technology to Stay Organized...42
13. How Equal Parenting Time Can Work Well 45
14. Avoiding Difficult Holidays Parenting Situations 48
15. Counting Parenting Days..52
16. Parenting Plan Provision Checklist...57
17. Tips for Working Out Long-Distance Parenting Plans 72
18. Who Pays Travel Expenses?...76
19. Tennessee Parent Relocation Law 79
20. Anti-Relocation Provisions...82
21. Dependency Deductions...85
22. Grandparent Visitation Rights 87
23. Stepparent Visitation Rights...90
24. Modifying the Primary Residential Parent Designation (Changing Custody) 91
25. Modifying Parenting Time..94
26. College Education Agreements Sample Language 97
27. Section 529 Plans..107

SECTION II: Tennessee Child Support

28. Tennessee Child Support Laws 111
29. Expenses Considered in Child Support Calculations 117
30. Needed Documents 120
31. Gross Income (and Not Income) 124
32. Commissions and Bonuses 126
33. Overtime 128
34. Self-Employed Parent's Income Determination 130
35. Cash Business Owners—What Can Be Done? 133
36. Income Averaging 135
37. Voluntarily Underemployed or Unemployed 137
38. Receiving Credit for Supporting Children Living in a Parent's Home 139
39. Receiving Credit for Supporting Children Not Living in a Parent's Home 141
40. Travel Expenses for Long-Distance Parenting 143
41. Special-Needs Children 145
42. Private School Tuition 146
43. College Tuition and Costs 148
44. Equal Parenting Time 150
45. Caps on Child Support for High-Income Parents 151
46. Ending Child Support 153
47. Modifying Child Support 156
48. Collecting Child Support 160
49. Strategic Advice about Child Support 162

SECTION III: Examples of Permanent Parenting Plans and Child Support Worksheets

INTRODUCTION 167
50. Alpha Family—80 Days per Year Parenting Time 169
51. Bravo Family—118 Days per Year Parenting Time 180
52. Charlie Family—141 Days per Year Parenting Time 189
53. Delta Family—170 Days per Year Parenting Time 202
54. Echo Family—182.5 Days per Year Equal Parenting Time 211
55. Foxtrot Family—182.5 Days per Year Equal Parenting Time 221
56. Golf Family—93 Days per Year Parenting Time: Out-of-Town Schedule 234
57. Hotel Family—113 Days per Year Parenting Time: Out-of-Town Schedule ...247
58. What is "Standard Visitation"? 257
59. Adams Child Support Example 260
60. Brown Child Support Example 264

BIBLIOGRAPHY 269
ABOUT THE AUTHOR 271

FOREWORD

Parenting plans include a lot of detail. They force divorcing parents to do something they naturally don't want to do—share their children. As a family lawyer, I help them navigate their future. Parenting plans I help create matter a great deal more than it may seem at the outset. Without a doubt, parenting plans are very important, but at times, I hate working on them.

After the parenting plan law came into effect, I created a training tool to help my clients with a resource to educate and inspire them. I created a tool parents could look at and use as a guide. For over a dozen years, I have assigned my clients to read much of the material in this book, and after that, we met, talked, planned, strategized, and hand-crafted solutions to their particular family's needs.

Divorcing parents can train. In the same sense a personal trainer helps people work smarter to lose weight and improve fitness, family lawyers help parents improve their lives by avoiding predictable disasters and smoothing out life's rough edges. Whether working with a personal trainer or family lawyer, you can work smarter. In the same amount of time and with less effort, you can get more work done.

In divorce, parents often never consider many important future aspects of parenting. Sure, the parenting plan form addresses many topics, but, for example, it does not discuss the right of first refusal or the prevention of girlfriends and boyfriends spending the night when the children are with that parent. These are only two examples of many provided in chapter 16's Parenting Plan Provision Checklist.

Read this book as you would a menu. Learn what the law says. See what others have done. Read over your options. Take notes. Write down lots of questions for your lawyer. Tell your lawyer what you want, what you fear, and what you want your family's future to be because your lawyer has never lived your life and cannot read your mind.

This book is designed to help put you in control of your parenting plan and the accuracy of your child support worksheets. The more specifically your parenting plan deals with the logistics of your life and those of your children, the less likely you are to return to court.

If you don't have an experienced family lawyer, hire one. Yes, this information is helpful, but it's only a start. Much of family law is counterintuitive. Your family lawyer will help you craft an individualized plan to negotiate the parenting plan you want because there is no "one size fits all" approach. Each negotiation is as unique as the parents and children involved. In every case, the first step is to communicate clearly what you want, and that's what this book will help divorcing parents do.

Mediation is a very important process. Every experienced family lawyer will tell you that many cases have resulted in settlements that both the lawyer and client initially thought were impossible. One never knows when a compromise can be reached regardless of what the other parent may have said about any particular issue. In such cases, trials can be avoided. Experienced and talented mediators can help parents find common ground. Working together, you and your lawyer can build the framework of a constructive parenting plan.

Experienced family lawyers advise what is possible, what is reasonable, and what is best to leave alone. For example, if the other parent refuses to agree to a particular proposed parenting plan provision and the trial judge is very unlikely to award it, maybe that issue should be conceded. On the other hand, if a parenting provision is very important and the other parent refuses to agree to a reasonable compromise, that's perhaps the time a parent should take an issue to court. Experienced family lawyers can help explain where you are and help guide you through the process.

If you are looking for a book to learn how to win a custody case, this ain't it. Contested custody case strategies are discussed in another book, *The Tennessee Divorce Client's Handbook*, available on Amazon and Kindle. There are also strategies for contested custody cases found on my website, MemphisDivorce.com. For updates to this book, Tennessee parenting plans, and child support laws, visit MemphisDivorce.com and its Tennessee Family Law Blog.

ACKNOWLEDGMENTS

To my clients, who have given me their confidence through the years.

To Lynn Massey, for letting me add her chapter on calculating parenting time and more.

To Kitty Bridges and Caren B. Nichol, J.D., for editing and checking my work.

To Martin McHugh, for patience and gentleness when editing this and my previous two books.

To Laura Valade, J.D., James J. Webb, J.D., Patrick Jones, and Taylor L. Fields, J.D.

To law clerks Elisabeth Courson, Carolan Deutch, Brad Reasonover, Jessica Bradley, Ryan J. Spickard, and Abigail M. Mabry for contributions, research, editing, and encouragement. All will make great lawyers.

To Judy and Betty McWillie, my great adopted sisters.

To Frank Mason, Patrick Mason, Alan Crone, Bruce Thompson, and John Snyder for their friendship and loyalty.

To the late Presiding Judge Joe B. Jones and Glenda Jones, my mother-in-law, for having so much grandparenting to make up and making it look effortless.

To Mom and Dad, we all miss you.

To my children, Anne, Miles Jr., and Abigail, my magical inspirations.

Always and forever, to my wife, Sharon.

Section I:

PARENTING PLANS

Chapter 1:

AN ACTION PLAN FOR PARENTS

WHY YOU NEED A PARENTING PLAN

If you have children and are contemplating or going through a divorce, you and your spouse will need to decide with whom the children will live and when the other parent will spend time with the children. In a Tennessee divorce involving children, concerns and complications related to child custody and parenting time take center stage and often create conflict and tension for everyone involved. While it will take some time for a divorce to be finalized, upon separation, parents need to immediately devise a parenting schedule that works for all involved.

Tennessee law requires divorcing parents to create parenting plans for good reason. A good parenting plan can help divorcing parents reduce the potential for disagreements and stress for themselves as well as their children, ultimately making the divorce process a little easier.

WHAT IS A PARENTING PLAN?

A parenting plan is a document that details a parenting schedule both parents have agreed to. As a general rule, a parenting plan should include the standard parenting schedule, which typically includes where the children will live during the week and weekends and who will be responsible for dropping them off and picking them up from school and other activities on certain days. In addition, the parenting plan can include a schedule for the holidays, summer vacations, and any other special days during the year. Examples are found in section III of this book.

Because family dynamics vary, there is no one-size-fits-all parenting plan that works well for all families. Your parenting plan should be tailored specifically to meet the needs of your family, and it should focus on what's in the best interests of your children. You may obtain information regarding parenting plans from your attorney or the court, but before you begin creating your own, it may be helpful to review some of the most common types of parenting schedules.

COMMON PARENTING SCHEDULES

Although parenting schedules vary from family to family, the following is a list of some of the most common parenting schedule templates.

The Standard

Probably the most common parenting plan for noncustodial parents is the alternate-weekend schedule, from Friday to Sunday, which often includes a Wednesday-night dinner. While the noncustodial parent would likely be granted more parenting time at trial, this schedule works well for parents with practical limitations because of their work schedule or the necessity for long-distance travel between households. Keep in mind that a midweek dinner may be disruptive for some children's evening routine, and the best interests of the children should always take precedence over the wants and feelings of the parents.

Alternate Weekends with an Extra Overnight

This parenting plan builds on the alternate weekend schedule by adding an extra overnight on Sunday or Thursday. This plan gives the noncustodial parent an opportunity for school pick-ups and drop-offs, allowing a parent who did not assume much responsibility for child rearing during the marriage to increase his or her participation in that. The quality of time a parent spends with his or her children is often just as important as the quantity of time, and school pick-ups and drop-offs are often excellent times for a parent to bond and communicate with their children.

More-Significant Timeshare

Short of a fifty-fifty parenting timeshare, an alternative plan allowing a noncustodial parent a more significant timeshare includes Thursday after school until Monday morning one week, and Thursday and Friday the next week, giving the noncustodial parent five out of every fourteen overnights. This schedule allows the less-involved parent longer blocks of time with the children on school days.

Most Weekends

When distance or other factors limit a noncustodial parent's ability to have physical custody during the week, a three-out-of-four or four-out-of-five weekend schedule is a good alternative schedule.

Equal Timeshare

Parents who have shared equal parenting responsibilities while married often prefer this parenting plan, which is most appropriate for parents who live reasonably close to their children's schools. The equal timeshare may be divided in a variety of ways. With younger children who have difficulty spending large amounts of time away from a primary caregiver parent, a common approach is for the children to spend Monday and Tuesday in one household, Wednesday and Thursday in another, alternating Friday-to-Monday weekends. However, with older children, alternating a week or two with each parent is less disruptive.

For more discussion and specific examples, see section III, Examples.

BEST INTERESTS OF THE CHILDREN

Although the unique life circumstances of each parent will always play a role in every parenting plan, the wants and needs of his or her children should always be the main priority. Some factors should be kept in mind when creating a parenting plan.

1) ## *Consistency Counts*

While it is understandable that a parent would want to spend as much time as possible with his or her children, sometimes a midweek dinner or extra overnight may be disrupting and unsettling to a child. Children, particularly younger ones, need predictability and consistency in their lives to feel secure. Take into consideration the individual temperaments of your children, and notice when a parenting schedule does not seem to be working well for them.

2) ## *The Burden Is on the Parents, Not the Children*

If commuting, juggling demands, and dealing with awkward scheduling changes are stressful for you, imagine what it must be like for your children. Too many transitions can be overwhelming to kids, so try to build transitions around natural breaks in your children's lives such as going to or leaving daycare or school. If it is at all possible, try to avoid transitions after dinner, when most children are likely to be tired. If a parenting schedule is going to inconvenience anyone, it should be the parents, not the children.

3) ## *Children's Preferences Matter*

Your family's parenting plan should take into account the unique temperaments, preferences, and activities of your children, even if that means one parent spends less time with them. Fairness between the parents should be thought of in the long term, not the short term. Remember that your children will grow, develop, and change over time, so you must remain flexible and open to adjusting your parenting plan when circumstances call for it.

STRATEGIES FOR CREATING A PARENTING PLAN

It would be wise to consult with an experienced Tennessee family law attorney before entering into any proposed parenting plan agreement so that you will understand the legal implications of the plan you have devised. If cooperation with your estranged spouse is a problem, you can create the parenting plan on your own and communicate it to your spouse or your spouse's attorney to see if it works for him or her. Mediation is always an option for parents having difficulty communicating and agreeing to a parenting plan.

The following are some suggestions for how to go about creating your parenting plan:

Make an attempt to get together with your spouse to discuss the proposed parenting plan.

Make sure to write down any decisions made, and be as specific as possible about them to reduce the likelihood of arguments once the plan is put into place. Make sure both you and the other parent are satisfied with the decisions, but also recognize that your plan needs to be flexible to accommodate the changing needs and circumstances of the children.

Decide on decision-making authority.

Typically, parents agree to split or share decision-making authority regarding their children's education, nonemergency health care, and religious and extracurricular activities. For example, the father may have final decision-making authority on extracurricular activities and religion, leaving the mother the other two categories.

Create a parenting time calendar.

Choose a schedule that works for the children, especially when it comes to school, including arrangements regarding holidays, school breaks, and vacations, and create a calendar that spells out the plan. Remember that parental convenience is not the primary purpose of a parenting plan, and you should try to avoid as much disruption to your children's lives as possible.

Outline the details regarding financial responsibilities.

Although a preliminary parenting plan is not an official child support order, the plan may include any agreements related to financial support if one parent has primary custody of the children. It is also a good idea to determine how other expenses such as sports, lessons, tutoring sessions, uninsured medical expenses, and copays will be handled. Make a list of all the expenses child support does not cover and decide which parent will be responsible for paying them.

Decide how you will be dealing with school-related issues.

Discuss what strategy you will take regarding receiving information and grades from the school. You may wish to arrange for one person to receive everything and make copies for the other, or you can share log-ins and passwords to look at school records.

What about parent-teacher conferences? Each parent may want to take turns attending, or both parents could attend together. Some teachers may be willing to make arrangements for each parent to attend all the conferences separately. One way or another, make sure you communicate about school events so at least one of you is attending.

Include instructions regarding your children's medical care.

Who will attend doctor's appointments? If you and the other parent work, you may want to take turns. Also, it is a good idea to have a medical emergency strategy for your children in place *before* an emergency arises. Both parents should have a list of emergency phone numbers and their child's medical and insurance information.

Come to an agreement about childcare.

Determine whether you and the other parent will use the same babysitter. Also, make a rule about contacting the other parent to watch the children before calling a sitter. This is commonly called a "right of first refusal."

Set up a communication plan.

It is essential for the welfare of your children that you regularly communicate with the other parent about your children's discipline, routines, chores, and medical and any behavioral problems. Come to an agreement about when and how you wish to communicate about these matters. Email can be a good method of communication, especially for parents prone to arguments. Online programs specifically designed for divorced parents that can function as safe and effective methods of communication (see chapter 12 for information and links about some of these).

Determine what you want, and have your attorney review your plan.

Before signing anything, get your lawyer to answer any questions you may have, review your proposed plan, and make suggestions and comments.

Parents, especially divorced parents, will always face challenges when raising their children. However, a detailed, clear, and flexible parenting plan can definitely make the difficult job of parenting a lot easier.

Child Custody Factors in Tennessee Law

Understanding Tennessee law can help avoid conflict. In the event a judge will be required to decide which parent will serve as the primary residential parent, the courts will consider the following factors:

(a) In a suit for annulment, divorce, separate maintenance, or in any other proceeding requiring the court to make a custody determination regarding a minor child, the determination shall be made on the basis of the best interest of the child. In taking into account the child's best interest, the court shall order a custody arrangement that permits both parents to enjoy the maximum participation possible in the life of the child consistent with the factors set out in subdivisions (a)(1)-(10), the location of the residences of the parents, the child's need for stability and all other relevant factors. The court shall consider all relevant factors, including the following, where applicable:

(1)   The love, affection and emotional ties existing between the parents or caregivers and the child;

(2)   The disposition of the parents or caregivers to provide the child with food, clothing, medical care, education and other necessary care and the degree to which a parent or caregiver has been the primary caregiver;

(3)   The importance of continuity in the child's life and the length of time the child has lived in a stable, satisfactory environment; provided, that, where there is a finding, under subdivision (a)(8), of child abuse, as defined in § 39-15-401 or § 39-15-402, or child sexual abuse, as defined in § 37-1-602, by one (1) parent, and that a nonperpetrating parent or caregiver has relocated in order to flee the perpetrating parent, that the relocation shall not weigh against an award of custody;

(4)   The stability of the family unit of the parents or caregivers;

(5)   The mental and physical health of the parents or caregivers;

(6)   The home, school and community record of the child;

(7)   (A) The reasonable preference of the child, if twelve (12) years of age or older; (B) The court may hear the preference of a younger child on request. The preferences of older children should normally be given greater weight than those of younger children;

(8)   Evidence of physical or emotional abuse to the child, to the other parent or to any other person; provided, that, where there are allegations that one (1) parent has committed child abuse, as defined in § 39-15-401 or § 39-15-402, or child sexual abuse, as defined in § 37-1-602, against a family member, the court shall consider all evidence relevant to the physical and emotional safety of the child, and determine, by a clear preponderance of the evidence, whether such abuse has occurred. The court shall include in its decision a written finding of all evidence, and all findings of facts connected to the evidence. In addition, the court shall, where appropriate, refer any issues of abuse to the juvenile court for further proceedings;

(9) The character and behavior of any other person who resides in or frequents the home of a parent or caregiver and the person's interactions with the child; and

(10) Each parent's or caregiver's past and potential for future performance of parenting responsibilities, including the willingness and ability of each of the parents and caregivers to facilitate and encourage a close and continuing parent-child relationship between the child and both of the child's parents, consistent with the best interest of the child. In determining the willingness of each of the parents and caregivers to facilitate and encourage a close and continuing parent-child relationship between the child and both of the child's parents, the court shall consider the likelihood of each parent and caregiver to honor and facilitate court ordered parenting arrangements and rights, and the court shall further consider any history of either parent or any caregiver denying parenting time to either parent in violation of a court order.

Tennessee Code Annotated § 36-6-106 (2013).

Chapter 2:

TENNESSEE'S PARENTING PLAN LAW

Divorcing parents should remember that more than two people will be affected by their decision to end their marriage. Children's needs are sometimes deferred when parents get caught up in their own anger, frustration, or worry. In worst-case scenarios, children may be used by divorcing parents as negotiating tools, but this will ultimately hurt the children and damage their relationships with their parents.

Tennessee's Parenting Plan Statute applies to all divorcing parents with children under age eighteen. The law was designed to help parents maintain a positive, communicative relationship after divorce to provide for the best interests of their children. The statute requires all divorcing parents to create a parenting plan that details the responsibilities and protects the rights of each parent and their children, provides for a way of settling disagreements between the parents when they arise, and keeps in mind the emotional and physical well-being of the children.

A good parenting plan should be very detailed and keep the children in mind at all times. Children's needs can differ depending on their ages, personalities, and abilities, and the parenting plan should take such individual needs into consideration. The plan should also recognize that needs will change as the children grow and should take anticipated changes into consideration as well to limit the need for modification of the parent plan.

The law was created with the hope that parents could make this plan by themselves, with no court interference. If parents can't come to an agreement, they are required to mediate disputes and make a good-faith effort at reaching an agreement. If the parents still cannot agree on a plan, they must each file a proposed plan, and the court will decide on a permanent parenting plan for the parents, taking their plans into consideration.

 A parent's proposed plan is written out on a standardized court form and must be submitted at least forty-five days before the divorce trial.

SHARED RESPONSIBILITY AND A RESIDENTIAL SCHEDULE

Children need to have quality time with both parents unless there is an overriding consideration such as violence or abuse. For this reason, the Parenting Plan Statute eliminates the idea of "sole custody" and "visitations." There can be one "primary residential parent," but both parents are responsible for their children and are entitled to "parenting time" or "residential time." One part of this responsibility, and one of the main requirements of the law, is setting up a residential schedule for the children.

When creating a residential schedule, parents must detail which parent the children will be with every day of the year. This means deciding where the children will be during the school week, on weekends, school vacations, and holidays. It is very detailed and even includes transportation arrangements. It also looks to the future so disputes can be avoided and the need for modifications to the plan can be limited. For example, parents are asked to indicate in which years (odd or even) each parent will get the children for each holiday.

When applicable, parents will also need to include where supervision of parenting time will take place, with whom, and which parent will cover the cost of the supervision. While it's easy to get stuck in the details, parents should remember that the children are at the center of the plan. They need enough time with both parents to provide them with emotional support and development.

If parents cannot agree on a parenting schedule, the court may intervene. It will take into consideration a number of factors, including each parent's current relationship with the children, the ability of each parent to provide for the economic and emotional needs of the children, the parents' schedules, and matters relating to continuity and stability.

The court may also consider the children's own preferences but only if they are at least age twelve. In addition to the very comprehensive list of considerations, the court may consider any other factors it deems appropriate in determining the residential schedule.

DETAILING FINANCIAL INFORMATION AND SUPPORT

The financial obligations and rights of each parent are important parts of the plan. The law requires parents to annually exchange documentation of their prior years' incomes as well as health, dental, and life insurance information. The plan also requires detailed information on child support, including the amount and how and when one parent will pay it to the other. The question of which parent is entitled to the tax exemption for their children comes up frequently, so the plan also requires this information to be detailed to resolve the matter ahead of time and avoid going to court. Child support worksheets are required to be attached.

WHO GETS TO DECIDE?

The plan must establish the authority each parent has over the children as well as the responsibilities each parent has for them. When the children are with a parent, that parent will make day-to-day decisions. For younger children, this includes breakfast, bathing, homework, activities, and bedtime. For older children, this may include computer usage, cell phone time, dating, and curfews.

The plan also needs to consider the larger, long-term issues involved in child raising and should give clear decision-making authority to either one or both parents on matters of their children's education, health care, extracurricular activities, and religious upbringing. Keeping in mind the necessity of looking toward the future, parents can also include an agreement related to the child's growth in these or other areas. The parents may also agree that regardless of how decision making is divided, either parent is allowed to make emergency decisions regarding the children's health or safety.

RIGHTS OF THE PARENTS

The law helps ensure that both parents remain active, involved, and committed to their children regardless of the division of decision-making authority. For this reason, the law guarantees that both parents are kept informed about their child's education and activities and are made aware of their children's health issues. For example, both parents must be updated about what's going on with their children at school (report cards, attendance, special activities, and events) and in extracurricular activities. Also, both parents are notified when there are medical issues involving the children.

Each parent is also protected from unfair or inappropriate behavior by the other parent. A parent has the right, for example, to speak to his or her children by phone at least twice a week for a reasonable period of time and send mail to the children without the other parent reading the letters. This helps guarantee the relationship between a parent and a child will be viable and healthy. The law goes so far as to provide that no parent may speak negatively about the other parent (or his or her family) to the children. These rights, while protecting both parents, help maintain a good relationship between the parents so they can do what is best for their children.

The plan also notes when a parent's rights are limited. In some cases, supervised visitation may be required. Parents in this category must list this information in the parenting plan and attach any court orders regarding the children.

RESOLVING DISPUTES AND MAKING CHANGES

Some amount of disagreement is foreseeable and may necessitate changes to a parenting plan. The children's school schedules and activities will evolve over time, and this will happen at times in unforeseeable ways. Before going to court, parents are required to make a good-faith effort and turn to an alternative dispute resolution process, usually mediation. Mediation is preferred because it can allow both parents to be heard and the mediator can help the parents handcraft a solution that satisfies everyone to the extent it is possible.

During any dispute, preference will generally be given to the terms of the original parenting plan, but modifications can almost always be made by mutual agreement. If the parents are able to agree, modifications are written up, signed by each parent, and submitted to the court for approval and entry as a court order.

The law requiring mediation aims at keeping the courts out of the process unless necessary and giving parents the opportunity to resolve their differences on their own. The court will usually intervene only if there is a serious question regarding the children's well-being. Attending alternate dispute resolution proceedings is required, so the court can impose financial sanctions on a parent who intentionally fails to appear and participate in good faith.

PARENTAL RELOCATION

The law regarding a parent's desire to relocate is addressed in the standardized parenting plan forms. Tennessee's Parent Relocation law requires a parent who spends time with the child and who wishes to move either out of state or more than fifty miles away to notify the other parent sixty days prior to the proposed move. It also gives the other parent the right to oppose the move. This helps protect the nonprimary residential parent from being denied access to his or her child. There are specific time limitations for modification of the intent to move and for filing an objection.

PARENTING CLASSES REQUIRED

The law requires both parents to attend parenting classes. Courts have different rules about when a parent must attend the class, at times prior to, or at times after the parenting plan is approved. Some judges may require both parents to complete the parenting class before they submit a parenting plan for approval, which is required for a divorce to be granted. Parenting class attendance demonstrates a seriousness and commitment on the part of the parents to learn how to coparent after divorce.

The parenting classes focus on showing parents the possible effects of divorce on the children, various parental arrangements, and techniques for communication, and they encourage parents to focus on the children, not on themselves. Classes are about four hours long and are taught by certified professionals. Once the course is completed, a certificate is issued to each parent and must be filed as part of the court action.

EVERYBODY WINS

Divorce is often unpleasant and can bring out the worst in both parents, but those who can suffer the most are the children. The Parenting Plan statute, enacted in 2001, aims at helping parents see beyond their individual emotions and do what's best for their children.

Family lawyers in Tennessee agree that the requirements of a permanent parenting plan help in most divorce cases. Experience has taught family lawyers and judges that the more details parents agree on, the less likely they are to return to court, which will save them legal fees and emotional stress. Avoiding such emotional costs always benefits children of divorced parents.

The act of formulating the plan itself also benefits everyone involved by helping parents learn how to work together for the sake of their children once they are divorced and what the parents can expect from each other. While it can't resolve all problems in custody cases, the Parenting Plan law goes a long way to improving the relationship of the divorcing parents and thereby helping their children. In the end, it's a win-win situation.

Chapter 3:
WHAT TO TELL THE KIDS

Probably the only thing more painful than the parents' recognition that their marriage is over is actually telling their children they are separating. While reconciliation may be possible, children need to be informed that one of their parents will be moving out of the marital home, and they need to be psychologically prepared for an ultimate divorce.

It's natural for parents to feel uncertain and anxious about talking to their children about divorce, so it's best for them to be prepared for what they will tell their children. The way parents break the news to their children will set the tone for how well they deal with the divorce down the road, so knowing what can be said and done to make things easier on the children is essential.

BREAKING THE NEWS

If it's at all possible, you should consult with your spouse before speaking to the children so the two of you can agree on what exactly you will tell them. Your children need a basic understanding of why their parents are divorcing and what will happen to them. Failure to give your children this information may lead to their confusion, anxiety, and loss of trust. Don't underestimate the importance of this discussion.

While things may be tense between you and your spouse at this time, if you don't have this conversation before talking to the kids, you may wind up having it in front of them. It would be best to put your feelings aside and make joint decisions about what you'll need to tell your children. If you and your spouse are not on speaking terms, you may want to consider consulting a counselor or mediator to help both of you work out the details.

Ideally, you and your spouse should break the news to the children together. Telling the children about the divorce together sends an important message to the kids that you and your spouse are on the same page and are going to work together to take care of the family. Make an attempt to incorporate the word "we" into your discussion with the children frequently to reinforce the notion of parental agreement.

You should have a discussion with all the children at the same time so each child hears the same story from you and your spouse and not a secondhand version of it from a sibling. The explanation for the divorce should be appropriate for their ages and their intellectual and emotional stages because young children can become confused by too many details.

While it's not necessary or even appropriate to share with the kids the specific details underlying the reasons for the divorce, older children usually have a more realistic understanding of their parents' marriage and will often want a more detailed explanation than younger children will, so be prepared for that. If your children are different ages, share only the basic information initially and then follow up with the older children later if and as you feel it's appropriate.

It's vitally important that you and your spouse remain calm during this conversation. Always try to resist the temptation to place blame or discuss who's at fault in the situation. Parents should take a tone of respect for one another.

Since it's not unusual for children to blame themselves for their parent's divorce, make a specific point of repeatedly reinforcing to the children that your decision to divorce has nothing to do with them, that it is not their fault, and that they are still deeply loved by both parents. Reassure the kids that although you and your spouse can no longer remain married, you both will continue to take care of and support them.

NOW WHAT?

Divorce can be a disruptive and scary experience for kids. You can reassure your children and make them feel safe and secure by providing them with the specific details, if you know them at that point, about changes that will be occurring in their lives. If you know, let them know where they will live and with whom.

You and your spouse also need to agree to a parenting plan and visitation schedule as soon as possible and make the children aware of it. Ask your children for their feedback on the parenting and visitation schedule only if they are mature enough. Parents will ultimately be responsible for decisions, so avoid making your children feel they must decide.

If you or your spouse has plans to move out, notifying the children about it in advance can make it easier for them to cope with such a change. The more information you can give your kids about where the departing parent will be living as well as when they will be able to visit that parent, the better they will feel about the situation. Post the visitation schedule in a prominent place in your home so your children can see when they will be visiting the other parent. Taking the children to visit their parent's new residence as soon as possible can also help relieve separation anxiety.

Being honest and up-front with your children about what you know and don't know in the beginning of the separation process can help psychologically prepare your children for the upcoming changes they will have to face. Assure your children that the two of you will do your best to disrupt their lives as little as possible, but don't make any long-range promises to your kids since the future can be very uncertain. Rather, stick with the assurances you can confidently make at the moment, and be extra-generous with your hugs and words of love and affection.

THE REACTION

Be sensitive to how your children react to the news of the divorce. The news may be no surprise to some children but an unexpected shock to others. The initial emotional reaction children have in response to a parental divorce can range from weeping and disbelief to anger and resentment. Don't be surprised, however, if your child seems to have no reaction at all. This does not necessarily indicate lack of feelings but shock or the inability to express intense emotions appropriately. It may take some time for the reality of the situation to sink in to your children before they will be able to articulate their feelings.

You should assume that the children will be upset, so be prepared to reassure them and answer questions or concerns with age-appropriate responses. Most likely, your children will have many questions to ask you and your spouse. However, you need to make the children aware that the situation will continue to unfold and that the topic will be revisited many times as new questions and concerns arise. Avoid conversations about what might happen—share only final decisions, not speculation.

Make a point of reassuring your children that their wants, needs, and feelings are important to you so they don't feel afraid to express themselves. Foster open communication among all members of the family, and tell the children they are entitled to their emotions about their new family situation.

Explain to your children that their emotions are neither right nor wrong and don't need to be judged but that you expect them to control their behavior and express their emotions in constructive, not destructive, ways. Children should also be encouraged to problem solve in their relationships to find solutions rather than feel helpless and complain.

WHEN UNEXPECTED PROBLEMS ARISE

Just as you realize, children also need to realize that as time goes on, there will likely be bumps in the road caused by parenting and visitation schedule changes. Do your best to give your children honest but simple explanations for the disruptions without placing blame. Try to explain to them that you and their other parent are doing your best to iron out conflicts. While you should do everything possible to maintain consistency in your children's lives, most children can adjust to minor differences in routine.

MOVING ON

At some point, either you or your ex may get involved in new romantic relationships or remarry. While it's normal for divorced parents to move on to new partners, that can create some turmoil for the children, who then have to get accustomed to new relationships their parents have. Introduce new partners into your children's lives slowly, but if someone is planning on remarrying, the children need to be told well in advance so they can adjust to the fact gradually.

In some instances, there may be family members who are not adjusting well to changes after the divorce. Be sensitive to signs of more-serious psychological problems such as emotional outbursts, withdrawal, prolonged periods of sadness, or acting-out behaviors. Express your concern and show your support for the family member in crisis, but be careful not to make the person feel ashamed. Individual or family counseling can be helpful when these issues aren't going away as part of the natural adjustment process.

Talking to your children about divorce and the resulting emotions and problems in the aftermath is going to be hard. Parents need to remember that while children need to be informed about the divorce, being too honest can make children believe they have input, making them feel "caught in the middle." Share decisions made, but keep the kids out of the decision-making process as much as possible.

Chapter 4:
COPARENTING DOS AND DON'TS

Like it or not, if you have children, your relationship with your ex will continue after the divorce due to the need for you two to have interaction and communication regarding your children. For some people, the thought of coparenting with an ex may seem overwhelming. Challenges will most likely arise, but some tips can help divorced parents coparent their children more effectively.

CREATE A DETAILED PARENTING PLAN

Upon separation, the first and most important thing you and your ex should do is agree to a parenting plan and visitation schedule that works for your whole family. The written parenting plan should set out the parenting and visitation schedule, including where the children will live during the week and weekends, and which parent will be responsible for dropping off and picking them up from school and other activities on certain days. Be sure to make the children aware of the parenting plan schedule, and post it in a prominent place in both parental homes.

A parenting plan and visitation schedule is very important for maintaining stability and continuity in your children's lives as well as reducing the likelihood of problems stemming from confusion about parental responsibilities. You can nip potential conflicts in the bud by openly communicating with the other parent about any changes in the parenting plan or visitation schedule.

However, try not to become too rigidly attached to the plan, since the children's circumstances will change as they get older, requiring both parents to be flexible enough to make parenting plan adjustments. Devising a detailed but flexible parenting plan in which each parent participates equally in the children's extracurricular activities, helps with schoolwork, and so on, will ultimately make life easier for the kids.

BE COOPERATIVE WITH THE OTHER PARENT

While it may be easier said than done, you should do your best to be as courteous and cooperative as possible when communicating with your ex about the children. Treat him or her as you would a business acquaintance by being professional and responsible in your interactions. If you're going to miss a visit with your children or are going to be late picking them up or dropping them off for visitation, notify the other parent in advance. Try not to wait until the last minute.

Take responsibility for your feelings and behavior, and don't blame the other parent for all your children's problems. If you have resentful feelings toward your ex and find you just can't let it go, or if you have conflicts with your ex regarding the children that you can't seem to resolve, consider getting professional assistance such as individual counseling or mediation.

Your ability and willingness to cooperate with your ex for the sake of the children is the single strongest predictor of a successful coparenting relationship. Regardless of how you feel about your ex, remember that the best interests of your children are more important than your personal resentments and conflicts.

SUPPORT HEALTHY FAMILY RELATIONSHIPS

Children need healthy relationships with both parents, so do your best to foster open communication among all family members. Give your children permission to love their other parent by facilitating and supporting that relationship.

It's not unusual for children to complain about or refuse visitation with their other parent for a variety of reasons. While you should listen and try to empathize with your children, they should also be encouraged to resolve relationship problems themselves by openly communicating their grievances to their parents and attempting to find solutions or strike compromises.

Be careful not to put the children in the middle of conflicts between you and your ex. This will only make your children feel they are expected to take sides. If you have an issue with your ex, politely communicate directly with him or her. Don't use your children to relay messages, and don't interrogate your children for information about your ex.

You should especially refrain from making derogatory remarks about your ex to your children or even in front of them. Taking a respectful attitude toward your ex is one of the most influential things you can do to support a healthy relationship between your children and their other parent.

FOCUS ON PARENTING

Raising children is not always easy, and after a divorce, it can become even more difficult. Guilt about the divorce and limited time with the children can motivate some parents to overcompensate or compete with their children's other parent.

In spite of whatever emotions you may have resulting from your divorce, you need to remain focused on being a good parent to your children. They need you to be their parent, not their "friend," and they need fair and consistent parental discipline. Don't feel you need to fill all the time you spend with your kids with special or fun activities. Time spent at home with you engaged in ordinary, real-life activities is more important. Rules, chores, and limits create much-needed security in the lives of your children.

Whether or not you have primary residential custody of the children, make sure your home is child-oriented and safe with adequate room and privacy for your kids. You should also become familiar with your children's medical history, doctors' names, and health insurance information in case of emergencies.

Put your effort into spending time alone with each of your children to let them know they are special and to learn what's going on in their lives. Make the most of the limited time you spend with your kids by making a special effort to get involved in their lives by showing an interest in their school and extracurricular activities, sports, clubs, friends, and hobbies. If your children's school has your children's grades, activities, and school events posted online, make sure you know the log-in name and password and check it regularly. Do your best to keep up with what's going on, show up to school and sports events, and be polite to your children's other parent.

It also may be helpful to continue to educate yourself on divorce, childhood development, and parenting to learn how to deal with the unique challenges divorced parents face. Always keep in mind that visitation or parenting time is supposed to be for the benefit of the children, not the parents.

FIND EFFECTIVE COPING STRATEGIES

You know the emotional toll your impending or completed divorce has taken on you, so you can assume your children have also been emotionally affected even though some may be good at hiding it. Parents and children will need to learn healthy strategies to cope with the emotional aftermath of divorce.

You should accept the fact that your children will be upset about the divorce, so they should be encouraged and allowed to talk openly about their feelings. Be empathetic to your children's feelings, but try not to get overly emotional when they express their distress about the divorce and how it has affected them. Be on the lookout for warning signs of depression or other psychological problems in your children such as social withdrawal, poor academic performance, or increased aggression, as these can indicate a need for counseling.

While you should do your best to not put down your ex, if there were serious problems in the marriage such as addiction or domestic violence, there may be times when you'll need to give your children a realistic view of their other parent. Be honest and realistic with your children about the divorce, but don't discuss adult issues such as finances or divorce litigation with them.

All family members are likely to feel vulnerable and stressed after a divorce, making emotional support from other people even more essential. Don't feel you have to be strong and bear the burden of your emotions privately. Doing so will only increase your stress and likely worsen your problems.

However, don't burden your children by inappropriately turning them into your confidantes. Instead, put the effort into finding a good support system for yourself and your kids such as support groups for divorced parents and their children. You also may want to consider counseling for your children, yourself, or the whole family.

DON'T RUSH THINGS

Accept the fact that it's going to take time for your children and you to adjust to your new lives after a divorce even under the best of circumstances. Sudden change can be very difficult for children to cope with, and too much change in a short time can be overwhelming. Keep this in mind when making decisions that will affect the kids. Try to avoid relocating for a year after the divorce.

Parental dating or remarriage is another source of stress for children, so take your time to gradually introduce new relationships to your children. If you are going to get remarried, tell the children well in advance, since new steprelatives will definitely impact their lives.

Successful coparenting after a divorce does not happen automatically. Both parents must make their best attempts to cooperate with one another and put the best interests and well-being of their children ahead of themselves. However, divorced parents can take heart in knowing that they don't have to be alone in their struggles and that it's possible to raise healthy and happy children with their exes even after painful divorces.

Chapter 5:

INFANTS AND YOUNG CHILDREN—
AGE-APPROPRIATE PLANS

It's no secret that the stress of divorce takes a toll on children. This is one of the reasons why divorcing spouses with children are required by Tennessee law to create a parenting plan that contains the details related to child custody and parenting time. While the reasons for creating a parenting plan are usually clear to divorcing parents, how to create one appropriate for any one child's age may not be so clear.

Because children have different needs depending on their ages and stages of development, divorcing parents must have a general understanding of how infants and young children form bonds and attachments to their parents and how they respond to disruptions in their living arrangements and routines.

ATTACHMENT IS IMPORTANT

Developing healthy attachments to parents during infancy and early childhood is crucial to a child's psychological development. The first three years of a child's life are critical to development, and it is essential that children receive safe and consistent caretaking from each parent during this time.

Small children who don't attach to or bond sufficiently with their parents may develop Reactive Attachment Disorder (RAD), making the child excessively inhibited, hypervigilant, or highly ambivalent toward primary or secondary caregivers. RAD can ultimately interfere with a child's ability to initiate and form satisfactory relationships later in life.

With a healthy parental attachment, a child feels secure in exploring the world as long as the primary caretaker parent is close enough to provide comfort as soon as the child becomes frightened or uncomfortable. When a primary attachment figure such as a parent is consistently unavailable, the child will feel fearful and perceive the world as inconsistent, unpredictable, and threatening.

As time goes on, the child may become depressed, withdrawn, anxious, and insecure. The child learns to distrust the environment and turns inward for security. This could have the consequence of inhibiting the child's ability to bond with others, and this may result in more acting out later in adolescence and/or adulthood.

WHAT IS AN APPROPRIATE PARENTING PLAN?

When parents are separated or divorced, an infant may find attaching to both parents a real challenge. When infants or very young children are involved, the issues raised regarding custody and parenting time can be confusing, contentious, and anxiety provoking. Which parent should have primary residential parent status? How much time should the residential alternate parent spend with the child to ensure proper attachment? Are overnight stays appropriate for infants and young children? These questions are not always easy to answer since the circumstances of each family will strongly influence what would be in the best interests of the child.

Before the 1970s, the legal standard in determining child custody in divorce was the "tender years" doctrine, which assumed that mothers were more-appropriate caregivers for very young children than were fathers. The "best interests of the child" standard, however, makes no presumptions about the caretaking abilities of mothers or fathers. It focuses on the best interests of the child. However, some family law judges still make custody decisions involving very young children assuming that the child is better off with the mother unless there is evidence indicating otherwise.

PARENTING SCHEDULES FOR INFANTS

Research suggests that an infant should have contact with each parent at least every three days for the first two years of life to facilitate the formation of proper attachments to each parent. It is recommended that infants under a year live with one parent acting as primary caregiver, with the alternate residential parent frequently spending time with the child for short periods, perhaps four to five times a week for two to three hours at a time. These contacts should ideally be at different times of the day to allow the alternate residential parent to participate in a variety of caretaking activities such as playing, feeding, bathing, and putting the child to bed so the infant's bond with him or her can strengthen.

The two- to three-hour frequent visits can take place where the child lives or where the other parent lives. This parenting arrangement is likely to be inconvenient and especially unappealing to parents who have difficulty getting along, so waiting until the child is older before starting overnight visits could benefit the child.

IS AN OVERNIGHT VISIT APPROPRIATE FOR AN INFANT?

While there is no consensus on right or wrong in regard to overnight visits for young children, one school of thought holds that infants up to twelve months are old enough to tolerate overnight stays with the alternate residential parent. The child's temperament, caretaking history, and level of conflict between the parents among other factors may influence how much time away from the primary residential parent the child can tolerate.

However, some experienced child custody experts recommend that while an occasional overnight visit with the alternate residential parent will not damage the child's attachment to the primary residential parent, overnight visits should not be regularly scheduled for the first year of a child's life.

Some experts suggest that overnights should be only for one night away from the primary caregiver for children up to age two. After that, overnights can be regularly scheduled and the number of consecutive overnights can increase, but they should not exceed three nights in a row until a child is at least four.

When parents with infants or toddlers live in different cities, the situation gets more difficult. Ideally, the primary residential parent should accompany the child for any overnight stays until the baby is at least one. Even then, the best interests of the child should always come first. It may be difficult for parents to be objective about the situation, which is why it is necessary for parents to put effort into having open communication regarding a child's development.

An example of parenting time age-appropriate suggestions for infants can be: First year: no regularly scheduled overnight visits. Second year: regularly scheduled overnight visits for no more than three consecutive nights, assuming the child is adequately attached to both parents.

Other factors should be considered in determining whether a one- or two-year-old is ready for overnight stays. Is child outgoing or reserved? How appropriately attached is the child to the custodial parent? Is the child secure? How far apart do the parents live? How well do the parents get along with each other?

TODDLERS AND OLDER CHILDREN

Younger toddlers can typically tolerate only about one to two days away from each parent, while older toddlers may be able to deal with three days. By the time they are in preschool, most children can tolerate three to four days away from a parent depending on their temperaments. However, parents need to be sensitive to the needs of their child rather than rigidly adhering to what "experts" say.

By the time children reach elementary school, they can usually tolerate alternate weeks with each parent. Some children are comfortable with midweek overnight stays while others may consider them disruptive. Again, the specific temperament of a child needs to be taken into consideration and put before the wants and needs of the parents.

The goal is to allow children access to their parents while creating as little disruption to their lives as possible. Recent literature about childhood brain development indicates that infants and toddlers who have healthy, competent parents deal well with spending a night with either parent as long as there is a consistent, predicable schedule for such visits. When small children do have difficulty adjusting to overnight stays with the alternate residential parent, it is usually because of the anxiety the parents have about the situation.

CREATING A PARENTING PLAN THAT WORKS FOR YOUR FAMILY

Since parents know their children and family situation better than any family law judge ever could, divorcing parents should agree to a parenting schedule rather than ask the court to make a decision for them. If the parents can't agree, mediation is an option that is much better than going to court. In addition, they can seek counseling from a competent mental health professional to work out developmentally sensitive parenting plans.

All those contemplating or going through divorce should seek counsel from an experienced Tennessee family law attorney for legal advice related to divorce and custody issues.

Chapter 6:

DIFFUSING TENSION IN A HIGH-CONFLICT DIVORCE

Divorce is major life change for spouses and especially their children. The entire family must adjust to changes in residence, finances, and lifestyle. High-conflict divorces are those that are more acrimonious than usual and are often characterized by:

- *ongoing, relentless hostility and arguing between spouses*
- *frequent, drawn-out court actions*
- *discovery wars*
- *contentious custody disputes*
- *allegations of domestic violence, physical abuse, sexual abuse, and/or addictions*
- *restraining orders*
- *inability of a couple to communicate effectively about their children*

Research indicates that up to 10 percent of divorces in the United States can be characterized as high-conflict divorces. Though relations between exes in high-conflict divorces generally improve as intense emotions simmer down after the divorce is finalized, other high-conflict divorcing spouses will always have difficult relationships. They can spend much time in arguments over minor matters, communicating with lawyers, talking with therapists, undergoing repeated parenting evaluations, and attending court hearings.

WHY ALL THE TENSION?

There are often a variety of explanations for the stress and conflict before, during, and after a divorce. Financial concerns and unresolved feelings as well as mental health issues on the part of one or both divorcing parties can add tension to a high-conflict divorce scenario. When it comes to arguments concerning custody and parenting time with children, some common factors contribute to the conflicts.

Using the Children to Vie for Power and Control

A divorce can be deeply psychologically wounding to many people, leaving them humiliated, angry, and hungry for revenge. Some divorced or divorcing parents believe they will feel better if they can control the other parent's life. Unfortunately, many parents perceive custody, child support, and parenting time as a battle they want to "win" to make sure their ex "loses." They mistakenly think that if they spend more time with the children, they will finally have "proof" they are the better parent.

Some high-conflict parents will repeatedly make accusations of abuse, neglect, mental instability, and poor parenting to try to punish the other parent so they can feel in control. Sadly, this type of control battle in the courtroom is financially and emotionally costly to themselves, the other parent, and the children.

Differences in Parenting Styles

Different people have different parenting styles, but once a couple is no longer married, their parenting approaches tend to diverge even more. When divorced parents have differing rules regarding bedtimes, chores, and the like, conflict with the other parent is the usual result. The more one parent tries to make the rules for the other parent, the more high conflict the situation can become.

A New Significant Other

Once a divorced parent starts dating and introduces a new partner to the children, drama often ensues. It is not unusual for parents to feel uncomfortable when an unknown person is suddenly interacting with their children. Problems sometimes arise when a new person crosses boundaries and starts stepping into a parental role in a way that is threatening to the other parent. Sometimes, the children don't like a parent's new boyfriend or girlfriend, which creates tension in their relationship with that parent. Whatever the issue may be with the new significant other, the end result is often high conflict.

The Consequence to Children

Unfortunately, as one can imagine, children can pay a huge price for their parents' conflicts, a proposition confirmed by countless researchers. Parental conflict is the biggest predicator of unhappy and maladjusted children regardless of whether the parents are married or divorced.

One of the most destructive things that high-conflict divorcing or divorced parents do to their children is make them feel obligated to engage in the parental conflict as a confidante or messenger. This behavior makes children feel they must pick sides, and this is extremely stressful for them. High-conflict parents often become so preoccupied with their conflict and distress that they become unavailable to fulfill the needs of their children.

Because parental conflict is so devastating to children, parents should put as much effort as possible into learning how to effectively communicate and cooperate with their exes to minimize the potential for conflict.

Ways to Minimize Conflict

While personalities cannot be changed, some steps can be taken that can help diffuse tension in a high-conflict divorce.

- *Attempt to avoid arguments by limiting face-to-face communications with the other parent. For example, make transitions with the children in neutral settings instead of either home, and use email and other online technologies specifically designed for separated and divorced couples. Don't send on heated messages. Relax. Don't always write what you want. Try to be polite.*
- *Understand and manage your anger. Take responsibility for your own life, and try to avoid pointing the finger and blaming the other parent.*
- *Maintain healthy boundaries with your ex by limiting communications to just the children's issues. Try to develop a businesslike attitude when it comes to dealing with the other parent.*
- *Make sure you have a clear and complete parenting plan in place, and try to limit changes to it to emergencies only. If necessary, adjust your schedule to the parenting plan instead of the other way around. Consider creating mirrored parenting calendars showing parenting time a year in advance.*
- *Create a method for making decisions and resolving the disagreements that will inevitably arise as the children get older. Don't be afraid to give in every now and then.*
- *Consider using a mediator if you are unable to resolve disputes with the other parent.*
- *Keep your commitments, and stick to your financial agreements.*
- *Try to be flexible and open to doing things differently if your strategies for minimizing conflict are not working. Seek solutions instead of reverting to arguments.*

As always, it is a good idea to seek legal advice from an experienced Tennessee family law attorney. But with a good attitude and structured parenting plan in place, you may be able to diffuse some of the tension of a high-conflict divorce from the start.

Chapter 7:

WHAT TO DO WITH A CHILD RELUCTANT TO VISIT

You and your ex have finally agreed to a parenting plan and visitation schedule that looks like it will work for your family. Everything is running smoothly, that is, until your child starts crying and complaining when visitation time comes around.

While it is not unusual for children to express reluctance or even flat-out refusal to visit their other parent, it is still the responsibility of the primary residential parent to put the effort into complying with visitation orders and encouraging a healthy relationship between their children and the other parent. It is also not unusual for a child to express equal reluctance to the other parent prior to exchanges.

WHAT'S THE PROBLEM?

There are various explanations for why children can be reluctant to spend time with a parent, ranging from minor reasons related to a child's personality and preferences to more-serious issues such as parental neglect or abuse.

A child's age as well as differing household rules, personalities, and parenting styles, and parental conflicts are common reasons why a child may have a less-than-enthusiastic response to a parental visitation. While it's possible a child might be reacting to other pressures in his or her life such as problems with peers or in school, in some cases, there may be a significant relationship problem with one or both parents.

The situation becomes even more problematic for parents who have serious concerns about their ex-spouse's parenting skills and ability to adequately take care of their child's needs. While it's a frustrating and difficult situation to deal with, there are strategies to help parents when their children say no to a parental visitation.

TRY TO BE OBJECTIVE

While children may complain about their other parent, don't automatically assume your ex-spouse is to blame for your child's rejecting behavior. Children are usually aware of conflicts between their divorced parents and can sometimes try to manipulate the situation to their advantage, which is especially easy to do when both parents are quick to find fault with each other. While you should listen to what your child is saying, you should also give your ex the benefit of the doubt when your child complains or shows an unwillingness to visit his or her other parent.

It's your responsibility as a parent to identify what is really going on with your child. To do this, you need to be objective about the situation and consider other possible explanations for your child's negative attitude.

COMPLY WITH COURT ORDERS

Court orders regarding visitation and parenting time need to be obeyed or there will be legal consequences. While children's wants and needs are important, you don't want to communicate to them that laws don't need to be followed. Explain and demonstrate to your children that basic rules of social behavior should be followed even when they don't feel like doing so.

Structures, rules, and consistency make children feel more secure, and when you make a point of encouraging respect for the law as well as your ex, the impact on your child's life can be immediate and powerful.

Your child's concerns may be resolved without ignoring the parenting plan, violating the court order, or initiating legal action. Parents should put effort into complying with child custody and visitation orders while at the same time communicating with their children and the other parent to resolve the underlying issue.

ENCOURAGE PROBLEM SOLVING

When children express problems with a parent, they should be encouraged to openly communicate with that parent to solve the problems themselves.

While it's normal for children to want to avoid problems, healthy problem-solving skills can help them resolve conflicts in their relationships. Healthy relationship problem-solving skills require children to learn how to identify their feelings, directly communicate them, and listen to what another person has to say in response.

Encourage your child to attempt to resolve any differences with the other parent during visitation. The focus of attention should be on the child's feelings and issues, not on complying with the court order, which may put a child in the middle of a parental legal battle.

BE OPEN TO PROFESSIONAL ASSISTANCE

Professional counseling may not always be necessary, but early intervention can help quickly resolve problems and promote family cooperation, so be open to any professional assistance that may be necessary or helpful.

If you have a legitimate reason to believe your child may be in danger as a result of neglect or abuse by the other parent, you need to seek emergency assistance from an experienced family law attorney in addition to seeking psychological counseling for your child.

While there are no guarantees for family happiness, good-faith attempts by parents and children to solve problems can make a big difference in supporting healthy family relationships after a divorce.

Chapter 8:

TEENS AND DIVORCE

Because divorce is a notoriously difficult experience for children, decisions related to child custody are probably the most important and complex issues divorcing couples and family law courts face. Some couples are able to easily agree on child custody and parenting plans that work well for their families. However, in more-contentious divorces in which spouses cannot agree on the issue, child custody determinations are made by a family law judge.

Most courts will take into consideration the preferences of older children, especially teenagers, when deciding which divorcing parent receives primary residential custody. But whether the parents agree to a custody arrangement or the custody issue is decided by the court, the question still remains, how much weight should be given to a teenager's preferences when deciding child custody?

MENTAL AND SOCIAL DEVELOPMENT

Since child custody decisions should always be based primarily on the "best interests of the child" standard, the issue boils down to whether teenagers are capable of making decisions in their best interests. Understanding the stages of your teenager's mental and social development can help shed light on the subject.

Recent research on adolescent brain development indicates that logical reasoning and basic information-processing abilities mature before social maturity and good judgment develops. While the thinking ability of a sixteen-year-old is practically indistinguishable from that of an adult, his or her social functioning and decision-making abilities can be significantly less mature than that of young adults in their early twenties. As a result, teenagers have a tendency to engage in risky behavior, making adolescence a time of heightened vulnerability.

Since susceptibility to peer pressure peaks at about age fourteen, the midteen years are an especially important and influential time in the life of your adolescent. While peers become an increasing influence in the lives of teenagers, parents continue to be an important source of guidance to their teens as well. Studies indicate that teens exposed to parental hostility exhibited lower self-esteem and academic achievement as well as more acting-out behavior, so don't underestimate the impact of your behavior on your teenager.

INFLUENCE OF PARENTING STYLE

Research on adolescent decision-making skills and abilities indicate that, as one would expect, parenting style plays a large role in a child's mental and emotional development, helping or hindering his or her ability to make appropriate, independent decisions.

Children of permissive parents who place few demands on their children, allowing them to regulate their own activities and behavior, often have difficulties respecting authority and obeying rules. Children who grow up in permissive households are at increased risk of drug and alcohol experimentation as well as minor delinquency and lack of engagement in school.

On the other end of the spectrum are children raised by authoritarian parents who take a more controlling approach to child rearing, imposing rigid rules on their children. Authoritarian parents value a child's willingness and ability to conform to their expectations more than their child's autonomy. Children who grow up in authoritarian households tend to have difficulty with independent decision making since they are accustomed to letting their authoritarian parents make decisions for them.

Striking a balance between the two extremes are "authoritative" parents who attempt to direct their children's behavior by imposing reasonable rules in a manner that values a child's autonomy and self-will. Children raised in such authoritative households who are allowed to make some independent life decisions have been found to show greater self-esteem and self-motivation than children with permissive or authoritarian parents.

EFFECT OF DIVORCE

In recent studies, 70 percent of children whose parents were divorcing felt uncomfortable with the divorce process and wanted to be included in the decision making process though they did not want to have the final say regarding custody. Teenagers want to feel they have some control over their lives and are not totally at the mercy of their parents' decisions. Yet understandably, choosing between parents is very stressful for children, and most kids don't want the burden of having to make that choice themselves.

So how can divorcing parents and family law courts determine how big a role a teenager's preferences should play in custody decisions? To make that determination, the parents need to accurately evaluate a teenager's mental and social development, independent decision-making skills, and other relevant needs.

However, this isn't always an easy judgment to make, and sometimes, genuine disagreements arise among parents regarding their children. In these instances, parents and family law courts often rely on the expert opinions of mental health care professionals who interview the children and come to a conclusion regarding their preferences, psychological health, and maturity levels. A mental health professional can offer an unbiased opinion of the situation, making child custody decisions and residential time a little easier on families.

Chapter 9:

SPECIAL-NEEDS CHILDREN

All children have needs their parents are responsible for fulfilling. A child with special needs, however, has unique medical or developmental difficulties that require greater attention than those of the average child. Studies show that 85 percent of parents of children with special needs get divorced. Since separated and divorced parents with special-needs children have more significant parental responsibilities, it is especially important that both parents participate in developing a parenting plan that effectively meets the extra needs of their child.

Parenting plans are documents outlining all the pertinent information regarding how parents will continue to care for their children after separation or divorce. While Tennessee, as is the case with many other states, has specific requirements for parenting plans, at the very minimum, a plan should cover the issues of custody and parenting time, including details regarding where the children will live during the week and weekends and which days each parent is responsible for school drop-offs and pick-ups. Often, parents also include in their plans information regarding child support and how the parents will make decisions regarding medical, educational, and religious issues concerning their children.

Devising a good parenting plan is crucial in assisting divorcing parents in raising their children together. However, when divorcing parents have a child with special needs, the parenting plan needs to be custom tailored to meet the unique needs of that child. Creating a successful parenting plan for a special-needs child may require a greater amount of cooperation and flexibility between parents than in most other divorce situations.

With special-needs children, additional factors such as the living circumstances of the child, medical care, therapy, insurance, child care, and special-educational needs all must be given particular attention by parents. The intricacy of the parenting plan will depend largely on the nature of a child's needs. Parents need to be willing and able to adapt their parenting plan as their child inevitability develops and changes as time goes on.

When devising a parenting plan for a special-needs child, it's important to realize that caring for a child with special needs may be too challenging for one parent to deal with singlehandedly. Consequently, both parents need come to an agreement about a living arrangement for their child that does not put the burden on one parent alone. Social science research suggests that it may be more difficult for special-needs children to move between two homes, and parents of a physically disabled child may also need to ensure that both households are equipped to meet their child's special needs.

However, if the child lives primarily with one parent, both parents should create a parenting schedule that gives the parent who is the primary caretaker some time off. Maybe the other parent can watch the child in the primary parent's home or take primary custody of the child for extended periods of time during the year. The parents may choose to hire someone to care for their child. If parents can decide on child care for their special-needs child, they need to agree on the qualified individual who will be caring for their child in addition to how the child care costs will be allocated.

Of course, medical care and insurance are enormous concerns for parents of special-needs children since they typically require extra medical care, therapy, and counseling. This means that parents will need to communicate about decisions regarding choice of health care professionals in addition to determining how they will share the responsibility of making decisions for their child. Both parents should examine their health insurance to help them decide the best way to handle the child's medical expenses.

Joint decision-making regarding a special-needs child's education will also likely require frequent, in-depth communication between parents. Establishing whether a child needs special education in a public school system will require parental input in addition to consultation with various professionals.

While divorce can be a time of stress, crisis, and conflict, parents need to realize how important it is to keep the best interests of their children their main priority during this process. For parents of special-needs children, it is even more critical that they don't allow their feelings related to their divorce to interfere with their ability to effectively communicate in a cooperative fashion with their ex-spouse to successfully coparent their children together.

Unfortunately, it is not always the case that parents are able to work in a collaborative manner. When there is a breakdown in communication, parents may benefit from retaining the services of a neutral third party such as a parenting coordinator or mediator to help facilitate the decision-making and communication process. A neutral third party familiar with the parenting plan, the family dynamics and needs, and the other professionals involved can often help reduce conflict between parents and resolve conflict more efficiently when it does arise.

Mediation can provide parents with an opportunity and process for problem solving in regard to their children. The mediation process offers parents the chance to learn the communication skills they need to work together for the present and the future of their special-needs child. These types of mediated parenting discussions also allow parents to address the challenging parental responsibilities involved in caring for a child with special needs.

By following this parenting plan template, parents with special-needs children should be able to devise a parenting plan that works well for them. Keep in mind, however, that every special-needs child faces unique medical, physical, educational, and social challenges. Parents must research what may be needed in the future and get advice from qualified professional caregivers experienced in their child's particular condition. Be prepared to educate your lawyer about everything that is likely to happen and also what could happen, even if it's unlikely. Hope for the best, but plan for the worst.

Chapter 10:
ADVICE FOR THE VERY ANGRY PARENT

Because going through a divorce is an emotional experience, temporary feelings of loss, sadness, and anger related to the dissolution of a marriage are normal, but they should dissipate over time. However, when two divorced people have children, the necessary ongoing involvement with each other can add fuel to any existing anger, which over time can become toxic, making parenting more difficult.

The most obvious explanation for anger toward an ex-spouse after a divorce is the leftover anger from the marriage. Typically, people get divorced in an attempt to put an end to the arguing and misery by "getting away" from a spouse. However, when two people have minor children together, there is no getting away from each other. Realistically, parents need to realize that simply getting divorced will not permanently resolve their conflicts. They still must put the effort into resolving differences in a civil manner to continue parenting their children together.

What can you do if your anger is affecting your ability to appropriately parent your children? While there are no magical solutions for overcoming difficult emotions, being aware of how your feelings affect your behavior and your relationships is the first step in avoiding the corrosive consequences of anger. You can then make a commitment to finding more-constructive ways of dealing with stress and conflict.

THE IMPACT ON YOUR CHILDREN

You need to be aware of the detrimental impact your anger can have on your children who, having already endured the disruption of divorce, desperately want and need security in their lives. Children can become disillusioned and depressed when anger and arguments between their parents cannot be resolved even after a divorce. The stress of dealing with the unending cycle of conflict between their parents can cause children to regress in development, become clingy or withdrawn, act out by throwing temper tantrums, develop problems in school, or develop long-term emotional and behavioral problems.

While no parent wants to inflict this type of emotional distress on a child, parents often unwittingly do so when they don't think about the consequences of their behavior. Parents must make the best interests of their children more of a priority than their own anger.

PARENTING CONFLICTS

A common source of tension in divorced families can be caused by the differing rules and parenting styles of the parents. It can be very difficult and confusing for children to adjust to two different sets of rules and expectations for each parent's household. To make life easier for the children, parents should make an attempt to "parallel parent" by establishing a parenting plan in which each parent equally participates in their children's extracurricular activities, helps with schoolwork, etc. Preferably, the parallel parenting plan should be agreed to before the divorce.

While parents should always do their best to put their differences aside for the welfare of their children, agreements about parenting don't always happen in spite of their best efforts. In an especially high-conflict divorce, anger toward an ex-spouse is typically expressed in relation to the children. Oftentimes, a parent's anger will take the form of criticizing an ex-spouse's parenting abilities and choices as well as blaming the other parent for their children's problems. In turn, this behavior usually provokes an angry reaction on the part of the other parent, prompting a counterattack, thereby perpetuating the vicious cycle of anger and conflict.

The most common complaints relate to children's bedtimes, when and what the children are fed, the types of activities the children are involved in, and how the children are disciplined. Rather than automatically reacting defensively to these complaints, a better approach would be to at least consider if maybe any complaint along these lines has some validity. For example, if a problem relates to the children's bedtimes, you may want to consider if the children are in fact getting a reasonable amount of sleep. Make the needs of the children the primary focus of attention.

When the criticism is baseless, however, you may be tempted to make a defensive emotional reaction, but that will only put your children in the middle of the conflict. Ignoring baseless criticisms and attacks may be the best option, but you should also make the effort to communicate with your children about the issue. Taking into consideration your children's thoughts and feelings will help them feel more empowered and secure while helping you to make better parental decisions.

LETTING GO OF ANGER

Check yourself. Each parent needs to look inward and make the effort to improve communication with their children as well as the other parent. Of course, you cannot control your ex-spouse's behavior. You may not even be able to control the fact you're angry, but you can control your behavior and how you choose to respond to your anger. Letting go of your grievances and forgiving your ex-spouse will make a world of difference in how effective your coparenting relationship will be after the divorce.

Here are some rules of thumb to help relieve your anger, reduce conflict with your ex-spouse, and be a better parent to your children.

- *Don't blame or get into control battles with your ex-spouse.*
- *Don't put down your ex in front of your children.*
- *Don't argue with your ex in front of your children.*
- *Do forgive your ex.*
- *Do take responsibility for your own feelings and behavior.*
- *Do make the best interests of your children your main priority.*

Divorce and its aftermath can be stressful for anyone, so don't be afraid to reach out to others for help. If you find you are unable to manage your anger on your own, consider counseling or parenting classes to help you deal with your emotions more effectively. Family, friends, and divorce/parenting support groups can also be of great assistance when you are feeling overwhelmed. Putting the effort into letting go of your anger will make you not only a better parent but also a much happier person.

Chapter 11:

TIPS FOR THE STEPPARENT

Getting married is one of life's most exciting and joyful experiences. The beginning of a marriage is typically a time of positive expectations for the future. However, when there are stepchildren involved, the situation can become a little more complicated. While being a stepparent can be both anxiety provoking and challenging at times, there are strategies stepparents can take to create healthy relationships with their stepchildren as well as decrease stress and tension, making family life a lot easier for everyone.

All the adults in this situation should be sensitive to how difficult this new family transition will likely be for the children. A parent's remarriage and all the life changes that go along with it are not developments most children would likely be excited about. After experiencing the disruption of divorce, they are faced with another significant life change, a new parent who will likely cause children to feel uncertain about what their new lives will be like and how the situation will effect relationships with their natural parents. Additionally, having to get along with any new stepsiblings they may not know well or may not even like can be an additional source of negativity and conflict.

BEFORE YOU GET MARRIED

While you and your partner may be filled with passion and optimism about the future of your new relationship, if there are children involved, it is a good idea not to rush into marriage, especially before an in-depth conversation about raising kids. It's best to wait two or more years after a divorce to remarry to give the children time to adjust to life changes more gradually. Preparing a stepparenting strategy before walking down the aisle will likely make the adjustment easier for them.

Take the time to get to know your partner's children before you consider marriage, and don't expect them to fall in love with you overnight. Trying to force a bond with children too soon can backfire. Put the effort into getting to know your partner's children in "real life" daily situations rather than thinking that if you take them to an amusement park every weekend, they might like you better. The main goal is for everyone to get used to one another, so it's best to be realistic in your approach from the beginning so there won't be any upsetting surprises down the road.

Before you get married, you and your partner need to discuss and come to an agreement on a coparenting strategy. As time goes on, if any problems arise, you can make adjustments to your parenting styles before you get married. This should make the transition smoother, and the kids won't become shocked and angry about sudden changes. You may also want to request to see your partner's written divorce and custody agreement. Understand that your spouse's family obligations will be yours as well.

AFTER YOU GET MARRIED

If you put the effort into laying a solid foundation with your future stepchildren before getting married, things shouldn't change significantly after marriage. However, as is the case with all families, your blended family will always be a work in progress, and you should accept the fact that there will be ups and downs in your relationships with the children.

As a general rule, in stepparenting situations, the biological parent should remain the primary disciplinarian until the stepparent has developed solid bonds with the kids. Even then, it may be best for the stepparent to play the role of adult counselor to the children rather than their disciplinarian.

It is also a good idea to create a list of family rules so everyone knows what is expected of them and the kids don't end up feeling as though they are being treated unfairly. Discuss the rules with the children and post them in a prominent place. If it's at all possible, try not to make abrupt changes to what the children are accustomed to, and attempt to keep the rules fairly consistent with what is expected of them at their other parent's residence.

Be prepared for change. As the children grow older, their wants, needs, and relationships will grow and change as well. You need to know what to expect from children of different ages to accommodate their changing needs. Children under ten are often more accepting of a stepparent because they have so many needs to be fulfilled. Adolescents between ten and fourteen may take longer to grow accustomed to a new adult in a disciplinarian role. Kids that age may not be as emotionally demonstrative as younger children, but they may be just as sensitive when it comes to needing love, support, discipline, and attention. Children fifteen and older tend to have less interest in family involvement and can sometimes be hostile toward parental authority, but they still need to feel loved and secure in their family too.

FAMILY COMMUNICATION

Communication is essential for any relationship, but it is especially important for stepparents because of the complications related to blended families. You and your spouse need to be on the same page about the children, so any disagreements related to the kids should be discussed and sorted out in private. You and your spouse need to be a united front in the eyes of the children.

Express to the children that you care about them, but let them know you are not trying to be a substitute for their biological parents. Allow the children to decide what they wish to call you, and make it a point of asking them for their input about your relationship with them. You'll be well aware of the problem of competing with the other parents, so it may be a good idea to have a discussion with your partner's ex-spouse to reassure him or her that while you want to love and care for the children, you don't intend to be a parental "replacement."

Given compassionate guidance and support, your stepchildren should gradually adjust to their new family. But remember, it is your responsibility to put the effort into meeting their needs, communicating openly, and allowing them the time to make a successful transition.

Chapter 12:

USING TECHNOLOGY TO STAY ORGANIZED

All parents know that raising children is often challenging. However, when parents are separated or divorced, many obstacles to communication can make parenting even more difficult. Tension and disagreements tend to make parents want to avoid interacting with one another, and keeping track of parenting time schedules and other details related to their children's lives can become a dizzying, stressful task for divorced parents.

For low-tech parents, one way to handle organizing the confusing mess that is a parenting plan is to buy two calendar organizers from an office supply store or Walgreens and a pink and blue highlighter. For an entire year in advance, color in nights with the mother in pink and nights with the father in blue. If there are no conflicts between the parents' understandings, make another version for the other parent.

High-tech parents can utilize a variety of online tools to get and stay organized. Many of these applications include scheduling calendars, messaging, tracking expenses, and other information related to the children. Pricing may vary over time.

POPULAR SCHEDULING APPLICATIONS

A variety of websites offer online and downloadable scheduling calendar software along with features divorced parents may find helpful.

- **OurFamilyWizard.com:** $99 per year/$179 for two years for each parent with free accounts for children. The main feature of this site is the parenting schedule calendar that can preschedule events up to three years in advance. Scheduling conflicts and schedule change requests are highlighted with exclamation marks. A great advantage of this program is the scheduling calendar's color-coding feature. To avoid any confusion, highlight the dad's parenting time in blue and the mom's in pink. Other handy applications on this site include:

  o a message board so parents can communicate with each other in a confidential forum the children can't see.
  o an option to be notified by email or text message when new information has been added to the site, for example, a scheduling change or health information update.

o   an information bank that allows parents to upload information regarding school, health insurance, immunization records, and contact numbers.

o   an expense log that automatically tracks expenses entered for each child, calculating each parent's share of the expenses while at the same time allowing the other parent to approve or disapprove of each expense.

o   security protections and encryption to protect personal data.

- **JointParents.com:** $9.95 per month/$99.50 per year for each parent with two free months. While a little less user-friendly than OurFamilyWizard.com, this site also has a scheduling calendar feature with the same convenient color codes as well as an expense log. One of the best advantages of this site is that it has a section for "virtual visitations" through the use of a webcam. Other helpful options include:

o   pages for photo albums, most frequent drop-off and pick-up locations, daily routine, contacts, and medical information.

o   a homepage containing an overview of all the pages, including a list of events for that day and upcoming events, log-in history of all users, updates for the last two weeks, and expense allocations for both parents.

o   a tool that calculates the number of nights each parent spends with the children.

- **ParentingTime.net:** $149.95 per year for each parent. This site also provides a scheduling calendar, messaging, and pages for important contacts, tasks, and file sharing as well as expense tracking. However, the best feature is an option that shows several charts tracking visitation totals for each parent, including the number of overnights and days spent with the children. This can be great evidence for court hearings about visitation disputes.

- **CustodyPlanner.com:** Free. While it does not offer expense or parenting time tracking, this simple, free online program allows parents to set up a scheduling calendar based on programmed custody rules and exceptions to those rules. The parenting time schedule as well as special events may be added to the calendar as well as messages and photos.

- **CustodyXChange.com:** $150–$400 for the software depending upon the version with a thirty-day free trial. This downloadable software program is simpler to use than OurFamilyWizard.com and JointParents.com, but it doesn't include messaging, expense tracking, or pages for information such as health insurance, school contacts, etc. However, the scheduling calendar automatically calculates the percentage of overnights for each parent and allows parents to include common parenting provisions.

- **SharedGroundonline.com:** $14.95 per month for the software with a free trial. With a user-friendly wizard to guide you through the family database setup, this downloadable program offers only a scheduling calendar. Each parent and child is given a color code, and parents can enter parenting time, school, vacation, and holiday schedules for each child. The program can show the percent of time each parent spends with the children, but the best feature is sample parenting plans that parents can use as templates to create their own.

- **CustodyToolBox.com:** $14.95 per month for the software with a fifteen-day free trial. This software program is used primarily for the parenting time scheduling calendar, but it also includes pages for an address book, to-do list, journal, minimal expense log, and mileage log.

OTHER HELPFUL TOOLS

- **Google.com** calendar has a simple function that can be used for parenting time scheduling.
- **Meetways.com** is a helpful tool if parents want to find a meeting place halfway between two points where they can meet to pick up or drop off the children.
- **Webcams** for virtual visitations work well for parents who travel or live far away from the other parent. Skype is the most popular.
- **Scanners** allow parents access to children's homework, report cards, artwork, and other documents.

Online parenting tools can be so effective in assisting divorced parents with their children that some courts order parents to use them. However, any parent can take advantage of the benefits these technologies offer to make life a little less hectic.

Chapter 13:

HOW EQUAL PARENTING TIME CAN WORK WELL

Some states' judicial systems presume that parents should be awarded equal parenting time. This is not the case in Tennessee, where no rule that says parents in Tennessee have a right to equal time. Family law judges and lawyers in our state believe that the only way equal parenting time works is if both parents agree and are committed to working together. Equal parenting time is often called "50/50 time" or "182.5 plans," referencing exactly one half of 365 days a year. "Shared parenting" is a vague term. Some may refer to "shared parenting" as precisely equal parenting time and others roughly equal time. Still others may mean coparenting in the sense that the parents share decision making. Here are some practical tips for parents sincerely committed to sharing parenting time equally.

A parenting plan is generally a document that contains the schedule of when the child will be with each parent and how child rearing decisions are to be made. The parenting plan may be developed solely by the parents. In some instances, it is created under the supervision of a mediator or a judge. A wealth of research has shown that the presence of specific qualities or factors aid significantly in joint-custody and shared-parenting arrangements. Those factors include families in which the parents are mature and insightful and have the ability to provide warm, compassionate, and responsive parenting. Such parents are committed to their shared-parenting plan and put the needs of the child before their own needs and emotions.

While not all these factors can be easily changed or are readily available in all circumstances, the chances of a shared-parenting plan's success are much better when they are present. Some the factors that can be changed are discussed below. These factors are also some of the most essential and critical to a shared-parenting plan.

A STRONG COMMITMENT TO A WORKABLE PLAN

Creating a very thorough, common-sense parenting plan is a significant investment of time, but it can be well worth the effort and will pay dividends with less conflict and a better environment for raising coparenting children. Both parents need to buy in to the plan and be ready and able to implement it and stick with it. A detailed, manageable parenting plan will promote consistency in the child's school life, friendships, and family relations. This helps the child with his or her confidence, integrity, and sense of stability.

TRUST AND COOPERATION BETWEEN THE PARENTS

Having trust in the other parent can go a long way toward establishing a pleasant working relationship. Both parents need to trust that the child is safe and well looked after when in the other parent's care.

Give your ex the benefit of the doubt, and remember that the best interests of your child is paramount. Try to take your emotions out of the mix, and don't allow any ill feelings toward your ex to factor into your negotiation and creation of the parenting plan.

Also, don't interfere with the other parent's time with your child or make a change without prior approval. Remember, a parenting plan is your team's playbook—it's what you will use to "win."

FLEXIBILITY

This quality goes hand in hand with trust and cooperation. Don't see everything in black and white—don't sweat the small stuff, and have some patience. Kids have crazy schedules, so don't call "foul" on something that is minor and can't be helped, like the other parent getting stuck in traffic or forgetting that a dentist appointment was *this* Monday. Build into your plan some buffer time, and work together to make sure you and your ex are doing the best thing for your child. If the schedule is one week on and one week off, understand that sometimes things happen beyond anyone's control.

PLAYING "NICE"

Reduce or eliminate the fighting and bad blood between you and the other parent. Parents who are angry, uncommunicative, and emotional with each other do nothing to help their child and his or her sense of security and self-worth. A child surrounded by negativity and parents who are constantly fighting has less ability and opportunity to thrive, be happy, content, and feel comfortable in either parent's household. Don't undermine the child's relationship with the other parent, and don't undermine the other parent's authority and parenting ability with the child.

These rules need to extend to the parent's relatives and friends—children should not hear negative comments from anyone in your circle about their other parent.

HEALTHY COMMUNICATION

Perhaps the most important and crucial component of a shared parenting plan is good communication. The communication must be positive—no email rants or screaming phone calls. Strip the emotion from this plan, and make sure you're working in concert with each other. For example, parents should copy the other parent on all email communications with teachers, health care workers, and other kids' parents. Make sure that your children do their homework even when they are moving from one house to the other. Long-term projects such as quarterly science fair projects or term papers should never be left to one parent to supervise unless that parent asks for the responsibility.

This healthy communication should also involve the child. Make sure the child has regular, meaningful contact with the other parent such as phone conversations and emails. Just because the child is with one parent doesn't mean he or she should be closed off from the other. Never be negative about the other parent when speaking to your child. Show him or her that you have respect for your ex and that the parenting is still being done by a team, not two separate players.

Several critical questions should be addressed with your ex-spouse prior to attempting to craft an equal time parenting plan. A successful and manageable parenting plan works with the schedules of the parents and takes into account the needs and activities of the children. For example, a very important factor is the amount of flexibility available in the parents' schedules. Others include,

- The child's age and maturity level
- The child's personality
- Whether there are special needs involved with the parents or child
- The logistics of the parents' homes and whether there will be regular, frequent contact
- Whether after-school care is required
- The significance of the child's and parents' cultural and religious practices
- The handling of school vacations and holidays
- Coordinating similar routines for mealtime, bedtime, and homework
- Comparable rules and discipline

Parental responsibilities must be defined and agreed upon in a 50/50 parenting plan. This must include support for the child's relationship with the other parent. A positive experience and relationship with both parents will enhance a child's emotional and social development, scholastic success, and overall upbringing.

Chapter 14:

AVOIDING DIFFICULT HOLIDAY PARENTING SITUATIONS

Imagine this scenario—it's Christmas, you're recently divorced, and your ex shows up to take the children for the holiday. You argue in front of the children—never a good thing to do at any time—that you already have plans for the kids and that those plans don't include your former spouse. Your ex leaves in a huff, the children are upset, you're upset, and the feelings linger for most of the holiday.

Another household has a similar scenario except that instead of giving in, the noncustodial parent tries to find a judge to hear the case that day. There are no judges available on Christmas, but the courts will be flooded with applications on the following business day by parents who believe they were unfairly deprived of time with their children. As a result, the custodial parent will soon be back in court.

How can you avoid these scenarios? The best answer is to plan ahead and to get your holiday schedule squared away in advance.

SCHEDULE YOUR HOLIDAY VISITATION NOW

Visitation in Tennessee is referred to as "parenting time" or "residential time." The word "visitation" is not a legal term but signifies what the average person understands to be his or her rights to be with the children following a divorce.

Courts now require use of a permanent parenting plan when there are children involved. It is not sufficient for the parenting plan to contain a general clause such as "visitation as the parties shall agree" or "reasonable visitation." The parenting plan must spell out the exact terms of parenting time for each parent. Your family lawyer can help you prepare the parenting-plan form. The goal is to get the best plan for your children while trying to protect your own rights as much as possible. The courts, however, are more concerned with what is in the best interests of the children.

WHY DO COURTS REQUIRE PARENTING PLANS?

Under Tennessee law, both parents are generally entitled to enjoy the maximum participation in their children's lives as long as it is in the children's best interests and there are no other factors present such as domestic violence or orders of protection. The goal of this law is to try to allow for equal parenting time in many cases. In some cases, the best interests of the children will not permit equal parenting time, but many cases will indeed permit parenting time that is as equal as practicable to the other parent's time.

It is crucial for parents to spell out their parenting time to prevent the scenarios mentioned above. While it's bad enough for former spouses to fight about parenting time, the children feel it even more. Open-ended or unscheduled parenting time hurts them and has the potential to ruin everyone's plans. This is especially so with holiday parenting time. However, if the holiday parenting time is spelled out, there will be no second-guessing who has the children on any particular day.

WHAT DO COURTS REQUIRE IN PARENTING PLANS?

While the parenting plan lists the most important holidays, with the parents often alternating years for each holiday, it is noteworthy that the Christmas holiday or winter vacation is listed as a separate entry. This particular holiday time is so important and one of the most litigated issues of parenting time that it deserves its own paragraph.

In the form, parents are allowed to choose when they will have the children during the holidays. Many times, divorcing parents may choose to split the holidays so one parent has the children for Christmas Eve until Christmas morning, and the other parent picks up the children midday on Christmas.

Another possible division of the holiday is for one parent to have Christmas Eve and Christmas Day one year while the other parent has both holidays the following year. Still another possibility is splitting the week of winter vacation in a way that will benefit the children and will be logistically sound for the parents.

IS THERE AN IDEAL HOLIDAY PARENTING PLAN?

No matter how the holidays—Christmas, Chanukah, or Kwanzaa—are split, it's unlikely that everyone is going to be a hundred percent happy. What works for one family may not work for another. There's no easy answer for splitting the holiday time. Whether you have to do drop-off or pick-up on Christmas Day or wait until the following year to be with your children on the holiday, there is no solution that works every time for everyone.

A parenting plan could provide for one parent to get parenting time with the children for both Christmas Eve and Christmas Day while the other parent gets the children for the rest of the winter vacation, including New Year's. However it is arranged, the idea is to get the holiday parenting schedule in writing so everyone knows with whom the children are supposed to be at any time. The key here is compromise.

Holiday time following a divorce can be difficult enough, and it will get only more difficult if you try to negotiate with a difficult ex on the spot. It's better to be prepared by arranging the schedule in advance even if it's not an ideal arrangement. The parenting plan will avoid many confrontations between you and your ex over where the children will be.

WHAT CAN PARENTS AND CHILDREN EXPECT DURING HOLIDAYS AFTER A DIVORCE?

The first year after a divorce is usually a difficult time for everyone. The children may refuse to go with the other parent, and that can make it difficult for that parent, especially the first time. Pick-ups and drop-offs could be a source of friction. You may want to have someone else present during pick-ups and drop-offs during this time to alleviate any source of tension.

Getting through the holidays after your divorce can be stressful, but the following tips can help you and your children enjoy the holidays even though the holidays will not be the same as before the divorce.

GETTING THROUGH THE HOLIDAYS

Among the hundreds of tips that can help divorcing parents and children survive the holidays are:

- Prepare for resistant children who will not want to go with the other parent. When a parenting plan goes into effect, you will have to ensure the children get into the other parent's car even if they cry and beg not to. Assure the children that they will have a wonderful time and that you have exciting things planned for them when they come back. This way, they will not feel they're missing out on something with you.

- Give the children something of yours so they can feel a connection to you if they're with the other parent during the holidays. It could be something like your scarf, a handkerchief, or better yet, a photo of you.

- Try to discuss gift-giving with your ex. The "one-upping" in gift giving is disastrous to children and parents because the children get more than they should and you will feel as if you always have to compete. Keep the gifts simple if possible. If the children are used to getting big gifts, perhaps the children can get two smaller gifts that will make them smile just as much as before.

- Try to keep old traditions in place. If that isn't possible because of the new schedule, come up with new traditions, such as opening presents under the tree on another day, or lighting Chanukah candles on a different night. Why not have special foods or traditions associated with the holiday ready for the children when they get back?

- Try to use the holidays to teach valuable lessons to your children, such as giving to people who are less fortunate. It may divert their attention from their own situation.

- Let the children feel involved in the holiday and not that everything is preplanned for them. Give them some tasks to make them feel their input is important. Let them come up with some ideas for celebrating.

- Explain to the children that they now get to celebrate the holiday twice if that's what the parenting plan provides.

- Don't bad-mouth your ex. Children should have two loving parents even if the parents are not together. The children will not love you any less if they still love the other parent. Allow the children to contact the other parent by phone, text, or email. If the other parent is doing a masterful job of bad-mouthing you, you may want to discuss this with your family lawyer.

- Be available for your children. They are going through a difficult time. Make sure you let them know you understand and are there for them. Let them tell you how they feel if they want to, and be sure to listen.

- If you are without the children for the holiday, make sure you have alternate plans. Be with family, friends, or both. Don't be alone if at all possible unless you really want the time to yourself. If so, enjoy it! Go to a movie or a concert. Read. Listen to music. Enjoy a long walk or a quiet bath.

With the right frame of mind and some good planning, you and your children will enjoy the holidays and look forward to celebrating them again next year.

Chapter 15:

COUNTING PARENTING DAYS

Lynn Massey, the senior paralegal at Miles Mason Family Law Group, PLC, has over twenty-five years of experience in the legal profession, particularly in the family law area.

Lynn has extensive experience drafting permanent parenting plans, and what follows is the Lynn Massey method of calculating parenting days. It is based on determining the parenting days in any year for the alternate residential (or noncustodial parent) (ARP) and subtracting that number from 365 to determine the parenting days for the primary residential parent (PRP).

A "day" is, in most cases, an "overnight." In most situations, if the child spends three hours with the parent, say from 5:30 to 8:30 on Wednesday evenings, that's not counted as a parenting day for child support calculation purposes.

Rule 1240-2-4-.02(10) of the Tennessee Child Support Guidelines defines "Days" as follows:

> A "day" of parenting time occurs when the child spends more than twelve (12) consecutive hours in a twenty-four (24) hour period under the care, control or direct supervision of one parent or caretaker. The twenty-four (24) hour period need not be the same as a twenty-four (24) hour calendar day. Accordingly, a "day" of parenting time may encompass either an overnight period or a daytime period, or a combination thereof.

Although technically, one could count a "day" as the child spending greater than twelve hours with a parent during the daylight hours (for example, 7:00 in the morning until 7:30 that evening), in the vast majority of situations, a child has to spend overnight with a parent for it to count as a "day." However, there are some variations on this rule. See "Extraordinary Circumstances Exception" below.

A. Counting Days

1. Determine Day-to-Day Schedule Parenting Days

Determine day-to-day parenting time without factoring in holidays and special occasions. For example:

- If the ARP has parenting time every other weekend from Friday night until Sunday night, that counts as 2 parenting days every 26 weeks, or 52 parenting days.

- If the ARP has 3 parenting days out of every 9 days, that would be 365 ÷ 9, or 40.56 9-day periods, multiplied by 3 parenting days for each 9-day period, 121.67 days total for the year.

2. Determine Holiday/Special-Occasion Parenting Time

The Permanent Parenting Plan lists certain specific holidays and special occasions:

New Year's Day
Martin Luther King Day
Presidents' Day
Easter Day
Passover Day
Mother's Day
Memorial Day
Father's Day
July 4
Labor Day
Halloween
Thanksgiving
Children's Birthdays
Other School-Free Days
Mother's Birthday
Father's Birthday
Fall Vacation
Winter Vacation
Spring Vacation
Summer Vacation

Count parenting days for each of the above holidays and special occasions, and follow these guidelines:

- If the child does not stay overnight or greater than 12 hours with the parent, it does not count as a parenting day. Therefore, if the child spends 3 hours on Thanksgiving Day with the ARP and then goes home to the PRP, that does not count as a parenting day for the ARP.

- If the ARP has a specific holiday only every other year, count each parenting day as half of a parenting day. For example, if the ARP has Martin Luther King Day every other year, that is half a parenting day.

- Check the children's school calendar to determine how many days the children have off for fall, winter, spring, and summer vacations and other holidays. Fall and spring vacations are usually 7 days each.

- The entire winter vacation is generally around 18 days. If the first part and second part of winter vacation alternates from year to year, it does not matter that some years the ARP gets fewer days than other years, because the average will be half of 18 days, or 9 days.

- Summer Vacation is 10 weeks for many schools.

- If the parents share a holiday and there is no overnight, that does not count as a parenting day. For example, the parents may agree that each will have parenting time with the child on the child's birthday, or one parent will take the child trick-or-treating on Halloween one year, the other parent the next year.

3.   Determine Overlap between Day-to-Day Schedule Parenting Time and Holiday/Special-Occasion Parenting Time

- If New Year's Day falls within the winter vacation, it does not count as a parenting day.

- If Memorial Day, July 4, or Labor Day *always* fall within the ARP's summer vacation time, these holidays don't count as parenting days.

- If Father's Day, Mother's Day, father's birthday, mother's birthday, or child's birthday *always* fall within a specific holiday or the day-to-day schedule, these special occasions are not counted as a parenting day. For example, if the ARP's birthday is June 15 and the ARP always gets the first month in summer, that does not count as a parenting day.

- If fall, winter, spring, or summer vacation overlap with the day-to-day schedule, deduct those days from the day-to-day schedule. For example, there are usually 3 weekends during winter vacation. If normally, one of those weekends would be part of the day-to-day schedule (in other words, the PRP has 2 parenting days every other weekend), subtract 2 parenting days from the day-to-day schedule.

Below is a sample chart showing how parenting time can be calculated:

ARP'S PARENTING TIME

Day-to-Day Schedule	2 days every other week (2 days x 26 weeks = 52 days) Less fall vacation overlap (one 2-day weekend every other year = 1 day) Less winter vacation overlap (one 2-day weekend every year = 2 days) Less spring vacation overlap (one 2-day weekend every other year = 1 day) Less summer vacation overlap (two 2-day weekends every year = 4 days) Net: 44 days	44
New Year's Day	None—overlap with winter vacation	0
Martin Luther King Day	1 day ÷ 2 (every other year)	0.5
Presidents' Day	1 day ÷ 2 (every other year)	0.5
Easter Day	No overnight	0
Passover Day	Not applicable	0
Mother's Day	1 day ÷ 2 (every other year)	0.5
Memorial Day	1 day ÷ 2 (every other year)	0.5
Father's Day	Every	1
July 4	Overlap with summer vacation (ARP gets every July)	0
Labor Day weekend	4 overnights (Friday evening to Monday morning)	4
Halloween	Shared—no overnight	0
Thanksgiving	2:30 p.m. – 8:30 p.m. every year—no overnight	0
Child's birthday	Shared	0
Other school-free days	Shared	0
Mother's birthday	None	0
Father's birthday	Every, but always falls within Labor Day weekend—ARP always gets Labor Day weekend	0
Fall vacation	Every other year (7 days ÷ 2 = 3.5 days)	3.5
Winter vacation	Half of holiday (18 days ÷ 2 = 9 days)	9
Spring vacation	Every other year (7 days ÷ 2 = 3.5 days)	3.5
Summer vacation	Every July	31
Total:		**98**

B.   Extraordinary Circumstances Exception: Partial Days

In certain situations, a "day" can be defined as other than a 12-hour period. Rule 1240-2-4-.04(7)(b)3 states:

> No more than one (1) day of credit for parenting time can be taken in any twenty-four (24) hour period, i.e., only one parent can take credit for parenting time in one twenty-four (24) hour period. **Except in extraordinary circumstances, as determined by the tribunal, partial days of parenting time that are not consistent with this definition shall not be considered a "day" under these Guidelines. An example of extraordinary circumstances would include a parenting situation where the ARP is scheduled to pick up the child after school three (3) or more days a week and keep the child until eight (8) o'clock p.m. This three (3) day period of routinely incurred parenting time of shorter duration may be cumulated as a single day for parenting time purposes.** [Emphasis added.]

In other words, if the ARP is *routinely* scheduled to spend a cumulative amount of time with the child in a week that exceeds 12 hours, even if those 12 hours are not all at one time, this cumulative total can be considered a "day," subject to the determination by the court that such is an "extraordinary circumstance."

C.   Calendar Method

Some courts require that the parenting days be marked out on a yearly calendar. In other words, every day the ARP is projected to have a parenting day during a one-year span is marked on the calendar, and the days are added up. To be more accurate, this should be done for a two-year span, especially because of alternating holidays. Although making a calendar is time consuming, it can be a more accurate calculation of parenting days.

Chapter 16:
PARENTING PLAN PROVISION CHECKLIST

In this chapter are permanent parenting plan optional provisions *not* included in the Tennessee standard parenting plan form. They have been collected from a variety of sources, including provisions required or suggested in other states' laws.

Few provisions can be considered "standard," but others can be tailored to address your particular situation. You may not want to add any of these clauses, or some may be opposite to what you wanted to happen in a given situation. They are provided here because parents generally like to know what is possible—like a menu.

Read through these sample clauses and let your lawyer know about which, if any, you have questions about or want to consider adding to your proposed parenting plan. Take this exercise very seriously. Many parents have found provisions in this chapter very valuable. Suggesting a provision to the other parent in a neutral manner can result in a mutually agreed upon parenting agreement regarding issues of great importance. Some parenting problems can be avoided just by setting ground rules early in the process before other routines are established.

Some clauses are provided in the alternative. Even though the same conduct may be addressed in more than one provision, subtle differences in application or tone may help a provision be accepted by the other parent rather than rejected outright. In addition, it is recommended that parents suggest provisions in terms that are neutral in effect, applying equally to both parents.

Some of the provisions are very restrictive and would not likely be ordered by a court or enforced by a court unless agreed upon by the parents. Some situations, however, may call for a much more restrictive provision. Sometimes, a parent can be overprotective concerning the activities of the other parent. Some of the simpler, less-restrictive provisions will never be agreed upon by some parents, while other parents may agree to very restrictive provisions. Parents never know until negotiations are over, so it is suggested that parents be flexible.

Remember that the term "custodial parent" has been replaced with "primary residential parent" and "visitation" has been replaced with either "parenting time" or "residential time" (except in Shelby County's Juvenile Court). Because some definitions can have different meanings to different judges and chancellors in different jurisdictions, ask questions concerning their meaning in the context of how they are used in your permanent parenting plan or appendix.

In addition, in what follows, you will see that certain words or terms such as "Parent" and "Nonprimary Residential Parent" are capitalized as these are words or terms that can be defined in legal documents such as Permanent Parenting Plans.

PARENTING RELATIONSHIP, LOVE, AND EMOTIONAL TIES

Neither Parent will "rewrite" or "rescript" facts the child knows to be different.

Neither Parent will punish the child physically or threaten such punishment to influence the child to adopt the Parent's negative program, if any, against the other Parent.

Each Parent shall refrain from discussing the conduct of the other Parent in the presence of the children except in laudatory or complimentary ways. Neither Parent will permit others to discuss the other Parent in the presence of the children except in laudatory or complimentary ways.

Parents should always avoid speaking negatively about the other and should firmly discourage such conduct by relatives or friends. The Parents should speak only in positive terms about the other Parent in the presence of the children. Each Parent should encourage the children to respect the other.

Neither Parent will trivialize or deny the existence of the other Parent to the child.

Neither party will make extravagant promises to minor children for the purposes of ingratiating himself or herself to them at the expense of the other party. Further, any reasonable promise to the children should be made with the full expectation of carrying it out.

Neither Parent shall threaten to withhold parenting time from the other for any reason.

Neither Parent shall threaten to prevent or delay the return of the children to the other Parent after a period of parenting time.

Both Parents shall, at all times, take all action necessary to promote the safety and well-being of the children, provide adequate care and supervision, mandate the use of seatbelts, and otherwise make the children's well-being and safety a paramount consideration at all times.

Both Parents will inform a future spouse of the provisions of this agreement and expect the new spouse to honor the terms of this Parenting Plan.

The Parents will acknowledge to the child that the child has two homes although the child may spend more time at one than the other.

The Parents shall cooperate to the greatest extent practicable in sharing time with the child.

Each Parent will permit the child to retain and allow easy access to correspondence, greeting cards, and other written materials received from the other Parent.

Each Parent will respect the physical integrity of items possessed by the child that depict the other Parent or remind the child of the other Parent.

Neither Parent will intercept, "lose," derail, "forget" or otherwise interfere with communications to the child from the other Parent.

The Primary Residential Parent shall provide the children with sufficient clothing and personal effects that may be required for the children's needs and comfort during each period of parenting time.

The parties will thoroughly discuss and consult with each other in regard to, and will be kept advised of, all decisions concerning the education, medical, and dental treatment, religious training, and dating of their children.

If a child becomes seriously ill or injured during the time he or she is with either Parent, that Parent shall notify the other as soon as possible. The other Parent shall be given the details of the illness or injury and the name and telephone number of the attending physicians, if any.

Neither Parent will remove the children from the jurisdiction of the court for more than one week without the written consent of the other party. If the Parents cannot agree, the removing Parent shall not remove the children without permission or leave of the court being granted. Such court permission may be granted only after notice to the other Parent, giving him or her opportunity for a hearing. If the Primary Residential Parent moves from the jurisdiction of this court, he or she will have the burden of showing that moving from the court's jurisdiction is in the best interests of the children. Violation of this section shall be deemed a change of circumstances sufficient to change status as Primary Residential Parent to the Parent who remains in this jurisdiction.

If either Parent plans to travel outside Shelby County, Tennessee, with the children for any period of time, that Parent shall notify the other Parent and provide him or her a telephone number before the trip.

 Either Parent may temporarily take the children to another state for vacation or for other good reason with reasonable notice to the other Parent. Reasonable notice is two weeks.

HOMEWORK, SCHOOL RECORDS, EXTRACURRICULAR ACTIVITIES, AND SCHEDULED EVENTS

All schoolwork for each child shall be saved and made available for review by the other Parent at the time the children are exchanged.

Parents shall provide adequate time for children to study and complete homework assignments even if the completion of work interferes with a Parent's plans for the children. Homework and studying come first.

Each Parent agrees to notify the other at least one week in advance of any special occasion or event for the minor children as to any religious, educational, or athletic event that shall include, without limitation, graduation, demonstration of acquired skills, recitals, or awards ceremonies. Each Parent shall have an equal right to attend these special occasions.

The Parent who receives a schedule of children's activities or other information regarding children's events will fax, mail, and/or email this information to the other Parent in a timely manner so the other Parent has the opportunity to plan for and attend those activities or events. This includes sports practices, games, scouting, music lessons, and performances of all kinds.

Regardless of where the children are residing, their continued participation in extracurricular activities, school-related or otherwise, should not be interrupted. The Parent with whom the children are residing shall be responsible for providing transportation to activities scheduled during residential time with that Parent. Each Parent shall provide the other Parent with notice of all extracurricular activities, complete with schedules, and the name, address, and telephone number of the activity leader if available.

The parties recognize that the children are involved in various extracurricular activities, including [*list activities such as t-ball and soccer*]. It is the Parents' desire that their children's lives be disrupted as little as possible by the divorce, so the Nonprimary Residential Parent will use best efforts to take the children to regularly scheduled extracurricular activities if they occur during that Parent's parenting time.

The Primary Residential Parent is responsible for providing the Nonprimary Residential Parent all of the school assignments and books.

Summer school that is necessary for a child must be attended, regardless of which Parent has the child during the summer school period.

The Parent who receives a child's report card will copy, fax, mail, or email it to the other Parent within twenty-four hours of receipt of the report card.

If grades are communicated by Internet, the Primary Residential Parent will communicate the Parent's log-in name and password to the other Parent so the other Parent may access all educational records online.

The parties will also discuss and be advised of a child's participation in driving, sports, or other dangerous activities.

PARAMOURS (BOYFRIENDS AND GIRLFRIENDS)

During the times the Mother and Father are exercising parenting time with their child, neither will have a member of the opposite sex who is not related by blood or marriage stay overnight.

Both Parents agree to a mutual consent injunction to the effect that neither party will allow adult members of the opposite sex who are not family members or to whom he or she is not married spend the night in the presence of or in the same residence of the minor children of the parties.

When a Parent is dating one person exclusively, the person the Parent is dating may spend the night with that Parent when the children are in that Parent's care provided that discretion is exercised.

Unless the Parent is formally engaged to a person, the Parent will not openly passionately kiss or otherwise act in a sexual manner with that person in the presence of the children. Further, that person shall not establish his or her primary residence with the Parent until such time as that person is married to the Parent.

PUNISHMENT

The Parents are to discuss the discipline of their children, and any corporal punishment is to be administered only by each Parent when the children are in his or her care and custody and not by a stepparent, paramour, or other child care person.

Neither Parent shall administer corporal punishment to the children.

PARENTING TIME LOCATION AND ENVIRONMENT

Parenting time shall take place in a suitable environment of each Parent's choosing.

Each Parent will permit the child to display photographs of the other Parent or both Parents in the child's room.

Each Parent will permit the child to carry gifts, toys, clothing, and other items belonging to the child with him or her to the residence of the other Parent or relatives or permit the child to take gifts, toys, clothing, and other items belonging to the child back to the residence of the other Parent, as the case may be, to facilitate the child having with him or her objects important to the child. The gifts, toys, clothing, and other items belonging to the child referred to here mean items that are reasonably transportable and do not include pets (if the Parents agree they are impractical to move about).

MEDICAL CARE, TREATMENTS

The Parents are also to advise each other concerning any medications or other "at home" medical treatment their children need.

The Nonprimary Residential Parent will be notified in advance of any prearranged medical or dental treatments, and in the event of an emergency, one Parent should notify the other as soon as possible.

COMMUNICATIONS

Both Parents shall keep the other party informed of his or her address and telephone number so either may call the children when the children are visiting or residing with the other Parent at reasonable intervals and at reasonable times. If either Parent takes the minor children out of town, he or she will notify the other Parent how to reach the children.

If a Parent plans to change his or her addresses, that Parent will notify the other in writing prior to the move with the new address and telephone number unless an order has been obtained from the court specifically exempting this requirement.

For all portions of this Permanent Parenting Plan, the definition of "telephone number" shall include, but is not limited to, land-based (traditional) telephone number, cellular phone number, child's cellular phone number (whether permanent or temporary), or any other voice communication method. For vacations or temporary residences for any reason, said numbers shall include contact numbers such as vacation rental homes.
Neither Parent shall deny the child reasonable use of a phone to call and receive calls from the other Parent and relatives.

Both Parents shall allow and encourage the children to maintain reasonable phone contact with the other party. Neither Parent shall withhold church attendance or phone conversations with the other Parent as a form of punishment.

RIGHT OF FIRST REFUSAL

When the children are with a Parent who cannot watch the children for any reason, the other Parent shall have first right of refusal for additional parenting time.

At any time in which a Parent plans to place the children in the care of a babysitter (including a friend, relative, or neighbor) without that Parent's presence for at least ten hours, the other Parent shall have the right of first refusal to care for the children during that time.

Grandparents may be asked to care for the children after the other Parent's right of first refusal has been offered and declined.

Prior to arranging for child care or babysitting of the children, each Parent will give the other the opportunity to perform such child care or babysitting services.

When it becomes necessary for a child to be cared for by a person other than a Parent or a family member, the Parent needing the child care shall first offer the other Parent the opportunity for additional parenting time. The other Parent is under no obligation to provide the child care. If the other Parent elects to provide this care, it shall be done at no cost.

If either Parent plans to be out of town while the children are scheduled to be in his or her care, that Parent shall provide a minimum notice of ten days to the Parent, who would then have the option of caring for the children. If during the time either Parent is out of town or a babysitter is required to be the sole guardian of the children for more than ten consecutive hours, the other Parent will be notified.

DEFINITION OF "FIRST WEEKEND"

The first weekend of the month is a weekend that includes both a Saturday and a Sunday.

The first weekend of the month is a weekend that includes Friday, Saturday, and Sunday.

SUMMER VACATION EXAMPLES

The Nonprimary Residential Parent shall have parenting time for five weeks, thirty-five days, each summer. Summer visitation shall be taken in increments of no greater than two weeks, fourteen days, or less than one week, seven days, unless otherwise agreed upon, and it shall not be extended because other parenting times fall within the chosen summer visitation weeks.

The Nonprimary Residential Parent shall give the Primary Residential Parent written notice of summer visitation plans between March 1 and April 1 each year. The Nonprimary Residential Parent has priority of choice of summer visitation dates if notice is given as required and unless the Residential Parent's vacation is an annual mandatory shutdown of the place of employment. If no notice is given by April 1, the Residential Parent has priority in the scheduling of any summer vacation plans, and the Nonprimary Residential Parent may choose only those weeks in which the Residential Parent is not scheduled to be out of town on vacation with the children.

The Residential Parent shall be entitled to up to two weeks for an actual vacation that shall not be interrupted by any conflicting visitation times. Each Parent shall provide the other Parent with destination, times of departure and arrival, and method of travel when taking the children outside the Parent's community.

DRUGS, ALCOHOL, SMOKING, GUNS, PORNOGRAPHY, CURSING, ANGER

Neither Parent will permit the child to be transported by a person who is intoxicated due to consumption of alcohol or illegal drugs.

If a Parent arrives to obtain the children for parenting time under the influence of alcohol or drugs, the visit may be considered forfeited on those grounds alone.

Neither Parent shall drink alcohol in the presence of the children.

Neither Parent may possess illegal drugs in his or her residence.

Neither Parent will drink alcoholic beverages openly in front of the children or allow others in their company to do so.

Neither party shall drive a vehicle with the children in it if he or she has drunk alcoholic beverages in the preceding eight hours.

Neither Parent will use tobacco products in the presence of the children or allow others in their company to do so.

Neither Parent will smoke tobacco materials inside structures or vehicles occupied at the time by the child.

Neither Parent will keep any firearms in their residence or allow others to do so.

Neither Parent will allow materials with adult content or of a sexually explicit nature where such materials are in any way accessible by the children. Should a Parent possess such materials, they will be locked up any time the children are in the home of or under the supervision of that Parent.

Neither Parent shall use foul language in front of the children.

In the event that any person exhibits abusive, angry, or violent behavior toward either of the children or the Parent, that person will no longer be allowed in the home with the children or to travel with the children.

TRANSPORTATION AND EXCHANGES

The Nonprimary Residential Parent has responsibility for transportation of the children to and from their home for residential time periods and may use another adult well known to the children for picking up or dropping off the children when necessary.

Any person transporting the children must not be under the influence of alcohol or drugs and must be a licensed, insured driver.

All child restraint and seat belt laws must be observed by the driver.
Car seats should be exchanged when required.

The Primary Residential Parent shall have the children ready for pick-up at the start of all residential time periods. The children and the Primary Residential Parent have no duty to wait for the Nonprimary Residential Parent to arrive for residential time more than thirty minutes unless notified. A Nonresidential Parent who arrives more than thirty minutes late without prior notification for a particular residential time forfeits that residential time unless the Primary Residential Parent agrees otherwise.

If the Nonprimary Residential Parent is more than one hour late for residential time, that residential time is forfeited.

The Nonprimary Residential Parent will not return the children early from parenting time unless the Parents agree to a different drop-off time in advance. The Primary Residential Parent or other adult well known to the children must be present when the children are returned from parenting time.

PARENTING TIME CONFLICTS

If the Nonprimary Residential Parent is unable to exercise his or her regular weekend parenting time, the parties must fully cooperate with each other in rearranging and rescheduling the parenting time so the parenting time may be made up.

If either Parent or child has plans that conflict with scheduled residential time and wishes to adjust that residential time, the parties should make arrangements for an adjustment acceptable to the schedules of everyone involved. Predetermined schedules are not written in stone, and both Parents should be flexible for the sake of the children.

Should the Nonprimary Residential Parent not exercise visitation as set out herein, that Parent shall notify the Primary Residential Parent (at least forty-eight hours before visitation) and pay such reasonable child care or babysitting expenses incurred.

Visitation arrangements and modifications will be worked out beforehand *between the Parents only* and without forcing the children to make choices and run the risk of parental displeasure. The children may be consulted only as it concerns their schedules.

Except in emergency situations, the Nonprimary Residential Parent must give at least twenty-four hours advance notice when canceling a visitation period.

If a Parent is unable to keep a scheduled parenting time, that Parent should give immediate notice to avoid subjecting the children to unnecessary apprehension and failure of expectations.

The Nonprimary Residential Parent shall advise the Primary Residential Parent as soon as possible if the Nonprimary Residential Parent is unable to keep a planned parenting time period with the children.

If parenting time does not occur through no fault of the Nonprimary Residential Parent, parenting time shall be arranged to be made up at a mutually convenient time.

OUT-OF-STATE RELOCATION

(Note: This provision may not be enforceable depending on the particular circumstances, applicable Tennessee law, and the particular judge's discretion.)

Both Parents agree not to relocate. The parental relocation law shall not apply. In the event the Primary Residential Parent seeks to move for any reason, the nonmoving Parent shall become the Primary Residential Parent.

Upon relocation of the children from the State of Tennessee, the Parents shall agree to a modified visitation schedule. If the Parents cannot agree, the Parent who is moving shall file a petition asking the court to modify the visitation schedule.

Both Parents are aware of their legal obligations pursuant to Tennessee's existing relocation law. If a Parent is relocating, both parties agree to comply with that law as the law requires as of the date of signing of this Permanent Parenting Plan by both parties in addition to complying with existing legal requirements at the time relocation is sought.

SUPPORT

Parenting time with the children shall not be withheld because of the nonpayment of child support. Child support shall not be withheld because of lack of parenting time.

"Good cause" exists so that the Nonprimary Residential Parent's income and wages are not assigned from the Nonprimary Residential Parent's wages.

CHILD SUPPORT INTEREST

Regarding interest on child support obligations, T.C.A. § 36-5-101(a)(5) reads in part as follows:

Any order for child support shall be a judgment entitled to be enforced as any other judgment of a court of this state and shall be entitled to full faith and credit in this state and in any other state. Such judgment shall not be subject to modification as to any time period or any amounts due prior to the date that an action for modification is filed and notice of the action has been mailed to the last known address of the opposing parties. **If the full amount of child support is not paid by the date upon which the ordered support is due, the unpaid amount is in arrears and shall become a judgment for the unpaid amounts and shall accrue interest from the date of the arrearage at the rate of twelve percent (12 percent) per annum.** All interest which accumulates on arrearages shall be considered child support. Computation of interest shall not be the responsibility of the clerk. (Emphasis added).

The Parents agree to share equally the cost of a midrange new or used motor vehicle for each child when that child turns sixteen and satisfactorily completes a driver safety course and further agrees to share equally the cost of insurance for that vehicle.

Adequate auto insurance for the children will be provided by *Father/Mother* with costs shared equally/pursuant to the child support worksheet's ratio of income. However, nothing herein shall require the Parents to provide auto insurance at an unusually increased cost of coverage if a child's driving record is such that there is reasonable cause to revoke the child's driving privileges.

The Nonprimary Residential Parent will pay an additional $_____ in August each year for school clothes for the children to the Primary Residential Parent.

Any payments made by either Parent at any time for any obligation under this agreement over and above the amounts required are not binding on that Parent. Any excess payments are not proof of or indication of the ability to make increased payments or of need for them. Any excess payments shall be credited to the amounts owed, and the party making the excess payments shall receive full credit for them even to the point of crediting them against money not yet due.

COLLEGE EDUCATION EXPENSES

Father/Mother shall pay/The parties will divide equally/according to the ratio of their incomes as determined by the Parent's previous year's income tax returns all college expenses of the parties' children until each child reaches age twenty-three or graduates from an accredited college, whichever occurs first. Said expenses include but are not limited to tuition, room, board, allowance, books, fees, and transportation to and from school. Any scholarships received will be credited against these expenses. The children must maintain a "C" or better average and be a full-time student making the normally scheduled progress toward a degree.

If a child fails to maintain the conditions required during majority, the payment shall cease for that child.

Father/Mother shall pay/The Parents will divide equally/according to the ratio of their incomes as determined by the previous year's income tax returns all listed college expenses of the parties' child until the child reaches age twenty-three or graduates with a bachelor's degree from an accredited college, whichever occurs first. Said expenses include but are not limited to tuition, room, board, and books.

Father's share of the expenses listed above are limited to and shall not exceed the equivalent costs listed or published for the same or similar education offered at the University of Tennessee at Knoxville for in-state students. If Father pays more than those equivalent costs for the University of Tennessee at Knoxville for in-state students in one year, he is not obligated to pay for those additional costs in any future year, and such excess payment shall be deemed a gift.

Any scholarships received will be credited against these expenses. The child must maintain a "C" or better average and be a full-time student making the normally scheduled progress for receiving a degree. If the child fails to maintain the conditions required during majority, this obligation shall cease for the child.

Father/Mother agrees and does hereby contract to pay one-half of the college education expenses for each child at a college or postsecondary school of Mother's choice. Father shall pay and does hereby contract that he shall reimburse Mother an amount equal to one half of the room, board, books, tuition, activity fees, and any and all other costs incident to the children's college matriculation.

Effective the year following the Parenting Plan, the Parents shall each contribute 3 percent of their gross annual earned income into one account to be jointly managed (and requiring both signatures for withdrawal) by the Parents for the children's college education. The Parents agree to each provide the other party copies of his or her federal income tax returns by October 31 of the year in which the return is due.

Each Parent agrees to make his or her respective contribution to the joint account by December 31 of each year. In the event that the money in the account is not completely used for college education, the money will be divided pro rata between the Parents based on contributions to the account upon the youngest child attaining age twenty-six. The Parents may also agree to invade the account in the event of any medical emergency expenses for a child.

Father/Mother agrees to bear all reasonable college expenses for the costs of a college education or a vocational education at the school or institution chosen by agreement of the Parents. Such education costs include expenses incurred by the children for tuition, fees, books, supplies, room and board, clothing, incidental living expenses, transportation to and from school, and any other expenses associated with the providing of a college or vocational education for said child.

It is the intent of the Parents that their children attend college if academically qualified, and both Parents agree to contribute thereto to the extent they are financially able to do so.

PRIVATE SCHOOL TUITION

Father shall pay/Mother shall pay/The Parents equally shall pay/The Parents shall pay in accordance with the ratio of their gross income as shown on the previous year's tax return all tuition and other expenses for the children to attend the private schools they are now attending and all reasonable successor institutions.

Father/Mother/The parties equally shall bear the expenses of private schools, should the need arise, for the benefit of the Parents' children. The selection of any private schooling shall be reasonable and appropriate and within the Nonprimary Residential Parent's financial ability to provide. The specific school selected shall be by mutual consent of the parties.

SPECIAL-EDUCATION OPPORTUNITIES

The Parents recognize that their children have special-educational needs and agree that where possible said needs will be met by reliance upon public sources such as public education. However, the parties also acknowledge that their children have special needs that may not be met by public sources such as camp, summer school, and tutoring. After Father and Mother consult on said special needs, Father/Mother agrees to pay the reasonable expenses of such reasonable and typical services as needed by their children.

The Parents agree to share equally the cost of a personal portable computer for each child suitable for that child's academic needs upon the child entering the ninth grade or at such time when the school program in which the child is enrolled requires such. The Parents agree to share equally the cost of an upgraded computer or laptop upon that child entering college.

OUT-OF-STATE PARENTING DETAILS

Father shall have the right to have parenting time as follows:

- Six weeks during each summer at a time to be selected by the Father, provided, however, that Father shall communicate by registered mail a written notice to the Mother of the dates of the intended visitation at least thirty days prior to such visitation.
- Each Christmas, beginning on December 26 at 9:00 a.m. and ending New Year's Day at 3:00 p.m.
- During the odd years, spring break vacation from 9:00 a.m. Saturday until the following Saturday at 6:00 p.m.
- During the even years, Thanksgiving vacation from 6:00 p.m. Wednesday until Sunday at 6:00 p.m.
- Any other reasonable times the Father is in the town in which the minor children reside. Father shall give forty-eight hours' notice, and the parenting time should be no longer than forty-eight hours.

During any periods of parenting time, after the children reach age twelve, the children may travel by commercial airliner, provided:

- The Father shall pay all air fares for the transportation of said children.
- The flights shall be either nonstop or direct, and no change of planes will be involved until the children reach age fourteen.
- All travel arrangements shall be made by the Father.
- The Father shall notify the Mother not less than ten days of the date of visitation, of the date, time, airline, and flight number of the proposed carrier.
- The Father shall send to the Mother the round-trip airline tickets or shall ensure they will be at the air terminal ready for said children at time of departure.
- The Mother shall be required to deliver the said children to the nearest commercial airport offering direct flight service to the airport at which the Father will receive the children, not to be in excess of 150 miles from Mother's residence. The Mother shall also pick up said children at the end of the parenting time.
- The Father shall ensure that either he or the children notifies the Mother of the arrival of the children as soon as possible after the children are met by the Father.
- At the end of the period of parenting time, the Father shall notify the Mother of the dates, time, carrier, and flight number of the children's return. The Father shall notify the Mother twenty-four hours prior to the time of departure.

- On the return of the children, the Mother shall ensure that either she or the children notify the Father of the children's return.
- Father shall enjoy the right of telephone contact or Skype each Thursday between the hours of 7:00 p.m. and 8:00 p.m. local time with the minor children at the Father's expense. The Mother shall neither interfere with nor listen in or be party to the telephone conversation or Skype conversation.

Chapter 17:

TIPS FOR WORKING OUT LONG-DISTANCE PARENTING PLANS

If you are the primary residential parent in Tennessee and the other is in another state, it's crucial that your Permanent Parenting Plan focuses on long-distance issues. The best way to achieve what is best for all parties, particularly the children, is through compromise. The travel agreements should take into account variables such as distance, type of travel involved, parents' job schedules, and the children's special needs, education, and activities.

There's no substitute for proper planning. Your lawyer will likely advise you to prepare for all situations that could arise in long-distance parenting. While no discussion of long-distance parenting can cover all scenarios, this overview will delve into many scenarios and how to address them before they happen. The purpose of the parenting plan is to use preventive maintenance before a situation gets out of control.

Depending on the circumstances, Tennessee can be generally liberal when it comes to parents and children relocating provided the primary parent is not moving for vindictive reasons. The primary parent must notify the other parent of the intended move if the move is outside the state or is more than fifty miles away in the state. The notice has to be given at least sixty days before the proposed relocation.

If you are the nonprimary parent and wish to challenge the move, you may file a petition with the court objecting to the relocation or even seeking to change who is designated as the primary parent, but you have to do so within thirty days of receiving the notice about relocating. Consult your lawyer so your challenge is done properly and in a timely fashion.

RESOLVING TRAVEL ISSUES BEFORE THEY BECOME PROBLEMATIC

One of the most important issues to include in a relocation parenting plan is how the children will travel—car, plane, bus, or train? Primary residential parents may not want their children going by plane alone, or distance may make driving infeasible. Discuss this with your lawyer, and make sure you have arguments ready if the other parent insists on a type of transportation to which you object. Consider your options, and search for a mutually agreeable travel companion for the children. Airlines will serve that function for young children or even teens flying alone, but both parents have to comply with the airline's rules. Carefully read the airline's policies and procedures for unaccompanied minors.

Which airport the children fly into could also be a consideration. One mother had the children fly into one airport because flights there were cheaper than the alternative, but the father had to drive several hours to and from that airport. This controversy could have been avoided by a specific mention about airports in the parenting plan.

A thorough parenting plan is a roadmap that contains instructions for travel, phone calls, and the length and dates of visits. It has to be followed unless both parties agree otherwise. If you want your children to fly without stopovers but that's not mentioned in the parenting plan, they could be changing planes, buses, or trains at the expense of your peace of mind.

The parenting plan should spell out how one parent notifies the other when the children arrive at the airport, train station—wherever. This could be through timely text messages, emails, or phones, but it should be mentioned in the parenting plan.

If you or your soon-to-be ex has issues with travel costs, this could call for some flexibility. Trains or buses may be an economical and safe alternative to planes for older children, for instance. One way or the other, agreeing up-front to transportation issues will go a long way toward preventing court battles about travel-expense matters.

If a relocation is from Tennessee to Kentucky, driving might be the best way to travel. But will the nonprimary parent do all the driving, or will it be shared? Such case-specific questions require both parties to be reasonable and perhaps split the driving duties, offer to spend make-up time with the children, or come up with a similar trade-off.

FIGURING OUT HOW MUCH PARENTING TIME IS FEASIBLE

One way to start designing a parenting plan is to consider how many days per year the nonprimary parent wants for parenting time. A lot may depend on questions of distance and method of travel. If, for example, you're two hours away rather than six, perhaps you would both be agreeable to more-frequent parenting time of shorter durations.

Determine how much parenting time you want if you're the nonprimary parent, factoring in transportation questions and factors. It's not in the children's best interests to do a lot of traveling because they need time to be with the primary parent, for extracurricular activities, and to be with friends. Parenting time will depend on work schedules, school schedules, distance, the feasibility of constant traveling during the year, and special traditions or occasions. Parents commonly alternate holidays, so one gets Thanksgiving with the kids while the other gets Christmas. A reasonable parenting time plan will take such factors into consideration, including long-distance travel.

One father measured in minutes how much time each parent had the children, and this was an example of micromanaging out of spite. Parenting times don't have to be equal, and in long-distance parenting plans, that probably won't be possible.

MAKE-UP PARENTING TIME AND FLEXIBILITY

What happens if the children get sick and can't go on a scheduled trip to Dad's? Does Dad lose out, or is there make-up time during the next holiday that would ordinarily be Mom's? It helps here to be flexible. Make-up time shouldn't be abused, but some of it may be a good idea depending on circumstances. Children need both parents, and parents ought to make such accommodations in fairness to all involved, even including them in the parenting plan.

While it's generally a good idea to specify how much advance notice is needed for unscheduled parenting time, sometimes this has to be worked out as you go along. With sufficient notice, both parents should show willingness to bend a bit.

DENIAL OF PARENTING TIME AND AN "OVERRIDE" OPTION

What if the primary residential parent says no to a proposed parenting schedule? The parenting plan may state that the parties need to go to mediation before going to court. Before someone resorts to mediation or the courts, he or she should consider whether the denial is reasonable. Is the child sick? Is the school holding a special event? Parenting time can be made up, so parents should deny parenting time only for valid reasons.

Make sure you honor your parenting plan unless something unforeseen or special comes up. If you're the nonprimary parent and the withholding of parenting time was unreasonable, talk to your lawyer about going to court to change the designation of primary residential parent.

Sometimes, the nonprimary parent will be unexpectedly in the area and want to see the children, but that may not afford the other parent enough time to rearrange his or her schedule. Some parents agree to an "override" provision, allowing parenting time at the last minute but only three or four times a year. This limitation can prevent abuse but at the same time encourage parenting time opportunities.

The primary parent should try not to withhold visitation with the children at such times due to little notice. The best practice is for each parent to allow unscheduled visitations if possible. Each parent should be able to spend some time with the children even if it's at the other parent's location as long as it's not being used in a spiteful way or is unmanageably frequent.

INCLUDING TIME OF DAY FOR TRAVEL AND WHAT TO DO IN THE EVENT OF A DELAY

Your lawyer will advise you spell out as much as possible in the parenting plan to avoid anger or trips to court. The plan may include what happens with delays due to a bad rush hour or work emergencies—perhaps prompt notification of one parent by the other, but never through the children. However you and your ex agree to communicate during a delay will probably be accepted by the court as long as the message gets to the other parent in a reasonable time.

SCHEDULING CONFLICTS, COMMUNICATION WITH CHILDREN, AND SPECIAL NEEDS

If the parenting plan does not discuss how scheduling conflicts are to be handled, the parents will have to come up with good compromises. No one can accurately prepare for every scenario that can come up in the years after a divorce. Again, the best way to deal with these unexpected issues is to be flexible and willing to swap out parenting time.

Parents should call each other at reasonable times but whenever necessary to find out or report where a child is. The parents must always know how to contact the children, and this should be in the plan. The children should be permitted to have undisturbed, private contact with the other parent by telephone.

A child who requires special care is entitled to get it from the residential and the nonresidential parent alike, which is easy if the parents are on the same page, but because medications or dosages may have changed, communication is critical.

A detailed roadmap of a parenting plan and flexibility will smooth the road ahead for divorcing parents and their children and keep them out of court. Only you know the reality of your situation, but your family lawyer can help you get the best parenting plan for the future.

Chapter 18:

WHO PAYS TRAVEL EXPENSES?

Tennessee law offers no set formula for payment of travel expenses for children in relocation cases, and such expenses can end up being a big bone of contention. Who pays? Can the costs be split? Should one pay more than the other or even all? Tennessee law offers very few guidelines.

Under Tennessee Child Support Guidelines entitled "Deviations from the Child Support Guidelines,"[1] if parenting time-related travel expenses are substantial because of distance, the court may order a deviation from the Presumptive Child Support Order. It may take into consideration the circumstances of the parties, which parent moved, which has the greater ability to pay, and the reason the move was made, but the guidelines don't require the court to award travel expenses.

The "Parent Relocation" section gives some mandates:[2]

> The court shall assess the costs of transporting the child for visitation and determine whether a deviation from child support guidelines should be considered in light of all factors including, but not limited to, additional costs incurred for transporting the child for visitation.

These two statutes are somewhat at odds with each other. One says the court may consider substantial costs of travel, while the other states that the court shall arrive at the transportation costs and determine whether to change the amount of child support based on these costs. The lawyers on both sides cannot be sure what the court will do when it comes to travel expenses.

One Tennessee case about travel-related expenses is Long v. Long, a 2008 Tennessee Court of Appeals decision. The father claimed he had relocated to Maryland without the children because the mother had been planning to move there with the children, but there was no proof of this. The father admitted part of his decision to move was because he wanted to be closer to his girlfriend. The father asked for a reduction of child support to offset his travel expenses for the children. The trial court denied his request and required him to pay all expenses.

The appeals court agreed with the trial court, following the language under the first statute above that said the court may order a change in child support. The appeals court found that the father had considerably more earning power than the mother and that the lower court correctly refused to lower the father's child support so that he was not given credit for travel expenses.

---

1   Rule 1240-2-4-.07(2)(c).
2   Section 36-6-108(b).

GETTING TIME OFF WORK AND KEEPING COSTS DOWN

The biggest problem of transporting children between exes is getting them to or picking them up from an airport or train station or driving them to and fro. One parent's inability to get time off work can cut down on visits with children unless the other parent does all the traveling.

The parents should agree to try to keep costs down even if the costs are paid by just one. Exes could use frequent-flier miles for this purpose. Keeping costs down will be the best thing for the children if this helps them visit more frequently.

Both parents should contribute to travel expenses if they can, which would allow both to be interested in keeping costs down.

MAKING SENSE OF THE STATUTES AND THE CASE LAW

Because the laws seem contradictory and because there is only one appeals case on the whole subject, it is not clear what a Tennessee court might do in any one case. The following arguments could be used, and it will depend on the court whether the arguments will be successful.

Scenario 1: Mom relocates with the children and cannot afford travel expenses.

The mother has relocated out of state or over 100 miles from the father with the children but cannot afford to pay for airfare or for driving the children. She asks for an increase in child support to pay for the additional travel expenses, but there's no guarantee a court would grant that. It might depend on how much the parents are earning and the reasons for relocating. Under the relocation statute, the court would consider all factors, such as additional costs of travel and other matters specific to her case, such as the needs of a special-needs child.

The father, on the other hand, may claim he can't afford these costs, or that the mother's move was unnecessary, or that she was making more than she claims. The court could order no increase in child support from the dad and order the mom to pay all travel expenses, or order partial payment from Dad, or order splitting the costs on a percentage basis, or order Dad to pay all of it. Here again, your family lawyer can help you figure out ways to navigate these matters.

Scenario 2: A nonresidential dad relocates without the children.

According to Long v. Long,[3] the reason a nonresidential father moves will be important, as will be his earning power. If a nonresidential father doesn't want to pay travel expenses, he will probably have to show a solid reason for the move and that perhaps the mother makes as much as he does or that she has other sources of income. The father will need assistance from a family lawyer, especially if he's earning more money.

---

3   M2006-02526-COA-R3-CV, 2008 WL 2649645 (Tenn. Ct. App. Jul. 3, 2008).

If he has a good reason for the move—he was offered a better job, for instance—that will be considered, and maybe the court would allow the costs to be split. However, since there's no set formula in Tennessee, the outcome could be anyone's guess. Having a good family lawyer is again crucial in this instance.

The mom in this scenario will want to point out that the dad could have gotten the same or a similar job in Tennessee and that the move was for his self-interest. She will also want to show that he can afford to at least split the costs if not pay them all.

Scenario 3: Mom relocates with the children out of spite.

If a mother relocates with the children out of spite, it can be argued that she would have to pay all the relocation costs no matter what her earning power is. The court will not look kindly on her putting distance between the children and their father. He, on the other hand, will want to establish that she relocated out of spite.

As you can imagine, there are thousands of different scenarios, so consult with a family lawyer for the best parenting plan for you and a strategy for dealing with travel costs. When parents work together on the logistics and the finances of travel expenses for visitation, the children will benefit, and that's the best result to shoot for.

Chapter 19:

TENNESSEE PARENT RELOCATION LAW

Tennessee family law requires divorcing parents to work together to come up with a permanent parenting plan. If the parents are unable to agree on a plan, they must go to mediation before going to court. This plan will include a residential schedule for the children, and it will also specify how parenting decisions will be made.

The parenting plan can have a big impact if one parent later decides to move with the children to another state (or a long distance away within Tennessee). Because the permanent parenting plan has such an impact on relocation, you should give the matter some thought if you believe relocation might ever become an issue for you. If you think you might want to move to another state with the children in the future, you should give some thought to preserving your rights to do so. If you believe the other parent might want to leave the state with the children against your wishes, there are some provisions you could suggest for the parenting plan that will make a move less likely.

The most important thing to know is that the rules governing parental relocation depend on whether the parents are spending "substantially equal time" with the children. In general, if both parents are spending substantially equal time with the children, it is more difficult for one parent to move the children if the other parent objects. Conversely, if the parents are not spending substantially equal time, it is easier for the primary residential parent to move with the children even if the other parent objects.

Therefore, if a court is called upon to decide whether a parent may move, it will first need to decide whether the parents have been spending substantially equal time with the children. In making this determination, the court will look at the *actual* amount of time the children spend with each parent. If the parenting plan called for a certain amount of time but the parents haven't been following the plan, the court will ignore the plan and base its decision on what the actual practice has been.

But the permanent parenting plan is legally enforceable, and if it calls for a certain amount of parenting time, either parent has the right to have the plan enforced. Therefore, to determine whether the time spent by the parents is substantially equal, the single most important document in the case will be the permanent parenting plan.

For this reason, if you think that parental relocation might become an issue in your case, you should give this issue some thought as you work on the permanent parenting plan. If you want to keep open the possibility of moving to another state, you will be in a much stronger position if the parenting plan does *not* call for parenting time to be substantially equal. If you want to make it less likely that the other parent can leave the state with the children, you should try to make the amounts of time in the parenting plan substantially equal.

The Tennessee courts have never given an exact definition of the words "substantially equal" other than to say that it does not need to be exactly equal. For example, in one case, a court found that a 57/43 split was substantially equal. But in another case, the same court held that a 60/40 split was not substantially equal.

It's also important to note that the court will look only at full days, and each day will be assigned to one parent. For example, if one parent spent eleven hours per day with the children every single day, that parent would probably not be credited with any individual day, and his or her percentage would be zero. On the other hand, if the same parent spent thirteen hours per day with the children for six months per year, that parent could be credited with 50 percent of the parenting time, even though the actual amount of time with the children was less than I the first example.

By keeping this in mind when you negotiate the permanent parenting plan, you can make your case stronger if the issue of parental relocation ever comes up. For example, if the other parent wants to spend large amounts of time with the children but you believe you might need to move to another state in the future, you can allow the other parent to have large blocks of time every day as long as you get credited with that day. For example, if the other parent has parenting time on a daily basis after school, he or she will be able to spend large amounts of time with the children, but as long as the children are living with you, you will get credit for each of those days. Therefore, the other parent may not successfully argue that his or her time was substantially equal. Discuss this with your family lawyer because partial days may be counted in certain circumstances.

On the other hand, if you want the option of more easily blocking a move by the other parent, you would be in a stronger position if you alternated weeks with the other parent rather than exercising your parenting time every day. You would get full credit for the seven days the children were with you, and you would be in a stronger position if you needed to claim your parenting time was substantially equal.

As discussed above, if a court is called upon to decide whether parenting time is substantially equal, it will base its decision on the *actual* amount of time rather than what the parenting plan specifies. Therefore, even if the other parent is not willing to "lock in" amounts of parenting time in the parenting plan, you would still be able to take advantage of any flexibility in the plan.

This is one area where a cooperative spirit can prove helpful. If the other parent is willing to depart from the plan perhaps because an emergency came up and he or she needs you to take over the parenting duties for a few days, those days will be credited to you if the issue of parental relocation ever arises.

REASONABLE PURPOSE FOR A MOVE

If the issue of parental relocation ever comes up, one key issue will be whether the move has a reasonable purpose. While it might not be possible to have a big impact, you should keep this in mind as you prepare the parenting plan. If you think you might need to oppose a future move, you should take a close look at the plan with this in mind. You should ask yourself whether there is anything in the plan that the other parent could point to and say that this would make it reasonable to move to another state.

Similarly, if you think you might need to move with the children, you should ask yourself whether there is anything in the plan that would make such a move unreasonable.

These issues might come into play if your children have special medical, educational, or social needs. If those needs are well addressed by the parenting plan, a court is more likely to say that a move is unreasonable. If those needs are not well addressed, the court is more likely to say that a move is reasonable.

If the issue of parental relocation arises in your family, it can lead to difficult decisions for everyone involved. It's not always possible to anticipate these issues at the time of a divorce. But if you give these issues some though when coming up with the permanent parenting plan, you can put yourself in a stronger position if they do need to be addressed.

For more information see, *Tennessee Parent Relocation Law* by Miles Mason, Sr., available on Amazon and Kindle.

Chapter 20:
ANTI-RELOCATION PROVISIONS

Divorce is frequently a very stressful, emotional, and painful experience, and it becomes even more so when children are involved. Divorcing couples in Tennessee create a parenting plan, a document that typically contains visitation schedules and how child rearing decisions will be made. The plan may be developed solely by the parents or in some instances under the supervision of a mediator or a judge, and it becomes an order of the court when approved. Some parties negotiate parenting plans that say the primary residential parent cannot relocate out of state or so many miles away with the children without the express written permission of the nonmoving parent. The legal question becomes whether the parents' agreement when properly recorded as part of a court order overrides or "trumps" the state's relocation statute.

As of 2013, Tennessee courts have not affirmatively stated whether an agreement of the parties will override the relocation statute. One argument that it does override state relocation law is that the parties agreed to it and the agreement was made a court order by the consent of the parties.

One argument that it does not is that the parties don't have the authority to change state law, even by agreement. The best interests of the children remain in the court's authority as long as the children are minors.

ANTI-MOVE PROVISIONS

Numerous states recognize "anti-move," "no-move," or "no-relocate" provisions. Some states have such provisions in their statutes, while others recognize them as binding contracts as part of divorce settlements or custody orders.

Anti-move language in divorce settlements or custody orders without a law in the jurisdiction is a little more fluid when it comes to enforcement. Whether the provision is enforceable and the effect of such a provision on a judge's decision to grant a residential parent's request to move out of state, or far away in state, depends on the judge and the jurisdiction.

Most states' relocation laws today deal with the notification of the nonresidential parent. Acceptable language states that each parent—or in some cases only the residential or custodial parent—is required to give the other parent reasonable notice before moving more than a specified number of miles away from that parent. Again, there are some variations with this language, especially if the term "reasonable notice" is used rather than a specific number of days, usually sixty or ninety. Also, the distance may be a certain number of miles, such as 100 or 200, or it may be moving out of state.

For instance, Arizona's statute requires the moving parent to give written notice to the other parent at least sixty days in advance of moving and permanently relocating a child. In Arizona, if the nonmoving parent objects, he or she can petition the court to prevent the move, and a hearing will be scheduled so the court can determine if the relocation is in the child's best interests. The court will typically forbid the move until the judge decides.

RATIONALE

The rationale behind the statutory language and that commonly used in divorce decrees and custody orders centers around the best interests of the child. The courts have some latitude in this matter, and some attorneys have pushed to have the terms altered to others more favorable to the parent who isn't moving. This includes reducing the geographic distance from 100 to 60 miles, preventing a child from being moved outside his or her current school district, or—a more arduous task—asking the moving parent to prove the move is in the child's best interests.

The time, expense, and stress of additional litigation are major considerations in these matters. If the relocation terms can be decided prior to the move, the issue is most likely to be dealt with in a more civilized and logical manner. Adding this provision promotes communication in advance of a move and, more important, can dissipate the anger and surprise that usually come up if a parent tries to conceal the move until the last minute.

Advance notice may also encourage the parents to calmly draft a new parenting plan. If so, the current arrangements would stay in effect until the issue or the parenting plan was settled.

A change in circumstances may be cause for an exception to the statute or provision. Divorce and second marriages are common, and a custodial or residential parent may remarry someone in another state and want to move there with the children. In many cases, permission will be granted by a court based on the rationale that the child will in some ways benefit from the custodial parent's new relationship and outlook. In addition, subsequent marriages might reflect a higher standard of living, which will also benefit the child.

SETTLEMENT PROVISION EXAMPLES

A few states permit the anti-move provisions in divorce actions or mention it in their statutes. Oregon's anti-move statute requires parents to give each other "reasonable" notice before moving more than sixty miles away from the other. Florida has a cutoff as to when laws went into effect. If parents were divorced before October 2006 with a settlement agreement that contains a relocation provision, this clause would continue to be in effect. If not, Florida law currently sets a radius of fifty miles from the parent's previous residence as the limit on how far the parent may relocate without consent of the nonresidential parent or the court.

North Carolina family law attorneys suggest including a relocation provision in settlement agreements and consent orders to prevent unnecessary litigation, and Texas is the same. Many California divorce judgments and marital settlement agreements contain similar language requiring the custodial parent to ask for the approval of the noncustodial parent or a judge for a move to a location far enough away to create a significant disruption in the noncustodial parent's visitation rights.

TENNESSEE AND ANTI-MOVE PROVISIONS

Unless the parents share roughly equal parenting time, Tennessee's relocation statute holds that if the parent wanting to move has had more time with the child, he or she will probably be allowed to move, but a new parenting plan will be needed. If parents have equal time with the child, the court will apply a "best-interest" test to determine if the child can relocate with the moving parent.

Section 36-6-108 of the Tennessee statutes says that if a parent wants to relocate outside the state or more than fifty miles from the other parent within the state, the relocating parent must give notice to the other sixty days before the move. The notice needs to contain a statement of the parent's intent to move, the location of the proposed new residence, reasons for the proposed relocation, and a statement that the other parent can file a petition opposing the move within thirty days of receipt of the notice.

The statute sets out additional criteria for the different scenarios that can take place with this issue, and the court is to consider all relevant factors. The statute makes it clear that the preferred method of handling the issues is for the parents to agree on a new visitation schedule.

Whether by statutory mandate or by agreement of the parties, parents and their children are best served when they can discuss the potential for relocation, examine the options, and come to an accord about the move and how it will be handled if it occurs.

Chapter 21:

DEPENDENCY DEDUCTIONS

The Tennessee parenting plan statute helps parents work together for the welfare of their children during a divorce. The plan contains everything related to the children—from educational issues and sleeping arrangements to financial considerations. Even the question of the federal tax exemption (often called the "dependency deduction") due to parents for their children is included in the plan. And here too, parents are given a good deal of room to make their own financial decisions.

According to federal law, parents can obtain a tax exemption for every child who is a "dependent." A child is considered a dependent if he or she is the parent's legal child, under age nineteen, lived with the parent for more than half the year, did not provide more than half of his or her own support during the year, and is not filing a joint tax return. If parents are divorced, the tax exemption for the child can be claimed by only one parent.

In most divorced families, the child can be claimed as a dependent by the primary residential parent (PRP—the IRS calls this person the "custodial" parent). The Tennessee Child Support Guidelines state that the "primary residential parent claims the tax exemptions for the child."

Federal tax law also grants the tax exemption to the primary residential parent since this is the person with whom the child lived for most of the year. According to federal law, the custodial parent is the one with whom the child lived for the greater number of nights during one year. In Tennessee, the parenting plan allows parents to evenly split child time. If the child spends the same number of nights with each parent during the year, the parent with the higher adjusted gross income is considered the custodial parent for federal income tax purposes.

There are, however, exceptions to this rule that allow the alternate residential parent (ARP) to receive the tax exemption. An ARP may receive the tax exemption for the dependent children if four conditions are met:

- The parents must be divorced or legally separated.
- The child had to receive over half of his or her support for the year from the parents.
- The child is in the custody of one or both parents for over half the year.
- The PRP spouse must sign a written declaration (IRS Form 8332 or a statement containing the same information as the form), that he or she releases the exemption to the ARP and will not claim the child as a dependent for that fiscal year.

That fourth condition requires cooperation between the parents. IRS Form 8332 and its instructions are available at IRS.gov. The ARP attaches this written declaration to his or her tax return. If the couple divorced after 1984 but before 2009, the ARP may be able to attach certain pages from the divorce decree or agreement rather than IRS Form 8332 but only if the decree or agreement states three things:

- that the noncustodial parent can claim the child as a dependent regardless of other conditions such as support payments,
- that the custodial parent agrees in writing not to claim the child as a dependent for that year, and
- that the years for which the noncustodial parent can claim the child as a dependent are recorded.

For parents divorcing or separating after 2008, only the IRS Form 8332 or a similar agreement is valid. It is *not* enough to attach the divorce decree or agreement.

The Tennessee parenting plan allows parents to choose who will get the tax exemption and when. Under the "Federal Income Tax Exemption" section, the parents must write whether the father or mother is receiving child support payments. They must also include which parent will receive the tax exemptions and for which children. Parents are allowed to negotiate who will receive the tax exemption regardless of who the primary residential parent is. The parents may even alternate years. For example, the father could claim the exemption in even years and the mother could claim it in odd years.

The conditions in the parenting plan also guarantee that each parent is protected against the other. If the parent paying child support wishes to receive the tax exemption, child support payments must be current, or paid up, by January 15 of the year in which the tax return is due. This prevents a parent from receiving a reward (the tax exemption) for payments that were never made. It also ensures that the obligated parent pays the child support. If not, there will be no tax exemption.

On the other side, the parenting plan also requires the primary residential parent to provide IRS Form 8332 to the other parent by February 15 of the year in which the tax return is due. This ensures that the parent paying child support receives the needed forms well before taxes are due. By balancing out the system for receiving the tax exemption, fights can be avoided, allowing divorced parents and their children to work together for everyone's benefit.

How much is the dependency deduction worth to a parent? It depends on the parents' comparative income. For some, whether high or low earners, there may be no value. Always consult a tax professional such as a CPA or tax attorney when considering this issue.

Chapter 22:

GRANDPARENT VISITATION RIGHTS

Grandparent visitation rights in Tennessee have changed over the last forty years to match the changing makeup of families. Families may comprise biological parents, stepparents, foster parents, and adoptive parents. The law changed as the needs of families changed. The law today covers many of these configurations and also gives the court enough room to take into account other important factors. Ultimately, the final determination is based on protecting the child from danger and doing what's best for him or her.

Grandparent visitations are not guaranteed. The parents of the child have the first say in whether the grandparents may see the children. In *Hawk v. Hawk,* a Tennessee Supreme Court case from 1993,[4] the court ruled that there is a parental right to privacy that limits the court's right to interfere with parents' decisions regarding their children. In that case, the parents decided to prohibit the father's parents from visiting the children. The grandparents went to court, using a 1971 law that guaranteed grandparents visitation rights if these were in the best interests of the child. In *Hawk*, the court added a new condition. When a couple is married, considered fit by the court, and have had continuous custody of their children, the parents have the right to decide about grandparent visitations, and the grandparents first must prove the children would be harmed by the denial of visitation rights. Only then will the court interfere with the parents' rights to make parental decisions.

In a later case,[5] a stepfather had adopted a child, and the court upheld the same standard. The parents cut off visitation between the biological father's parents and the child. The Supreme Court held that only if there is a finding of harm to the child will the court intervene and determine whether grandparent visitations are in the best interests of the child.

The law gives three very clear definitions of a grandparent for the purposes of this law only. They are the biological grandparents, the spouse of a biological grandparent, and the parent of an adoptive parent (this would include parents of a stepparent who adopted the child).

According to Tennessee law,[6] in certain cases only, grandparents who want visitation rights may request a court hearing if the visitations are being denied by the residential parent. Again, they may not request a hearing in the situation given above, in which the parents are still married to each other or in which there was a divorce and the stepparent adopted the child.

There are six situations that give grandparents the right to request a hearing. The first three situations relate to the parents themselves. They are cases in which either one parent died, the parents are separated or divorced or never married, or one parent has been missing for at least six months.

---

4   855 S.W.2d 573 (Tenn. 1993).

5   *Simmons v. Simmons*, 900 S.W.2d 682 (Tenn. 1995).

6   Tennessee Code Annotated § 36-6-307 (2012).

Two of the situations relate to the grandparents themselves. If the child lived with the grandparents for at least twelve months and was removed by the parent or parents, or if the child had a "significant existing relationship" with the grandparents prior to the relationship being severed by the parents (and there was no abuse or danger to the child by the grandparents), and severing the relationship may cause emotional harm to the child, the grandparents may request a hearing.

In the two situations in which the grandchild lived with the grandparents or in which one parent is deceased (and the deceased parent's parents are seeking visitation rights), the court presumes that denying visitation will endanger the child.

Finally, if a court in another state granted grandparent visitation rights, the grandparents also have a right to ask for a hearing.

After evidence is brought in the hearing, the court must decide if the child is in danger of substantial harm if the relationship with the grandparents is prohibited. The law says that there is a danger of substantial harm to the child in three cases. The first is a case in which the child had "such a significant existing relationship with the grandparent" that breaking off the relationship is likely to cause the child severe emotional harm. The second case is when the grandparent functioned as the child's primary caregiver. In such a case, ending the relationship could mean that the child's daily needs are not being met and therefore the child might be hurt both physically and emotionally. The third case is one in which the child had a significant existing relationship with the grandparent and ending that relationship may cause "other direct and substantial harm" to the child.

The law also defines a "significant existing relationship" as one existing between grandparent and child if the child lived with the grandparent *or* if the grandparent was the child's full-time caregiver for at least six consecutive months *or* if the grandparent had frequent visits with the child for a period of at least one year.

If the court rules there is no danger to the child if visitation is prohibited, the issue of visitation is left to the parents, and the court does not intervene. If, however, the court decides there is a "danger of substantial harm" to the child if grandparent visitations are denied, the court must then decide whether grandparent visitation is in the "best interests of the child."

The law lists ten factors the court can consider when making this determination of "best interest," but this list is not definitive. The court may take many other issues into consideration. The list includes such factors as the length and quality of the relationship between the child and the grandparent, the grandparent's role in the child's life, emotional ties between child and grandparent, the child's preferences (if the child is mature enough), the relationship between the grandparent and the parent, and whether the grandparent filed the petition in good faith.

It also gives consideration to situations of divorce in which a parent's visitation rights may be affected and cases in which one parent is deceased or missing. The court will also take into consideration any finding that a parent is unfit.

Generally, grandparents don't need to bring expert witnesses to show that there was a significant relationship with the grandchild or that the loss of the relationship might harm the child. The court has to look at these issues from the perspective of a "reasonable person."

If the court finds that it is in the best interests of the child to have visits with the grandparents, the court can order reasonable visitation.

Grandparents' rights are more limited if the child was removed from his parents' custody and placed in foster care or another child care agency. These are cases in which the home environment was a danger to the child and he or she was removed for safety's sake. In such cases, the grandparents can ask for reasonable visitation rights if three conditions are met:

- that the visitations are in the best interests of the child,
- that the grandparents will adequately protect the child from further abuse and intimidation by the perpetrator or another member of the family, and
- that the grandparents have not committed criminal offenses such as rape, sexual battery, and other violent crimes against the grandchild or their own children.

The laws above apply even in cases in which a relative or stepparent adopts a child. If the child is adopted by somebody other than a relative or stepparent, any visitation rights existing then automatically end.

Tennessee's grandparent law is not perfect. No doubt many grandparents will find the legal requirements overly burdensome and, some might argue, unfair and unjust. Parents for whatever reason may abuse their rights and deny a natural, normal relationship between grandparent and grandchild. The law and the courts recognize the possibilities for misuse of the law. The law and the procedure required by the court helps to weed out those cases that are harmful for the children and do what is really in their best interests.

Chapter 23:

STEPPARENT VISITATION RIGHTS

Tennessee law recognizes the changing nature of families by considering the role a stepparent may play in the life of a minor. If the biological parent permits visitation, there is no need to use the law or turn to the courts. If, however, the biological parent refuses visitation between the stepparent and the child, the stepparent has certain rights. The applicable law[7] permits the court to allow visitation to a stepparent when one spouse files a suit for divorce, annulment, or separate maintenance. The law, however, takes two factors into consideration when permitting visitation. The first condition requires that visitation by the stepparent is in the best interests of the child. The court, however, is limited by an additional economic factor. The stepparent is entitled to visitation rights only if she or he is providing or contributing to the support of the child.

The combination of these two conditions raises some interesting questions about the reasoning behind the legislation. Undoubtedly, there are cases in which a stepparent was essentially a "regular" parent for the child, perhaps even the only other parent the child has known. Even in cases in which there is still another biological parent, it can be assumed that children will form strong bonds with the stepparent with whom they lived. The law recognizes that prohibiting the continuation of this relationship might be detrimental to the child.

At the same time, the law emphasizes that if the relationship is indeed important enough to the stepparent to file an application with the court, that stepparent should also be willing to contribute financially. This will help weed out stepparents who are not interested in the child but rather just in getting even with the biological parent.

Recognizing there might be other circumstances, the second section of the law gives the court discretion to make changes or modifications "as the exigencies of the case require." For example, a biological parent may refuse visitation for selfish reasons, without considering the welfare of the child. Or there may be a stepparent who in fact cannot pay support. The court can consider all of these factors and make a final ruling that is truly in the child's best interest.

---

7   Tennessee Code Annotated § 36-6-303 (2012).

Chapter 24:

MODIFYING THE PRIMARY RESIDENTIAL PARENT DESIGNATION (CHANGING CUSTODY)

The key to understanding custody modification is knowing the difference between the legal standards that apply to an original custody determination and a modification of custody. In Tennessee, a custodial parent is designated as a primary residential parent (PRP) as a result of having more parenting time with the child than the other parent. The standard for an initial determination for the primary residential parent designation is the "best interests of the child," and the court has a list of ten factors to consider. Those factors are listed at the end of Chapter 1 and appear in Tenn. Code Ann. §36-6-106.

In the modification of primary residential parent case, the court has to work its way through a multipart analysis. First, the court must determine whether there has been a "material change in circumstances" and whether the change affects the well-being of the child. If the answer to the first question is yes, the court needs to determine whether the best interests of the child would be served by modifying the parent serving as the PRP. This has the court utilizing a list of factors listed in Tenn. Code Ann. §36-6-404(b) that are quite similar to those factors listed in Tenn. Code Ann. §36-6-106 but with an eye toward established routines and experience as a PRP.

The parent seeking to modify custody has the burden of proving the "threshold" question of whether there has been a material change in circumstances, and that is a hurdle with considerable height. The Supreme Court of Tennessee has laid out three subquestions on this issue: whether the change occurred after the entry of the order sought to be modified, whether a change was not known or reasonably anticipated when the order was entered, and whether a change is one that affects the child's well-being in a meaningful way.

Whether there has been a "material change in circumstances" can be difficult to establish even by the relatively low burden of proof known as "the preponderance of the evidence." Two cases of requested custody modification that did not succeed illustrate this point.

In the first case,[8] Stacy Wade Holt was a father who filed for modification of primary residential parent after the mother, Virginia Grace Massey-Holt, moved thirty-five miles away to accept a job, necessitating a change to the near-equal division of time the children were spending with each parent as well as a change of school enrollment. In his favor, the father had the Permanent Parenting Plan that was part of their 2004 divorce that provided for joint decision making on educational matters. Colliding with the terms of the parents' contract was a Tennessee statute allowing the primary residential parent to move up to a hundred miles away without consent of the other parent or court order.

---

8   *Massey-Holt vs. Holt*, M2006-02714-COA-R3-CV (Tenn. Ct. App. Oct. 31, 2007).

After three years of litigation, the Court of Appeals dismissed the father's application for failure to establish a material change in circumstances. While both parents agreed that the original parenting plan needed to change to reflect the mother's new residence and job, the Appellate Court did not consider that in itself a sufficient reason to even begin to consider whether the change to the schedule should qualify to consider changing the child's primary residential parent.

Another case with a long litigation history that was ultimately dismissed for failure to establish a material change in circumstances was *Scofield vs. Scofield.*[9] Divorced after seventeen years of marriage, the parents agreed to a Permanent Parenting Plan for their three children, including standard parenting time for the father and the designation of the mother as the primary residential parent.

The mother relocated three times after the divorce. The father, who had relocated the family during the marriage for his career with the army, decided to retire and settle in Huntsville, Alabama, as his permanent residence. But the father's case was dismissed at the end of a two-day trial involving testimony from the parents, two of the children, several teachers, and a law enforcement officer. To the trial court, the father made what appeared to be serious allegations in the initial petition ranging from alcohol and guns in the home and abusive corporal punishment to a decline in the children's grades, but these allegations simply did not measure up to the testimony and evidence that came out during the trial.

We can compare these two unsuccessful modification cases against a successful case that did result in the father being awarded a modification of primary residential parent of his two children. It took the father two petitions and seven years, but Edward Scott Combs successfully won his modification case against the mother, Melissa Combs Cranston.[10]

In the Combs case, the father demonstrated a material change in circumstances by proving that there was a change after the entry of the divorce order and a subsequent visitation modification order, that the change was not known or reasonably anticipated when the orders were entered, and that the change negatively impacted the children's well-being. The father presented evidence of persistent interference by the mother with all aspects of the father's relationship with the children, particularly his visitation and communication with them.

It can also be useful to focus some attention on witnesses who testify in primary residential parent modification cases. Because each parent is viewed as an interested party with a natural bias toward presenting himself or herself in the best light, independent witnesses in modification cases are given more weight by trial judges. Independent witnesses include teachers, school personnel, medical professionals, and members of the opposing parent's family.

Nonetheless, many cases involve the testimony of only the parents. When a parent brings in a witness, the result may not be what was anticipated. Consider, for example, the case of *Cosner vs. Cosner.*[11] The father ended up in the unusual situation of putting on his proof without the mother or her attorney being present in the courtroom. The father's testimony included allegations of inappropriate sexual conduct in the household, the mother's pregnancy with a child of a married man, and the mother's outbursts of anger against the father in the presence of the children.

---

9   No. M2006-00350-COA-R3-CV (Tenn. Ct. App. Feb. 28, 2007).
10   See *Combs-Cranston vs. Cranston*, No. M2000-02101-SC-R11-CV (Tenn. Ct. App. Feb. 4, 2003).
11   No. E2007-02031-COA-R3-CV (Tenn. Ct. App. Aug. 22, 2008).

The father called only one witness, the licensed clinical social worker who had provided counseling to the parties' daughter for approximately nine months. The social worker testified that the daughter was uncomfortable with the father's new wife. The social worker testified that the daughter "didn't speak very much about her mother's home at all."

While the trial court ruled in the father's favor, the Court of Appeals reversed. In its decision, the court emphasized that the testimony of the social worker had not supported the father's allegations.

A similar situation occurred in the case of *Kendrick vs. Kendrick Shoemake*.[12] The father and the mother submitted highly conflicting testimony. One of the father's witnesses was the mother's current husband's ex-wife. The witness previously submitted an affidavit to the court; however, her oral testimony in court was not as strong as her written allegations. Her in-court testimony was that she had "no first-hand knowledge that Mrs. Shoemake had been absent from her home, had visited any bars, or had otherwise neglected her children." The appeals court soundly stated, "We therefore afford very little weight to Ms. Bradley's accusations."

One tool that can be useful for primary residential parent modification is mediation. In the mediation setting, each parent presents various arguments with or without lawyers assisting. The mediator becomes the pivot point between the sides, looking for sensible and even creative solutions to help solve any problem.

If mediation does not result in a settlement, the process does not limit the rights of a parent to pursue a court case. Sometimes, however, a court case is put on hold to give the parents a chance to mediate. The upside to starting a case and then utilizing mediation is that each side has something to lose, and both face the same deadlines for results lest the court case proceed to trial. In Tennessee, all postdivorce parenting changes must be mediated before a court will hear a case.

---

12   90 S.W.3d 566 (Tenn. 2002).

Chapter 25:

MODIFYING PARENTING TIME

Whether we are dealing with a proposed modification of the primary residential parent role or a modification of the children's schedule between the parents' households, we are trying to determine whether a material change of circumstances has occurred that makes it in the best interests of the children to change the existing parenting plan.

There are two primary questions: Was there a material change in circumstances? Will that material change make it in the best interests of the children to modify the existing parenting plan?

The first question gets broken down into three parts: whether the change occurred after the entry of the current order, whether the change was not known or reasonably anticipated at the time the current order was entered, and whether the change is one that affects the children's well-being in a meaningful way. If the answer to any one of these three questions is no, the analysis does not advance and the petition is dismissed.

If a court case reaches the second question, Tennessee law provides a list of factors listed in Tenn. Code Ann. §36-6-404(b) (quite similar to those factors listed in Tenn. Code Ann. §36-6-106 found at the end of Chapter 1) that a judge should consider in determining the "best interests" of the children. However, there can be a significant difference in how these standards are applied, as a change to the children's visitation schedule requires less-significant events to persuade the court that a change of visitation would be appropriate.

In *Armbrister v. Armbrister,*[13] the Supreme Court of Tennessee dealt with the difference in application of the standard for modification of the primary residential parent designation and modification of the residency schedule. The father, after the original parenting plan was agreed upon, married the woman he had been dating at the time of the divorce, moved closer to the mother's home, and had more Fridays off work. The trial court denied the father's petition for a change of the primary residential parent designation. However, on its own initiative, the trial court modified the father's parenting time from 85 days to 143 days. The mother appealed this decision, and the Court of Appeals reversed the trial court's decision. The Court of Appeals read the father's petition for change of the primary residential parent designation narrowly, agreed with the trial court that the father had not met the burden of proof for a modification of the primary residential parent designation, and reversed the increase in his parenting time with the children.

Tennessee's Supreme Court, however, reversed the decision of the Court of Appeals. Although the standard for material change of circumstances to justify a change in the parenting plan was at one time very strict, the standard has been relaxed by the courts and legislature over time.

---

13   No. E2012-00018-R3-CV (Tenn. 2013).]

In 2004, the legislature amended the standards of what was considered a change of circumstances. The Supreme Court interpreted this amendment as a way to make it much easier to establish that a material change of circumstances had occurred when a party sought to modify a residential parenting schedule. The court concluded that the trial court had correctly modified the parenting plan schedule because, given the lower threshold applicable in the modification proceedings, the father had provided sufficient proof that there had been a material change in his circumstances.

Since 2004, Tennessee has had a statute with examples of a "material change of circumstances" in it. The statute sets out the following examples: "significant changes in the needs of the child over time, which may include changes relating to age, significant changes in a parent's living or working condition that significantly affect parenting, [and] failure to adhere to a parenting plan."[14]

Tennessee courts have also discussed certain examples. A common circumstance is a parent's remarriage following a divorce. In at least one case, the Court of Appeals found that if remarriage was the only event that did not constitute a "material change of circumstance" unless the new spouse "changes the home environment of the child." In *Riddick vs. Riddick*,[15] the Appellate Court wrote that "the character, attitude and general personality of other persons who would be in a position to influence the children" were important matters for the court to consider. The court also encouraged new spouses to testify in court, including their willingness for children to be in the home, their occupations, finances, and other stepparenting considerations.

Another common scenario relating to modification of the children's residential schedule is what happens when parents voluntarily change the schedule over time. It can happen for any number of reasons including but not limited to a child's involvement in extracurricular activities, a child's medical or academic needs, a change in a parent's work schedule, and an evolving relationship between a child and the alternate residential parent, particularly between sons and fathers during teenage years.

Over time, parents may change their day-to-day schedules, often deviating significantly from the written parenting plan. Until and unless the new schedule is written down, signed by both parents, and approved by a judge, the actual terms between the parents are only those written in the current court order. At any time, one parent or the other can pull out the signed order and insist upon a return to the schedule written in the order.

The question arises whether to go with the flow of a working coparental relationship or to seek judicial approval for a modified parenting plan. One middle approach worth mentioning is that of mediation. For parents with an evolving parenting schedule, it may be beneficial for the alternative residential parent in particular to explore changing the parenting plan and have it entered as an order. Especially when children are becoming teenagers (and teens are increasingly aware of interparental communication and strife), this can provide more stability by establishing a new but set schedule.

Another consideration on whether to memorialize informal changes being made to the children's schedule is the impact on child support. The increased time an alternate residential parent spends with the children beyond the existing schedule can result in a reduction in the child support owed to the primary residential parent.

---

14   See Tennessee Code Annotated §36-6-101(a)(2)(C).
15   497 S.W.2d 740 (Tenn. Ct. App. 1973).

The reduction of child support argument can also play out when the primary residential parent uses the other in a day care fashion three or more days per week. This may not have been the original parenting schedule, but it could easily arise when one parent is working standard hours and the other is not due to shift work, unemployment, or medical leave. In *Lowery vs. Womble,*[16] the trial court heard conflicting testimony from the father, who testified the children arrived at 6:30 a.m. each school day and were picked up at 8:00 p.m. by the mother, but the mother testified that she dropped off the children at 7:00 a.m. and picked them up at 4:00 p.m. The trial judge literally conducted a confidential interview with the children in his office to resolve credibility in favor of the father.

In the end, it may be that the analysis of whether to seek to create a written modification of a parenting plan comes down to the level of admissible evidence to establish precisely what schedule has been adopted by the parents and the children. The case of *Pace vs. Pace*[17] is an instructive decision particularly as the court expressed its own frustration with the lack of accurate records by either parent as to what was going on in the exchanges of the children. In its decision to hold the father to the original parenting plan and deny any modification of it for additional time the parents may have already been doing, the Court of Appeals used words such as,

> The exact amount of visitation time exercised by Mr. Pace is not clear ... Although neither party kept complete records of actual visitation, it appears from the calendar kept sporadically by Mr. **Pace** ... Not only is there insufficient evidence from which to determine the actual visitation exercised by the parties, but there is also insufficient evidence from which to conclude that the deviation either worked such a benefit, or a detriment, to the child as to justify modification of the schedule.

Just as a timecard is often important when it comes to getting paid, a thoughtful presentation of a request to modify a parenting schedule calls for calendar documentation of the actual hours the children are spending with the alternate residential parent, all the way down to the hours of pick-up and drop-off. Maintaining such a calendar also allows parents, their lawyers, and even mediators to thoroughly evaluate the schedule being followed, how it varies from the original parenting plan, and the duration of the new schedule. It will also put a parent further along the path of demonstrating the material change in circumstances that would warrant a modification of the current parenting order as being in the children's best interests.

---

16   No. M2010-01102-COA-R3-CV (Tenn. Ct. App. Jun. 28, 2011).
17   No. M2009-01037-COA-R3-CV (Tenn. Ct. App. Apr. 26, 2010).

Chapter 26:

COLLEGE EDUCATION AGREEMENTS
SAMPLE LANGUAGE

This chapter presents some sample college savings and costs language. College costs provisions must be tailored to individual parents' values and desire for control. Every parent has his or her perspective on the subject. Some parents want to maintain tight reins, while others can't wait for their young to leave the nest.

The college savings and costs road usually forks early, and it usually forks twice. First, even if parents want to pay for college, do they want to agree to become contractually obligated to save for it? Does either want to agree to pay for it? If so, parents must understand that a dollar paid for college tuition can't be used to pay alimony.

If one or more parents agree to pay for college in a Permanent Parenting Plan or marital dissolution agreement, that makes the children third-party beneficiaries to the agreement. Some dads like the idea of being able to tell the kids, "Hey, I got college." Some dads want to pay for college as a gift, retaining control over the situation over time.

To learn more about applicable Tennessee law, see chapter 43, "College Tuition and Costs." Below is sample language. Your family lawyer's experience will be invaluable here. Spelling out more detail is much better than relying on generic, vague language. At this stage, the more detail reduces the likelihood of having to return to court later to argue over interpretation of terms that did not address these issues.

INTENT

In any family law agreement, it's always a good idea to clearly state the parents' intent. If there is a dispute over the meaning of the terms, judges can look to the parties' stated intent to help decide a close call. Unfortunately, lots of family lawyers are scared to death to try to characterize in writing what the parties actually mean. Some lawyers are often afraid that the "intent" language could be used against them later, but careful family law practitioners shouldn't be afraid to document what the client really wants and why. Usually, both parents want their children to attend college. They expect to personally sacrifice as they would have had the marriage continued.

SAVINGS

Saving for college can be ordered by the courts as part of a Tennessee child support order for parents who earn more than $10,000 net income per month.[18] Otherwise, the parents must agree to save for college in order for it to be enforceable. Some parents agree that the supporting parent will contribute to an investment account, trust fund, or Section 529 account. If funds are to be held in trust and there is no trust document, one or both parents can become trustees of a constructive trust[19] with accountability and potential liability to the other parent and/or the beneficiaries. Some parents, on the other hand, agree to both contribute to separate accounts. The amount of funding should be enough to be meaningful but not so much that it impairs the monthly budget and affects the ability of a parent to save for emergencies.

Other than the amount to be paid, challenges to reaching an agreement most often relate to accountability and verification. What documentary evidence must be shared with the other parent, and how often? What will be done with the money if it's not needed to pay for college? Can another child use the money? Can a child use the money for an educational trip to Europe, a car after graduation, a down payment on a house, or a medical emergency?

In what follows, you will see that certain words or terms such as "Parent" and "College Costs" are capitalized as these are words or terms that can be defined in legal documents such as Permanent Parenting Plans.

COLLEGE SAVINGS: BOTH PARENTS CONTRIBUTE TO ONE JOINT ACCOUNT

Beginning January 1 following execution of this agreement, both Parents shall contribute $200 per month into an investment account[20] to be jointly managed and requiring both Parents' signatures for withdrawal held in trust for the children's college education. If mutually agreed upon, this shall be a 529 College Savings Account to reduce income taxes generated by its earnings.

---

18   A court can't order a parent to pay college expenses and tuition, but a court can order more-affluent parents contribute to a college trust fund. Tennessee Child Support Guidelines in 2014 state that a child support obligor who earns more than $10,000 per month net income may be required to have money "be placed in an educational or other trust fund for the benefit of the child"; Rule of Tenn. Dept. of Human Services 1240-2-4-.07(2)(g)(2)(iii).

19   A constructive trust is an equitable remedy resembling a trust imposed by a court to benefit a party. In college savings and costs cases, the benefit is usually a child. The child is a third-party beneficiary, and a parent may sue to enforce the contractual right imposed in the divorce settlement. Parents also have the option of creating an express written trust. There are many legal advantages to creating a detailed written trust, but most parents avoid this due to cost. Trusts can also create a fiduciary relationship to the child in addition to contractual liability to the other parent. If violated, this fiduciary relationship can create liability from the parent to the child.

20   If the parents agree to contribute based on relative earnings, some suggested language is: "The Parents agree to contribute a total of $2,400 per year to the joint account based on the relative percentage of each Parent's income. The Parents agree to exchange copies of his or her federal income tax returns by October 31 of the year in which the return was due. Each Parent agrees to make his or her respective contribution to the joint account by December 31 of each year."

In the event that the money in the account is not completely used for the children's college educations, the money will be divided pro rata between the Parents based on their contributions to the account upon the youngest child attaining age twenty-five. The Parents may also agree to invade the corpus of the account in the event of any medical emergency expenses for a child.

COLLEGE SAVINGS: BOTH PARENTS CONTRIBUTE TO SEPARATE ACCOUNTS

Effective January 1 following execution of this agreement, both Parents shall contribute $200 per month into an account solely in the control of the respective contributing Parent to be held in trust for the benefit of the children. This may be a 529 College Savings Account to reduce taxes. To the extent this account generates taxable income, the respective Parent will be required to pay applicable federal and state income taxes generated from the account. Funds in the account may be used to pay only that portion of taxes generated by the account's earnings.

Within thirty days of the request but not more often than annually, both Parents are required to provide documentation to the other Parent of the funding of, balances in, and withdrawals from the account adequate to prove compliance with this provision including but not limited to account statements, canceled checks, and supporting documentation.

COLLEGE COSTS

In general, there are two options when defining college costs: keep it simple, or define everything with specificity. Below is an example of one with more details listed. Reasonable limitations on total college costs are important. It makes more sense for most Parents to define a level of funding that can be relied upon than seeking an agreement on amounts that can never be realistically paid. Parents are often comfortable limiting the tuition costs to that of a state school such as the University of Tennessee at Knoxville or Middle Tennessee State University.

College means any accredited college, university, or community college but does not include a trade school, art school, or college with courses primarily presented over the Internet.

Parents mean both the Father and the Mother.

College Costs includes tuition, books, room and board (housing and food), course-required supplies, and education-related required fees and expenses for attending the College while seeking an undergraduate degree.

College Costs don't include the Monthly Allowance described below, fraternity or sorority dues and expenses, social event fees, funding for spring break vacations with or without family, travel to or from school to either Parent's home, or other educational travel.

Tuition expenses shall be limited to the amount required by the University of Tennessee at Knoxville as published on its website as "Schedule of Maintenance, Tuition and Fees" for twelve or more hours of courses taken for each semester for in-state students. This limitation shall be adjusted accordingly if the children's colleges hold trimesters or quarters.

The children are/are not required to apply for scholarships, grants, fellowships, and aid as financial assistance. College Costs shall be reduced by scholarships, grants, fellowships, and college-provided work-study income received but not student loans.

If one Parent is primarily assisting a child with application and enrollment, that Parent will use his or her best efforts to inform the other about the College Costs amounts and dates due for payments at least three months in advance. Parents are required to pay College Costs due no later than five business days before an amount becomes due.

Payments for College Costs may be paid directly to the school or the other Parent. For College Costs not required to be paid to the school directly, such as supplies and books, one Parent may seek reimbursement from the other following payment by that Parent. The Parent advancing the costs will seek reimbursement from the other Parent within sixty days of the actual payment having been made.

Reimbursement is due within fourteen days of the request for reimbursement and production of reasonable documentation of the payment such as an invoice or receipt (if available) and canceled check or credit card charge slip. If a reimbursement request is not made within sixty days of the payment, that request does not have to be paid by the other Parent.

MONTHLY ALLOWANCE

Financial advisor Dave Ramsey[21] advises putting children on budgets as early as high school. If college-age kids can't learn from their mistakes (e.g., getting nailed by bad-check charges), they will never have a chance as adults. Plus, they must learn that credit cards are a very serious responsibility.

In addition to the College Costs listed about, both Parents will pay directly to each child's checking account $1,800 per year payable $150 per month on the first of each month by direct deposit for living expenses in addition to meal plans included as part of room and board.

---

21   See www.daveramsey.com.

In general, this Monthly Allowance shall be used to pay for clothing, food in addition to a meal plan, entertainment, and travel expenses to and from College and one or both Parents' residences. This Monthly Allowance may be used without limitation or restriction for any expenses not otherwise required herein.

SAVINGS TO BE USED

If there are savings, how are they to be applied to college costs? Should they be used over time or used first? Here's suggested language requiring use of savings be allocated over a four- or five-year period.

To the extent any joint college savings (such as those held in a trust, college savings account, or Section 529 account) have been saved as required by this agreement, those funds shall be used to pay College Costs as evenly as possible over a four- or five-year period depending on the anticipated completion date.

For any other college savings designated as college funds held solely in that Parent's name only, those amounts may be utilized solely in that Parent's discretion without limitation.

THIRD-PARTY GIFTING

When one set of grandparents helps with college funding (by paying the required contribution for the parent), the other parent may resent that. While it arguably shouldn't be the case, the best way to prevent emotional fallout (and associated court action) can be to deal with this possibility in advance.

To the extent a Parent's parent(s) or other third party related to or associated with a Parent pays any amounts otherwise due by a particular Parent, that Parent shall receive credit for those payments made under this agreement.

LOANS

When it comes to student loans, parents' opinions and values differ. Some feel that children accepting student loans helps make children feel more invested in their education. On the other hand, other parents don't want their children financially and emotionally burdened by loans after graduation. For such reasons, college loans should be addressed in advance.

In most cases, loans and other need-based financial aid opportunities will require one or both parents to produce and disclose income tax returns. Here's one way to deal with the situation.

Children are not required to apply for loans or other need-based financial aid or scholarships but may do so at their discretion or upon request of both Parents. Upon reasonable request, both Parents agree to provide directly to the school or children required financial documentation or information including but not limited to federal and state income tax returns.

Parents shall also complete and execute required forms and applications so the children may apply for student loans, grants, scholarships, or need-based financial aid. This agreement does not prohibit or restrict children from applying for or accepting loans to supplement any amount due from the Parents whether paid or unpaid.

Neither Parent is required to become contractually obligated to be liable as a primary debtor or guarantor.

AMOUNT OF THE OBLIGATION

How much will the parents or a parent owe? They can share the expenses at least two ways:

To the extent payment for College Costs is not provided by any other source, the Parents shall share equally the College Costs for each child attending college/To the extent payment for College Costs is not provided by any other source, the Parents shall share pro rata according to the Parents' respective incomes for the prior year the College Costs for each child attending college.

The pro rata percentage of College Costs owed will be determined by each Parent's fraction of Income (the numerator) of the Parents' combined Income. Income means the Total Income from the respective Parents' IRS Form 1040, line 22 from the previous tax year's return, less earned income attributable to a Parent's future spouse.

To the extent there are investment earnings by a Parent at the time married to another person, those earnings will be included in the calculation only if earned by an account jointly titled in both spouses' names, but it will be excluded if the earnings are in an account in a Parent's spouse's name only.

Both Parents will exchange tax returns and needed supporting schedules and documentation as long as the obligation to pay College Costs exists to perform this calculation.

In the event of a dispute regarding this calculation, the Parents agree to choose an independent Certified Public Accountant to perform this calculation. The costs for the calculation shall also be shared pro rata according to the Parents' respective incomes from the prior year.

RESPONSIBILITY FOR TUITION CONTRACTS

Who signs the tuition contracts? One or both Parents?

To the extent at least one Parent is required to sign a contract for any part of College Costs, both Parents agree to execute the contract(s) and be legally liable to pay same.

LIMITATIONS

In general, limitations are limited only by the parents' imagination. Here are four to consider.

Either Parent's obligation to contribute toward a child's College Costs is limited by the following:

- Both Parents and child must agree on the College. Neither Parent shall unreasonably withhold consent for the child's College choice. [Alternate: Each child shall be permitted to attend the College of his or her choice free of either Parent's undue influence or pressure.]
- A child must attend College full-time, meaning twelve or more credit hours (or equivalent units) per semester, excluding summer.
- A child's scheduled courses and progress planned must result in the child attaining an undergraduate degree within five school years from graduation from high school.
- A child reaching his or her twenty-fourth birthday.

GPA MINIMUM

GPA minimums can be gut wrenching. On one hand, children should not be given free rides if they are not taking school seriously. On the other hand, if a child is seriously struggling, arbitrary minimums may be demoralizing or downright terrorizing, especially if the bar is set significantly above the college's standards. The question becomes where to draw the line—1.5? 2.5? If a child stumbles, can he or she rehabilitate the situation?

Each child must maintain a 2.0 cumulative grade point average on a 4.0 scale or its equivalent. If a child does not maintain a 2.0 cumulative grade point average for two consecutive semesters (or three consecutive trimesters), neither Parent shall have any obligation to pay College Costs.

If after a child fails to maintain the required minimum grade point average and that child remains in College and subsequently raises his or her grade point average above a 2.0 cumulative grade point average, both Parents' obligation resumes for future semesters not otherwise limited by other provisions in this agreement.

TAX-DEPENDENCY EXEMPTIONS

The parents should investigate and know federal income tax law applicable to dependency exemptions for adult children.[22]

Regardless of the amounts contributed by a Parent for College Costs, as long as the Mother/ Father otherwise qualifies for the dependency exemption for federal income tax purposes, he/

---

22   See IRS publication 504, Divorced or Separated Individuals, available at IRS.gov.

she may claim it. The Father/Mother will cooperate, execute, and deliver IRS Form 8332 to the Parent claiming the dependency exemption to the extent required.

ENFORCEMENT AND THIRD-PARTY BENEFICIARIES

To the extent possible under Tennessee law, some parents may want to disclaim the children's ability to sue as third-party beneficiaries.

This agreement to contribute to the children's college expenses is intended to directly benefit the children as third-party beneficiaries in addition to the other Parent. This agreement shall be enforceable by a Parent or a child.

[Alternate: The parties don't intend to create third-party beneficiary rights by entering into this agreement. This agreement is enforceable only by a Parent.]

MISCELLANEOUS

Here are miscellaneous clauses to consider.

The Husband/Wife shall pay the balance of any College Costs unpaid by the Wife/Husband and retains the right to initiate an action for collection.

In the event of future court action regarding college costs, reasonable attorney's fees and court costs shall be awarded to the prevailing Parent pursuant to this agreement.

The Parents reserve the right to amend this agreement by consent, but all changes must be in writing and signed by both Parents.

If a Parent pays more than the amount due pursuant to this agreement, that Parent shall not be obligated to pay for additional costs in any future year. Any such excess payments shall be deemed a gift to the child and may not be used to offset any future obligation.

OUT CLAUSES AND OTHER EQUIVOCATION

"Out clauses" are included here because some parents may want to limit or otherwise avoid legal liability even though one or both parents may still wish to agree in principle to the concept of paying college costs.

It is the intent of the Parents that their children attend college if academically qualified, and both Parents agree to contribute thereto only to the extent they are financially able to do so.
Each Parent's obligation is expressly limited by his or her financial ability to pay at the time during which the College Costs are due. Financial ability shall be judged in the context of how

much a reasonable and prudent parent in the same or similar financial circumstances would be able to pay.

The Parents, without legal obligation, will endeavor to provide for their children financial assistance besides financial obligations provided either is financially able to aid and assist their children in educational pursuits.

Either Parent/The Husband/The Wife is not required to pay for any specific amount of College Tuition if in good faith he/she determines the condition of his/her finances is such that he/she cannot provide full or partial payments of his/her share of College Costs.

If a Parent can no longer pay or otherwise refuses to pay for agreed-upon College Costs as described herein, that Parent must notify the other Parent and child of that determination in writing at least 180 days in advance of the upcoming semester to allow for appropriate advance planning.

ACCOUNTING AND SHARING DOCUMENTATION

For some parents, this may need to be spelled out too.

Upon written request, within thirty days, a Parent shall exchange with the other Parent requested financial information, documentation, and/or accountings of related College Costs incurred, amounts paid, financial aid awarded or received, child's earnings, and expenses reimbursed including but not limited to account statements, receipts, invoices, statements, canceled checks, or credit card receipts.

LIVING AT HOME?

What if a child attends college but lives with a parent?

If a child resides with a Parent in his or her home while attending College, the other Parent will contribute up to $2,400 per year payable $200 per month to the Parent housing the child to reimburse the Parent for each child's housing and food regardless of the actual costs associated therewith.

COLLEGE CAR CONTRIBUTION

Road trip! Whatever parents agree about cars, insurance, gas, repairs, maintenance, and speeding and parking tickets could also be spelled out. Often, though, these terms are never spelled out, and friction results. Here is a sample.

Either Parent may provide a reasonably priced car to a child for use in college. The Parents must agree that one Parent shall be primarily responsible for the associated costs therewith.

To the extent the Parents agree a child may use a car during college, the Parents will share equally the costs of the operation of the car, including its purchase, auto insurance, driver's insurance, maintenance, and repairs, but not gas. Gas expense should be paid with funds available from the Monthly Allowance provision.

Each month, the Parent primarily responsible for the car's costs will inform the other of amounts paid monthly. The other Parent will pay the Parent primarily responsible for the car's costs his or her contribution toward the amounts paid the month prior.

[Alternative: If a Parent provides a car to a child for use at college, the other Parent will pay $100 per month to the Parent providing the car's operation costs to assist with the cost of purchasing, maintaining, and insuring the car and insuring the child as a driver.]

To the extent a child obtains a DUI, wrecks a car more than once, or obtains more than one speeding ticket per year in any twelve-month period, either Parent can choose to discontinue paying this college car contribution.

APARTMENT LEASE DISCLAIMER

Apartment leases can be expensive. Sometimes, apartments can cost a great deal more than traditional student housing, and financial options might be limited.

Neither Parent is required to be liable and sign as a guarantor for any apartment lease or nonstudent housing.

DISCLOSURE

Who gets to know about this agreement?

The terms of this agreement as they relate to college savings and costs may be shared with each child as they approach college age for appropriate planning purposes only.

Chapter 27:

SECTION 529 PLANS

A Qualified Tuition Plan (QTP) is commonly called a 529 Plan since it is governed by Section 529 of the Internal Revenue Code. A 529 Plan allows a parent to save for college or prepay tuition. The main advantage of a 529 Plan is that it allows money to grow tax free, and as long as the money is used for educational expenses, the money is not taxable when withdrawn.

529 Plans also keep the money under a parent's control until it is used for college expenses. When a 529 Plan is set up, the parent names the beneficiary, generally the person who will benefit. However, that person has no ownership in the money, and the original donor calls the shots as to how the money is spent. The original donor has the option to transfer the account to another relative or even withdraw the money for other uses (though taxes would probably be due in that case).

Money invested in a 529 Plan is not tax deductible on the parent's federal tax return in the year in which it is invested. However, some states allow the parent to deduct contributions to state-run plans from state income taxes in the year in which the contribution is made. (Such contributions are not tax deductible in Tennessee.)

A state or an eligible educational institution will manage a 529 Plan. The state-run program in Tennessee is TNStars, which is offered by the Tennessee Treasury Department.

There are two types of 529 Plans. The first is a prepaid tuition plan. Under a prepaid plan, a student's family pays tuition (normally pegged at the tuition rate of the state university) at today's tuition rates. When the student attends college, the tuition will already have been paid. Since tuition rates have been increasing faster than inflation, this can result in large savings. Even though the amount of tuition is usually pegged to the rate of the state university in that particular state, the money can usually be used at other institutions.

Currently, only a few states offer prepaid tuition plans. Tennessee's prepaid tuition plan was called the Baccalaureate Education System Trust (BEST). However, this prepaid plan was closed to investment in 2010. Some public universities, however, still offer prepaid tuition plans. The Private College 529 Plan is a prepaid tuition plan offered by 270 private colleges and universities. Under this plan, the participant pays for one semester of tuition at today's rates. If the beneficiary attends one of the participating schools, the tuition has already been paid. If the beneficiary does not attend one of the participating schools, the money can be rolled over into a state-operated plan.

The other type of 529 Plan is the savings-type plan. The current Tennessee 529 Plan, TNStars, is one such savings plan. It is not pegged specifically to tuition prices. Instead, the growth of the investment is based on market performance of the plan's assets.

The main tax advantage of either type of 529 Plan is that when money is paid out in a qualified distribution for higher education expenses, the distribution is exempt from federal income tax. In many states, these distributions are also exempt from state income tax. In some states, this is limited to the state's plan even though most states allow residents of other states to participate in a 529 Plan. However, in most cases, the distribution would be subject to state income tax if the 529 Plan was in a different state.

Tennessee does not offer a tax deduction or credit for distributions from a 529 Plan, so distributions from a 529 are subject to Tennessee income tax. This means that in Tennessee, the tax consequences of the distribution would be the same for TNStars as they would be for a plan offered by another state.

Because most state plans are available to nonresidents, parents residing in a state such as Tennessee without a state tax deduction or credit should shop around and consider 529 Plans offered by other states.

The money from a 529 Plan can be used for educational expenses such as tuition and fees, books, and required supplies and equipment. This money can be used at any accredited college, university, or vocational school in the United States and at some foreign universities. The money can be used for room and board as long as the student is at least a half-time student. If the money is not used for educational expenses, it is generally subject to income tax and may also be subject to a 10 percent early-distribution penalty.

Since most 529 Plans are now savings plans, there is always the possibility the investment will lose value. One advantage of the 529 Plan is that losses may still be deductible. After all of the money has been distributed, a parent is entitled to a deduction if the total distributions were less than the total amount of contributions. (This deduction is limited to 2 percent of the parent's adjusted gross income.) In this way, a 529 Plan can be used to hedge your bets. As long as the money is used for educational expenses, the distributions are not taxable. However, if there were losses, then the losses are deductible.

A 529 Plan is set up for a particular beneficiary. Normally, a parent can set up a plan for each child. If one child doesn't attend college, it is possible to transfer the money to a 529 Plan set up for another child as long as he or she is a family member of the original beneficiary. This could include another child, the child's spouse, their parent or stepparent, or even a first cousin.

Federal and state income tax laws change. Parents should always consult a trusted certified public accountant and/or a financial advisor regarding important details and possible changes in IRS regulations and tax law.

Section II:

TENNESSEE CHILD SUPPORT

Chapter 28:

TENNESSEE CHILD SUPPORT LAWS

Tennessee's Child Support Guidelines are rules put out by the Tennessee Department of Human Services, Child Support Division, and they are modified every few years. Always check to make sure you have the current set of guidelines.

In 2005, the rules dramatically changed to the Income Shares model, taking into account the income of both parents, the number of overnights enjoyed by each parent, and other key expenses such as health insurance and child care. The guidelines are lengthy, detailed, and complex, so the discussion here is a general overview. Note that exceptions may apply to any situation. To get the answer to a specific question, consult with an experienced family law attorney.

Interpretations of the guidelines will be determined by the Tennessee Court of Appeals and the Supreme Court of Tennessee. But because some of the guidelines' provisions are relatively new, some important interpretations may not come out for years.

The parent who pays child support is the alternative residential parent (ARP), and the parent who receives child support is the primary residential parent (PRP). The child support worksheets are forms and a calculator used to input a lot of information to determine the amount of support.

In theory, Tennessee's Child Support Guidelines are to be reviewed and updated every three years or so. As of writing this book, that hasn't happened in a while, so Tennesseans can expect one coming. For a copy of the current Child Support Guidelines, links to the calculator, and updated information and analysis, visit MemphisDivorce.com, its "Child Support" pages, and its Tennessee Family Law blog.

BASIC CHILD SUPPORT OBLIGATION

Determining child support begins with determining the basic child support obligation (BCSO), the expenses child support is designed to cover. Expenses include an average amount to cover child rearing expenses including housing, food, and transportation. The share of total expenditures devoted to clothing and entertainment is also included in the BCSO, but it's relatively small compared to the other three items. Basic educational expenses based on a public school education (such as fees, books, and local field trips) are also included in the BCSO. Private school tuition and costs and any educational expenses beyond high school are not intended to be covered by the BCSO. They are handled separately.

The BCSO does not include health insurance premiums for the children, work-related child care costs, a child's uninsured medical expenses, special expenses, or extraordinary educational expenses because of how much these can vary among different families.

The first step to calculate the BCSO is to obtain the gross income of each parent. Gross income includes all income from any source before taxes and other deductions whether earned or unearned.

It includes just about all income. See chapter 31: Gross Income (and Not Income). Gross income is a very broad category. The wealth of a stepparent or other person residing with a child is not considered in setting child support awards.

The second step is to calculate the adjusted gross income (AGI) of each parent by subtracting "credits" from the gross income of each parent. Credits allow a parent to reduce the amount of gross income used to calculate the BCSO. These credits are self-employment tax, a child supported in the parent's home, a child supported by the parent under a child support case, and a child who does not live in the parent's home and is receiving support from the other parent but not pursuant to a court order.

Credits are available for children under preexisting and subsequent orders. For credit purposes, preexisting orders are directly deducted from the gross income of a parent, who received full credit for it. No credit is given for overdue payments. To receive credit for children who are under a support order, a parent must prove he or she is actually providing support for those children. To receive credit for children not under a support order, the parent claiming the credit must prove he or she has a legal obligation to support the child and is doing so.

Documented proof of support includes evidence of payments to a child's caretaker (such as canceled checks or money orders), evidence of payment of child support under another child support order, and evidence of "in kind" payments (such as food, clothing, diapers, or formula that have been given a dollar value).

The available credit against gross income for either parent's qualified "not in home" children is the actual amount averaged to a monthly amount of support paid over the most recent twelve-month period to a maximum of 75 percent of a theoretical support order calculated according to these guidelines. None of these credits is available for stepchildren.

The third step, after calculating each parent's monthly adjusted gross income by deducting credits, is to total the amount of AGI each parent has and cross-reference the amount with the Child Support Schedule, which gives the monthly total obligation or BCSO both parents must provide.

The fourth step is to take the monthly BCSO and divide it by each parent's adjusted gross income. Each parent's share, called the percentage of income (PI), is determined by prorating the BCSO between parents. More steps follow.

PARENTING TIME ADJUSTMENT

An adjustment to the BCSO is based on parenting time. In equal parenting situations, the adjustment is based on each parent exercising 182.5 days, a half year, of parenting time.

Except as applied to equal parenting situations, the adjustment is based on the ARP's number of days of parenting time with the children. Only one parent can take credit for parenting time in any one twenty-four-hour period. A "day" of parenting time occurs when the child spends more than twelve consecutive hours in a twenty-four-hour period under the care, control, or direct supervision of one parent or caretaker. The twenty-four-hour period need not be the same as a twenty-four-hour calendar day. Accordingly, a day of parenting time may encompass an overnight period, a daytime period, or a combination of these.

Except in extraordinary circumstances, partial days of parenting time not consistent with this definition shall be considered a "day" under these guidelines. For example, let's say an ARP picks up a child after school three or more days a week and keeps the child until eight in the evening. The three days of routinely incurred parenting time of shorter duration may be added up and counted as a single day for parenting time purposes.

MORE TIME WITH CHILDREN

If the alternative residential parent spends ninety-two or more days per calendar year with a child, the assumption is that he or she is making greater expenditures on the child during parenting time for costs such as food and perhaps is paying child rearing expenses for items duplicated between the two households such as beds and clothing. A reduction to the ARP's child support obligation may be made to account for these transferred and duplicated expenses.

The amount of the additional expense is determined by using a mathematical formula that changes according to the number of days the ARP spends with the child and the amount of the BCSO. This mathematical formula is called a "variable multiplier."

Conversely, parents who have parenting time less than sixty-eight nights will have to pay an increased amount of support due to the other parent's increased expenses.

"Split parenting" can occur in a child support case only if there are two or more children of the same parents and one parent is the primary residential parent for at least one child and the other is the primary residential parent for another. Split parenting situations are calculated differently under the new Child Support Guidelines so that both parents are given credit for having more than 50 percent of the time with at least one child.

HEALTH CARE COSTS AND ADD-ONS

Under the Child Support Guidelines, the cost of medical insurance premiums (which can include dental insurance) for the children and the costs of work-related child care are included in the calculation for the support order. The parents must divide these expenses according to each parent's percentage of income, and every court order under the guidelines must address these expenses.

Uninsured medical expenses are added to the BCSO. These expenses must be routinely incurred so a specific monthly amount can be reasonably established and added to the BCSO. Parents must divide these expenses according to their percentages of income regardless of whether they are routinely incurred and added to the BCSO. Uninsured medical expenses may include deductibles, copays, dental, orthodontic, counseling, psychiatric, vision, hearing, and other medical needs not covered by insurance.

After calculating the BCSO and adding health insurance costs and work-related child support expenses, educational expenses for private or special schooling for children can be considered as a deviation from the presumed amount of support. The court may consider other special expenses such as music lessons, summer camps, travel, and other activities that may contribute to the child's cultural, social, artistic, or athletic development as deviations from the child support order and added to the child support amount.

These add-on expenses are not mandated under the Child Support Guidelines and must exceed 7 percent of the BCSO to create a deviation before they're added to the BCSO.

PAYING CHILD SUPPORT

Keep in mind that the guidelines are minimum requirements. Child support can be set above the guidelines' minimum requirements when warranted. One such instance could be a hardship deviation. Specific rules apply to a very narrowly defined hardship exception.

Courts can order an employer to deduct child support from the supporting parent's salary and pay it directly to the receiving parent. This is called a wage assignment. In Tennessee, the court should order it unless there is a good reason not to. This works extremely well. However, if the supporting parent is self-employed and gets much of his or her income in cash or is on a straight commission without a draw, this process might not be helpful.

A supporting parent may be ordered to pay child support through the state's collection agency. In many cases, such payments simplify the process for the custodial parent, who need not enter into confrontations with the supporting parent or use the children as collection agents. The agency maintains the record of payment, and when a parent fails to pay child support, the proof of the amount is much easier to obtain.

If the supporting parent moves out of state, the child support order may be enforced through both states' collection agencies. Armed with your state's court orders, you can go to the other state's court (often handled through the local district attorney or your local juvenile court) to enforce the wage assignment.

Child support is owed even if the supporting parent files for bankruptcy. Also, child support payments are not taxable income for the recipient parent or deductible by the paying parent. If your former spouse is not making child support payments after filing for bankruptcy, check with your lawyer immediately for advice.

Parents can agree to allow the parent paying child support (the ARP) to have the benefit of child dependency deduction as long as the recipient parent (PRP) completes and signs IRS Form 8332, which must be filed with the ARP's tax return. This is addressed in the Permanent Parenting Plan form.

INCOME DETERMINATION CHALLENGES

When a parent's income cannot be ascertained, the Child Support Guidelines read:

> When establishing an initial order and the obligor fails to produce evidence of income (such as tax returns for prior years, check stubs, or other information for determining current ability to support or ability to support in prior years), and the court has no other reliable evidence of the obligor's income or income potential, gross income for the current and prior years should be determined by imputing annual income of $36,369 for male parents and $26,989 for female parents.

After the initial order, for situations in which the court has no reliable evidence of a parent's income or income potential, then the court shall enter an order to increase the child support obligation of the parent failing or refusing to produce evidence of income by an increment not to exceed ten percent (10 percent) per year of that parent's share of the basic child support obligation for each year since the support order was entered or last modified.

RETROACTIVE SUPPORT OWED

In paternity cases, retroactive support may be ordered from birth and can include reasonable birth-related medical expenses. The court may also award child support retroactively to the date of separation of a married couple, abandonment of a child, or physical custody of a parent or nonparent caretaker. Retroactive support is generally calculated using the average income of the parties over the previous two years. Other provisions may apply if a parent has intentionally hidden a child to prevent visitation.

RUNNING YOUR OWN CHILD SUPPORT WORKSHEETS

Are you wondering how to fill out your Tennessee child support worksheets to determine support obligations for your kids? You can start by making two downloads directly from the Tennessee Department of Human Services. The Child Support Guidelines can be found at tn.gov/humanserv/is/isdownloads.html.

The first download offered on the state's website is the automated web-style calculator, ideal for crunching numbers under the Income Shares guidelines applicable in Tennessee child support cases.

The second download is for the child support and credit worksheets in Excel (versions are available for Windows and Mac). Line-by-line worksheet instructions are included. To make this a lot easier, the child support worksheet takes you through six key steps:

1. Identification

After you identify yourself, the other parent, and each of your children, you provide the number of days each child spends with you, with the other parent, and with a caretaker. That may take some reflection, but the information is very important to the child support case. The time each child spends with a parent or caregiver can vary depending on the circumstances. Consider the minor's age and stage of development. Does the child have special needs, a disability, or an ongoing medical condition? Do both parents work outside the home, requiring regular child care from a provider? Has one of you always been the primary caregiver?

2. Adjusted Gross Income

Both parents' monthly gross income is reported and adjusted. Income in the form of federal benefits received for a child is added to gross, while deductions are made for self-employment tax and child credits. The result is a combined monthly adjusted gross income (AGI) for the parents. There is no need to fret about figuring out child credits. Included in the DHS download is the worksheet you will use to calculate credits for both in-home and not-in-home children.

3. Parents' Share of BCSO

There is a basic child support obligation (BCSO) shared by both parents. You don't need to add the BCSO. Excel will automatically insert the figure using your combined monthly AGI, number of children, and basic child support amount from the Tennessee schedule (also included with this DHS download).

Depending on your circumstances, an adjustment may be appropriate for parenting time that could increase or decrease the amount owed to the primary residential parent (PRP). Most commonly, the PRP will receive a portion of the BCSO from the alternate residential parent (ARP). The total BCSO is rounded up to the nearest $50, so don't let that throw you off.

Are you and your ex sharing parenting time equally? Then you may need to make an important parenting time adjustment to your basic child support obligation.

4. Additional Expenses

The kinds of additional expenses that can increase child support include health insurance relating specifically to the children's coverage, any recurring medical costs not covered by insurance, and child care costs incurred while you and the other parent are at work. When additional expenses are added to the BCSO, the result is an adjusted support obligation (ASO).

5. Presumptive Child Support Order:

There is a maximum for the presumptive child support order (PCSO), depending upon the number of children in the family being supported. If you are seeking a child support modification, indicate on your worksheet the significant variance required from the original support order and whether you are a low-income provider.

6. Deviations and FCSO

Deviations from the presumptive amount of child support are not granted willy-nilly. The court-ordered reason for any increase or decrease from the PCSO needs to be included in step six. The result is the final child support order (FCSO), and Excel will automatically insert that amount into the worksheet for you upon completion of all the previous steps.

You can add a pertinent comment, detail your calculations, or provide a rebuttal to the child support schedule at the end of the worksheet. Before submitting your worksheet, though, consider seeking competent legal advice from a Tennessee lawyer experienced working in the area of child support.

Chapter 29:

EXPENSES CONSIDERED IN CHILD
SUPPORT CALCULATIONS

The Tennessee Child Support Guidelines are based on the Income Shares model. This means that both parents contribute to the support of the children in proportion to their actual available income. Under the guidelines, the total cost of raising a child is computed. Part of this computation is based on the income of the parents, and this amount is treated as the basic amount for most expenses such as housing, food, and transportation. Other expenses such as child care and medical expenses are highly variable. For these expenses, the guidelines look at the actual amount of the expenses.

To make the child support calculation, the court first computes the Basic Child Support Obligation (BCSO). This amount is based on the combined adjusted gross income of both parents and the number of children. Once this figure is determined, it is adjusted based on the additional expenses discussed in this chapter. After the BCSO is calculated, the additional expenses are added to the BCSO. The result of this computation is the Adjusted Support Obligation (ASO). This figure, along with the amount of parenting time by each parent, is used to compute the actual amount of child support.

The expenses used to compute the ASO include each parent's share of the children's health insurance and medical expenses. They also include work-related child care. Finally, in some situations, certain add-on expenses such as summer camp, music lessons, or athletics may be considered. In all, the BCSO is the amount of money the guidelines presume is necessary for everything the children need other than health care and work-related child care.

The ASO, on the other hand, covers everything: it is the BCSO plus the cost of health care and work-related child care. The reason why these two expenses are treated separately is because they can vary so much from family to family. For expenses such as food, clothing, and transportation, it is easiest simply to use a percentage of income. But for health care and child care expenses, the actual dollar amounts are used.

The rules governing each of these expense categories can be complicated, and this chapter explains how these expenses work into the child support calculation.

HEALTH INSURANCE PREMIUMS

The general rule for insurance premiums is that if the medical and/or dental needs of the children can be obtained by a parent at a reasonable cost, the amount of that cost must be included in the ASO. In applying the guidelines, the court will look at the amount of the insurance premium attributable to the child. The costs of insurance for others (the parent or children from another marriage) are not included. This is an easy calculation if the insurance premium is broken down by person.

However, in many cases, it's not possible to verify the exact amount for each child. Many employers offer health insurance for an entire family without specific additional amounts for each child. In this case, the total premium would be divided by the total number of people, and this amount would be the cost per child.

Once computed, the cost of the children's medical insurance is added to the BCSO and becomes part of the ASO. If the health care expense is completely paid by someone other than the parent, the amount paid is not added to the BCSO.

TennCare and Medicaid are not considered "insurance" for the purposes of the Tennessee Child Support Guidelines. Therefore, a court cannot order participation in either of these programs to provide for the children's health care needs.

WORK-RELATED CHILD CARE

Child care expenses are added to the BCSO if those expenses are necessary for a parent's employment, education, or vocational training. Before taking these expenses into consideration, the court must determine that the employment or education is appropriate. Also, the child care expenses must be appropriate to the parents' financial abilities and lifestyle of the child. The goal of the guidelines is to provide the same level of support as if the parents were living together. Therefore, to determine whether the expenses are appropriate, the court will look at whether they would have been appropriate if the parents and child were indeed living together.

For child care expenses, the amount used is the actual amount incurred by the parent. If the amount varies from month to month, the average monthly amount is used. If the child care is subsidized by a public assistance program, only the amount paid by the parent or caretaker is included in the calculation.

UNINSURED MEDICAL EXPENSES

All medical expenses should be taken into consideration when calculating the ASO. Since insurance premiums are generally in the same amount every month, they are dealt with separately above. But uninsured medical expenses also need to be considered. These include deductibles, copays, orthodontic expenses, counseling expenses, and vision and hearing care. If these expenses are incurred routinely, the monthly amount should be added to the BCSO in the same way insurance premiums are added. If these expenses are not routinely incurred, they are not included as part of the child support calculation. Instead, the court order should specify that these expenses must be paid by the parents. The division of these expenses would normally be based on the percentage of each parent's income, although the court might order some other type of division. If one parent fails to pay his or her portion of these expenses, enforcement can be pursued.

ADD-ONS

The court is required to take into consideration the expenses discussed above (health insurance, child care, and medical expenses). In some cases, however, the court may decide that certain "add-on" expenses can also be taken into consideration. These are called "special expenses" in the guidelines and include expenses for such things such as summer camp, music or art lessons, travel, and school extracurricular activities such as band or sports. If your child travels to play a competitive sport, here is a chance to include the costs and fees and the expenses for uniforms, gear, gas, and overnight accommodations. In most cases, these expenses are not taken into consideration because the guidelines look at them as being part of the ordinary costs of parenting, which are already included in the BCSO. However, if these expenses are more than 7 percent of the BCSO, the court will determine whether there should be a deviation from the Child Support Guidelines in that particular case.

Chapter 30:

NEEDED DOCUMENTS

In general, divorces require many different documents. For a very thorough list, see chapter 12 of the *Tennessee Divorce Client's Handbook: What Every Spouse Really Needs to Know*. For just child support or child support modification, the list can be much shorter as it just depends on the situation. If one of the parents owns a business, the list can be much more complicated because such a case may require one parent to produce business financials for two or more years and the other parent may need the assistance of a forensic accountant to review all of the documentation.

Note that the Tennessee parenting plan form (which is or becomes a court order when approved and signed a judge) requires each parent to send proof of income to the other parent for the prior calendar year as follows:

- IRS Forms W-2 and 1099 shall be sent to the other parent on or before February 15.

- A copy of his or her federal income tax return shall be sent to the other parent on or before April 15 or any later date when it is due because of an extension of time for filing.

- The completed form required by the Department of Human Services shall be sent to the Department on or before the date the federal income tax return is due by the parent paying child support. *This requirement applies only if a parent is receiving benefits from the Department for a child.*

- The parent paying work-related child care expenses shall send proof of expenses to the other parent for the prior calendar year and an estimate for the next calendar year, on or before February 15.

However, experience shows that for whatever reasons, unless specifically requested of one parent by the other, most parents don't seem to comply with this particular requirement. But before litigating these issues, a parent may choose to assemble this information and agree to exchange it, review it, and see if a modification is possible. For more discussion of child support modification, see chapter 47.

How many years of income information and documentation will you really need? In many situations, only the most recently completed two-year period plus the current year to date. But if a parent earns uneven commissions or bonuses or has some other reason to average income over a several-year period, the parent receiving child support may need up to five full years of financial documentation. Among the documents a parent receiving child support may need to review include, but are not limited to, the following:

- Most-recent pay stub summarizing earnings to date
- Income tax returns
    - state and federal
    - W-2s
    - 1099s
    - K-1s
    - supporting schedules
    - attachments, receipts, or schedules
    - depreciation schedules
- Financial statements (possibly prepared for mortgage or loan applications)
    - statements of net worth
    - balance sheets
    - income statements
    - profit-and-loss statements
    - statements of cash flow
- Business ownership records—if a parent is self-employed
    - stock certificates
    - charters
    - corporate minutes
    - operating agreements
    - trusts
    - joint venture agreements
- Resumes—if unemployed or underemployed
- Employment records, contracts, and explanations of benefits
    - employment agreement
    - documentation of compensation
    - bonuses, commissions, raises, promotions
    - expense accounts and other benefits or deductions
    - employment handbook or manual
- Stock options
    - detailed plan descriptions or plan summaries
    - benefit statements
    - employment contracts
    - schedules of vested and unvested granted stock options
        1. numbers of options
        2. exercise dates

       3.   exercise prices

       4.   expiration dates

       5.   vesting dates

- employment manuals
- brochures
- handbooks
- memoranda
- reload and replacement provisions

If your ex is claiming an income below what is expected or otherwise unrealistic for his or her spending level, you may want to consider imputing income to him or her based on that spending level and not the claimed amount of income to the IRS. If this is the case, you and your lawyer must handcraft a solution to this particular problem. But it may include requesting (or issuing subpoenas) for bank statements, investment account statements, credit card statements, and other documentation of assets and spending.

Under the Tennessee Child Support Guidelines, certain expenses are treated uniquely. The two most common are children's health insurance premiums and child care, including after-school child care. Both of these expenses are almost always addressed as part of the child support worksheets. Many employers lump health insurance premiums for a parent and the children into one figure. You may need documentation from the human resources department that breaks those figures out. You can ask human resources to let you know what you would be paying just for yourself; the difference between that and what you're paying can thus be attributed to your child or children.

Child care expenses can vary from month to month. You may want to assemble all the canceled checks for the most recent six months or school year and simply average the total. It is shockingly expensive to raise children. Often, neither parent, even the one paying the bills, knows how much it all costs. Take the time to come up with this figure; it may help to have that documentation and information ready.

Other common expenses or "add-ons" include:

- Private school tuition
- Tutoring
- Special-education needs
- Ongoing medical treatments not covered by insurance
- Psychological counseling
- Camps, scouting, competitive sports, music, and other activities
- Orthodontia
- Other routine or anticipated expenses

You may be required to document expenses as part of negotiations, mediation, or a court hearing. To negotiate for assistance with payments for some of these add-ons, you should be prepared to share the information and documentation with the other parent. If you know your daughter is going to need braces next spring, call your dental insurance and orthodontist for written statements or estimates of how much will be required to be paid and when. Avoid surprises whenever possible.

Parents can include additional routine and anticipated expenses in the child support calculation and have them paid pro rata in accordance with the ratio of the parents' income, or the parents can agree to share the expenses fifty-fifty or on some other basis. These fixed ratios could be "outside the calculation" or shared separately from the child support calculation. Depending on the circumstances, this may be considered an "upward deviation." In any event, as long as the child support calculation is correct and the parents are treating the additional expenses in a reasonable manner, almost all judges will approve the manner of payment agreed upon by the parents.

When lawyers say "documents," they mean the paper copies (or hard copies), the electronic versions, or both. Today, almost all scanned documents will be in Adobe Acrobat's PDF format. Bank statements can be mailed to you, but you may also be able to download them online, usually in PDF format. Personal financial management programs such as Quicken or Quickbooks may generate reports of monthly income and expenses. These reports may be printed on paper or stored in PDF format on your computer. Your lawyer may prefer to have the electronic versions of these files, and he or she may ask you to obtain a personal finance software program as well.

If you can, get hard copies and electronic copies. Save the electronic versions of the documents to a thumb drive, burn them to a CD, or email them to your lawyer. Because making copies of documents can be costly, you may want to avoid copying. However, skip photocopying only if you are absolutely sure the electronic versions are exactly the same.

Chapter 31:

GROSS INCOME (AND NOT INCOME)

The easiest way to think about "gross" income is to add up all income, taxable or not. The court ruled in a 1911 Tennessee case that a parent must provide support "in a manner commensurate with his means and station in life."[23] This philosophy of children benefiting from the financial success of their parents is the force behind Tennessee child support statutes and court decisions on everything from W-2 wages to sales of stock options.

Under the Tennessee Child Support Guidelines,[24] a long list of examples of income must be included in the computation of child support income:

wages

salaries

commissions, fees, and tips

bonuses

overtime pay

severance pay

self-employment income as an independent contractor, partner, or owner

net rental income less appropriate expenses

retained earnings

disability benefits

workers' compensation benefits

unemployment insurance

judgments recovered for personal injuries

interest income

dividend income

trust income

pensions and other retirement pay including but not limited to Social Security benefits

mandatory retirement account withdrawals

lottery winnings

Another source of financial benefits that can be included in the computation of child support is "fringe benefits." The Tennessee Child Support Guidelines[25] defines "fringe benefits" as income or in-kind payments in exchange for work if the benefit reduces personal living expenses. Examples of fringe

---

23   *Evans vs. Evans*, 140 S.W.745 (Tenn. 1911).

24   Rule 1240-2-4-.04(3).

25   Rule 1240-2-4-.04(3)(a)(4).

benefits that can be quantified and included in the gross income of the parent are a company car, housing, and meals.

The logic of the Tennessee legislature and courts in taking this inclusive approach to the calculation of gross income is that children should enjoy the higher standard of living the parents enjoy whether they are in a single household or are in separate households. When parents receive more money, even if it is a one-time event such as a bonus, judges generally include it in the computation of gross income for purposes of the child support calculation.

Tennessee offers a technique of income "averaging" that can be applied in certain circumstances. If a parent's income spikes or dips for unique reasons such as a particularly strong year in sales or the sale of a business, the court can average such windfalls over two or more years of income. This method can even out unusual financial occurrences and arrive at a more accurate financial picture of a parent's average income.

The court can also review multiple years of income and, even in the presence of changes of employment, find that from year to year, the gross income has been relatively consistent. One example of such a case was *Pace vs. Pace*.[26] The father, who was the child support payor, worked from 2005 to 2007 as an automobile broker. In 2006, he sold his ownership interest in the automotive dealership. He then dabbled in real estate investments until 2007, when he became partial owner of a different company. For purposes of computing the father's gross income, the court included all moneys received by the father in 2005 ($201,036), 2006 ($241,360), and 2007 ($242,278), and as these amounts were relatively consistent, the court used the father's 2007 gross income to calculate child support.

By contrast, what is not included in gross income is a very specific list in the Tennessee Child Support Guidelines.[27] The list includes such things as child support payments received to benefit children not of the parents to the pending case, TANF benefits, food stamps, SSI benefits, SSDI benefits, LIHEAP benefits, adoption-assistance subsidies, and income of the child. These excluded monetary benefits can be characterized as "means-tested benefits," benefits received as a result of low income to provide essential sustenance to the child and/or family.

When you are approaching a child support calculation of gross income, it is important to have complete copies of all tax filings for the past three to five years. Going through income tax returns and highlighting all figures declared whether taxable or not will result in a more thorough list of income from all sources. This inventory from Form 1040 to Schedule C will also be the starting point for the court as it adds up all moneys to be considered part of gross income for the purpose of calculating child support.

---

26 No. M2009-01037-COA-R3-CV (Tenn. Ct. App. Apr. 26, 2010).
27 Rule 1240-2-4-.04(3)(c).

Chapter 32:

COMMISSIONS AND BONUSES

Tennessee law requires that child support calculations be based on the gross income of both parents. The Tennessee Child Support Guidelines, a set of administrative rules on child support, work on the "income shares" model, that is, that both parents contribute to the support of the children in proportion to each of their incomes. The guidelines further explain,

> The Income Shares model for determining the amount of child support is predicated on the concept that the child should receive support at the same level that the child would receive if the parents were living together.

When considering the actual income of a parent, Tennessee, like most states, includes commissions and bonuses as part of the gross income of the parents. The guidelines define gross income as including "all income from any source … whether earned or unearned, and includes but is not limited to, the following: wages, salaries, commissions, bonuses, overtime payments …" The courts will consider past commissions and bonuses when determining how much child support a parent must pay based on the assumption that the best predictor of future income is past income.

On the flip side, judges are frequently told that commissions and bonuses are never guaranteed. Many factors come into play that determine bonuses or commissions paid to someone. In some work places, bonuses and commissions may be based on the work ethic of the employee, in others on the actual work completed, and in still others based purely on the business's profit. Many external influences have an impact on how big (or small) a bonus the employee receives. Did a recession slow business down? Did something change in the market that increased sales? If indeed so many factors unrelated to the individual's performance determine the payment of bonuses and commissions, is it fair to base child support on a parent's past gross income without considering possible future changes?

In *Stacey v. Stacey*,[28] the court ruled that a fixed amount of child support must be determined, including bonuses and commissions, for several reasons:

- A fixed payment based on previously earned income—including bonuses and commissions—allows both the noncustodial and custodial parent to plan accordingly for the households' finances.
- If the noncustodial parent is permitted to determine how much of his or her bonuses and commissions are included, needless time and energy are wasted and tensions between parents increases.

---

28   *Stacey v. Stacey*, 1999 WL 1097975 (Tenn. Ct. App. Oct. 6, 1999).

- Setting a definite amount allows the court to determine if the obliged parent is complying with court orders.

But this still doesn't solve the problem for the obliged parent who finds himself or herself without an expected bonus and thus unable to pay the court-determined child support. To prevent this situation, the courts and the parents need to take an active, creative role in determining child support and look beyond the pure mathematical calculation created by the guidelines.

HOW TO CALCULATE BONUSES AND COMMISSIONS FAIRLY

Rather than calculating income based only on one year (in which a large bonus may have been earned), the courts can review gross income over a two- or three-year period to best determine what the parent can expect to receive in wages over the coming years.

Courts can consider whether a bonus is speculative or predictable. When a parent receives a routine bonus of a certain percentage of his or her salary or has a *predictable* pattern of commissions, it is appropriate for the court to average the bonus or commissions over twelve months and include it in the parent's annual gross income.

If, however, the bonus or commission is not predictable, the court might consider excluding it from gross income. In *Velez v. Velez,*[29] for example, the Court of Appeals of Tennessee at Nashville did not include the father's bonus in the child support calculation because "the evidence in the record only indicated that Father had received a few bonuses and that these bonuses were not guaranteed in the future."

Tennessee parenting plans require parents to exchange income information annually. Tennessee law expects parents to seek to modify the child support on a regular basis. Unfortunately, the modification process can be more expensive than it should be. But by requiring the exchange of information, it is more likely that the money will be distributed fairly between the parties. One parent does not arbitrarily determine how much she or he will pay when there is a change in income (for the noncustodial parent), and alternatively, the receiving parent cannot make unfair demands. If the original child support is fair and takes into account unknowns, these modification requests will be unnecessary and used only when no alternative means can be found.

The Appellate Court held in Velez that "broad discretion is afforded the trial court in its child support determinations, and that discretion is bounded on all sides by the child support guidelines." In other words, bonuses and commissions must be included when calculating gross income for purposes of determining child support, but they must be considered in a way that ensures fairness to both parents while guaranteeing that every child's needs are met.

---

29   No. M2011-01949-COA-R3-CV (Tenn. Ct. App. Jul. 31, 2012).

Chapter 33:
OVERTIME

The subject of overtime income can lead to grief during child support calculations because, like claiming a child as a dependency/exemption for income tax purposes, overtime pay carries emotional attachment for the parent who worked the extra hours. The question for the court becomes finding a fair way to take any overtime pay into consideration so the child benefits from the additional income just as would be the case if the parents were cohabiting.

As always, one starts the child support question with a strict computation of child support in accordance with Tennessee's Child Support Guidelines, which make it clear that all income from all sources must be put into the calculation, and this includes overtime income.

The issue arises that the guidelines are equally clear that "variable income," which can include overtime pay, commissions, bonuses, and dividends, should be averaged over a period of time consistent with the facts of the case. Such variable income is added to routine wages or salary to calculate a parent's gross income for child support purposes.

The approach set out in the guidelines creates an opportunity for both parents to make arguments relative to overtime earnings. Arguments could be made for someone who worked overtime that it was a unique event, that it had not occurred in previous years, that it will not occur again, that there is no guarantee the overtime will continue, or that the overtime was not desired or sought but was imposed under special circumstances due to layoffs or hiring freezes.

For the employee working overtime, a successful argument against the strict inclusion of all overtime in the child support calculation, the battle is fact-intensive, may require a hearing, and will require documentation and third-party witnesses such as an employer or supervisor. One scenario might be a limited amount of overtime for the completion of a single project. Another might be a temporary overtime to cover responsibilities for an injured coworker. The burden of proof will be on the parent who worked overtime, and it will require detailed proof as to dates, wages, and circumstances.

The primary residential parent, however, has a chance to respond with information about a longer employment history, including overtime known to be worked while married or cohabiting, media reports about the employer for things such as increased production and government contract awards, or even presentation of rebuttal witnesses who may be fellow employees.

The issue of overtime pay in child support calculations is ultimately at the discretion of the court. A judge may determine it is appropriate to capture all the overtime pay but to smooth it out through income averaging over a period of two or more years. In a case involving a request for a modification, the court may find that the income modification threshold was not met because it was a unique, not an ongoing, event.

In one case[30] that included the issue of overtime pay, the father himself provided the essential testimony that sealed the decision that his overtime pay should be included in the child support calculation. The father testified that he had not received overtime pay for the preceding two weeks, but he later responded to questions whether overtime would be starting again by saying, "It always does."

This case illustrates how a fact-intensive matter such as the inclusion of overtime pay in a child support calculation often comes down to the responses to one or two questions that give the judge all the facts he or she needs.

---

30   *Widener vs. Widener*, No. M2010-02435-COA-R3-CV (Tenn. Ct. App. Aug. 12, 2011).

Chapter 34:

SELF-EMPLOYED PARENT'S INCOME
DETERMINATION

A child support case involving a self-employed parent who pays child support is going to be more difficult—every time—than a paycheck-collecting employee.

In Tennessee, the child support computation begins with a determination of a parent's "gross income," which includes income from "all sources," including self-employment income. Self-employment income is also defined in the Tennessee Child Support Guidelines as

> income from, but not limited to, business operations, work as an independent contractor or consultant, sales of goods or services, and rental properties, etc., less ordinary and reasonable expenses necessary to produce such income.[31]

It is helpful to cover this topic in light of federal income tax return documents. A person can be characterized as self-employed based on the type of income tax returns he or she files as well as year-end income documents received from the business.

A "sole proprietor" annually files a Schedule C to the IRS Form 1040. This tax return may even be completed by hand, using a shoebox of receipts and some bank statements. Simply because a sole proprietor had a tax preparer complete and file the return does not mean the accountant has reviewed any records or confirmed any figures; such is the role of an auditor. A sole proprietor might not have any annual income statement issued by the business, but a sole proprietor may have Form 1099s from persons or businesses that hired him to perform work and paid him at or over $600 during the year.

"Partners" are also self-employed. At year's end, each receives a federal Form K-1 to quantify their portion of the income, loss, and deductions of the partnership. This information flows onto a person's individual income tax return, much in the way that an employee W-2 Wage and Benefit Information flows onto a different line of the federal Form 1040. The partnership's tax return is assembled on Form 1065.

A person who owns a corporation are also considered self-employed. You might learn it is a C-corp, an S-corp, an LLC or PC or other variations of a corporation. These variations have to do with the annual earnings of the business and the owner's financial liability. The S-corp and LLC business owner also receives a Form K-1. These annual statements issued from a business go to the owner as well as to federal and state tax authorities.[32]

---

31   1240-2-4.04(3)(3)(i)
32   C-corp and PC owners file separate returns for the business and generally receive W-2s showing salary income.

One additional category of self-employment that routinely arises is that of income from rental property that is found on IRS Schedule E.

While an employee receives periodic paychecks from an employer, the self-employed person might receive a paycheck but also take a "draw" of money, defer income, or receive income disguised as company perks. Any benefits that are in excess of reasonable and customary business expenses might be excluded from deductions for the computation of child support.

Depreciation deductions taken on business tax returns are not allowed as part of business expenses for purposes of child support calculations. Any amount taken on an income tax return as a depreciation deduction is added back into income for child support calculations, although certain exceptions to this provision are in Tennessee appellate opinions.

As you can see just from this brief overview of tax documents related to self-employment, it is important to know what to ask for and how to read it or the child support calculation will be incorrect.

When a primary residential parent fears or can demonstrate that the parent paying child support has underreported income for tax purposes or otherwise hidden income, it may be time to involve an expert witness, a forensic accountant, in the review of the financial records of the self-employed parent. In rare cases, courts can even appoint an independent auditor to review the financial records of a company.

The real question in child support cases involving a self-employed parent is whether that parent is forthcoming with financial records to permit a reasonably accurate income and expense analysis. Whenever there is resistance to disclosing the requested books and the supporting documentation, one can essentially assume there is a problem with the bookkeeping and its accuracy or completeness.

Once the records are in hand, focus should be put on the gross receipts of the business. The revenue received by the business and whether it is accurately reported to the government on tax returns is a threshold question in a child support case. If you can prove that gross receipts were underreported, you will have gone a long way to making the argument that child support should be calculated at an amount higher than a strict computation using income tax returns.

One case that helps us to understand these principles is *Pace vs. Pace*.[33] The father was an automobile broker and a partial owner of Global Motor Sports. He sold that ownership interest and became partial owner of a different company, Dixie Motors. The father provided income tax records for 2005–2007, showing income of over $200,000 per year. Even though he claimed his income went down in 2008 to $32,750, the father failed to provide any proof of that 2008 income—no paystubs, tax returns, or anything else. Without any documentation of such recent decreased income, the court discredited the father's testimony and used the earlier income figures from his filed tax returns.

Another illustration from a self-employment child support case is *Parris vs. Parris*.[34] The father claimed he was a poet and construction company owner who also owned rental properties. He claimed his income from Harmony Industries for 2004–2006 was "negative zero." It turned out that bank deposits during the period April 2005 to April 2006 were $237,692, of which $191,109 was business income. The father claimed the money was spent. The court determined there were expenses of only

---

33   No. M2009-01037-COA-R3-CV (Tenn. Ct. App. Apr. 26, 2010).
34   No. M2006-02068-COA-R3-CV (Tenn. Ct. App. Sept. 18, 2007).

$41,880 attributed a net income to the father of $149,228, and computed his child support obligation to be $1,646 per month.

The "lifestyle audit" or the "net worth method" is another approach to a determination of the income of the self-employed parent that is particularly useful when documents are not forthcoming. Developed by the IRS, the lifestyle audit takes into consideration what one can see and value, e.g., a house, cars, motorized toys, trips, household help, and so on. The argument is then made that the only way someone could afford this level of living was to earn a certain amount of money per year over so many years.

Chapter 35:

CASH BUSINESS OWNERS—WHAT CAN BE DONE?

A self-employed parent who owns a business that routinely takes in cash is generally viewed by lawyers as the most difficult type of child support case. What has worked in favor of parents seeking child support is that so little cash is used any more in the modern economy that these cases tend to be less frequent, but the problem still comes up. Because not all the cash received may be recorded by owners of such a cash business, the income reported on tax returns and for child support likely represents only a small portion of the true sales of the business.

Typical business owners primarily paid in cash include retail sales, restaurants, bars, lawn cutting and landscaping services, and construction subcontractors such as painters or those who hang sheetrock. Some contractors may even provide an incentive to be paid in cash by general contractors by offering substantial discounts for payments in cash. Some cash business owners may even refuse any form of payment other than cash from customers.

A simple checklist of documents in self-employment cases begins with all income tax documents that can be obtained, from the Schedule C (Sole Proprietorship) to the Form K-1 (partnerships, corporations) to the Schedule E (rental property). One can also seek W-2 Wage and Tax Statements in addition to all Form 1099 Miscellaneous Income.

If the information contained in these tax-related documents would yield an unsatisfactory child support computation, one must stop and ask whether there is any possibility of actually proving unreported cash income. One might hear a story about a safe or a safety deposit box, but the odds of seizing those items via a court order in a timely fashion is slim. Or one might hear about a stash of cash taped behind file cabinet drawers or above a rafter or drainpipe, but rarely if ever can a parent seize the cash to bring to trial as proof.

Yet another problem surrounding cash freely floating into a parent's pocket is that if the other parent is a spouse and is knowledgeable of cash flow, or was a spouse who knew about this in the past, both parents could face false income tax reporting charges. The "innocent spouse" defense is hard to prove to the IRS when a parent now wants to vilify the self-employed parent who created the lifestyle the family was enjoying.

All debate aside, the first step in any child support case is the calculation of base child support starting with each parent's income. Courts generally start with income as last reported on income tax returns. For the self-employed parent with cash transactions, this is generally the IRS Schedule C, beginning with the bottom line for net income or loss.

One could almost view the reported net income as the least amount of income when a parent is self-employed. Some states such as New York presume that the self-employed routinely underreport income by at least 20 percent. Again, the question is whether one can find any evidence of cash in the form of deposits to a personal instead of a business account, checks being cashed but not recorded, or similar schemes.

As stated by the Tennessee Supreme Court,

> These self-employment guidelines are fashioned in such a way as to authorize the trial court to address the potential of a self-employed obligor to manipulate income for the purpose of avoiding payment of child support.[35]

An ex of a self-employed person should begin with tax-related information and the strict computation and then apply such additional elbow grease and wisdom as the credibility of the self-employed parent demands.

An excellent illustration of the kind of work required to attack the claims of a self-employed parent is *Parris vs. Parris*, discussed at the end of the last chapter. Expert accountants determined that his claim of earning only about $32,000 one year was not credible in light of the fact he had earned over $200,000 the three previous years, and the court based its determination of how much he owed in child support on this information.

The analysis conducted in Parris is a standard approach, but there are others. One is similar to the IRS "lifestyle audit" or "net asset method" (mentioned at the end of the last chapter), and another uses data from the Bureau of Labor Statistics "Wage Data by Area and Occupation" to show the court the average earnings in a given field, location, and education as indicative of the earnings potential of the self-employed parent.

Forensic accountants are often called to investigate and testify in situations like these. As expert witnesses, forensic accountants are experienced with many methodologies, techniques, and the law concerning cash-business owners who underreport or hide income. These special CPAs review tax returns and other financial statements, including bank statements, to gain a sense of the overall lifestyle and personal spending history of the business owner spouse. From there, the forensic accountant can work with the client and family lawyer to develop a plan to make sure that as much of the cash business owner's income as possible is included for calculation of child support.

---

35 *Taylor vs. Fezell*, 158 S.W.3d 352 (Tenn. 2005).

Chapter 36:

INCOME AVERAGING

Tennessee presumes the strict computation of child support is correct, but this is rebuttable. The analysis always begins with the strict computation, using each parent's gross income from all sources. But Tennessee leaves open the possibility that recent income is not indicative of the earnings history or the earnings capacity of a parent, and this allows the primary residential parent to argue that the income figure that should be used for child support calculations should be higher than one based solely current income.

One way to get an income higher than that reported on income tax returns taken into consideration is using "income averaging"—the court should average the reported income of the child support paying parent over a period of years. There is sufficient flexibility in this approach to make the argument for any length of years going into the averaging equation.[36] This possibility is dependent on the facts and circumstances of a given parent.

There are several scenarios in which an income averaging approach might be appropriate, including, for example, when a parent is reaching the natural winding down of his or her career due to age. In the case of *Berryhill vs. Rhodes*,[37] the mother successfully argued that to use only the two prior years' income of the father would be unjust or inappropriate given his career as a doctor who had been practicing since 1963 but who had been winding down his career.

While the mother did not have complete income information, she was able to demonstrate a wide variation in the father's income during the prior ten-year period. The range of income had a high of $333,856 and a low of $30,388. Because there were some gaps, the Supreme Court remanded the case back to the trial court to complete the information gathering and to determine the appropriate number of years to use in the averaging.

By contrast, consideration of case where a request for a longer duration of income averaging was lost allows us to see how the credibility of the parent paying child support factors into the judicial decision-making process. In *Richardson vs. Spanos*,[38] the Court of Appeals reviewed a trial court decision, including the trial court calculation of the income of the physician father for his child support obligation.

The earnings history in 2001 and 2002 of the father included earnings up to $100 per hour for contract work through West Tennessee Health Care, including annual income information. The father explained through his testimony how that contract had concluded without renewal and, through his employment search efforts, he was able to secure a comparable position at $65 per hour at Jackson-

---

36 In most cases, though, the averaging is usually two years and rarely will go greater than five years income averaged.

37 21 S.W.3d 188 (Tenn. 2000).

38 No. M2003-01139-COA-R3-CV (Tenn. Ct. App. Oct. 5, 2005).

Madison County General Hospital. Evidence was presented of the father's income during the first three months of 2003 under this new contract.

Affirming the two-year income averaging approach of the trial court, the Court of Appeals expressed its belief from the record on appeal that the father had not taken any affirmative steps to result in a situation of being underemployed. On that basis, it declined to reach further back into the father's earnings history to create a higher average gross income for purposes of the child support calculation.

Another example of income averaging is presented through the case of *Von Tagen vs. Von Tagen*.[39] The Appellate Court affirmed the approach of the trial court, which used income averaging to smooth out a one-time influx of income. The specific financial event in this case was the father's sale of a business that resulting in a one-time capital gain. The income figures were significant: in 2007, the father had an income of $395,930, compared to 2008 and 2009 income of $50,000. By averaging three years of income, the court set the father's income for purposes of child support computation at $165,300 per year.

---

39   No. M2009-00850-COA-R3-CV (Tenn. Ct. App. Mar. 12, 2010).

Chapter 37:

VOLUNTARILY UNDEREMPLOYED

OR UNEMPLOYED

When you consider that the Tennessee Child Support Guidelines is a mathematical formula, the calculation of basic child support sounds easy. You take the child support calculator and worksheets, you insert numbers such as each parent's income, the program does a little multiplication, a little division, and you have the matter solved, down to the last penny. Right?

Maybe not, if the support-paying parent isn't earning as much as the primary residential parent believes he or she should, could, or ought to be earning. In Tennessee, parents are to fulfill their financial responsibility to their children by exercising their earning capacity whether or not a parent has a relationship with his or her children.

In Tennessee, parents can make a claim that the other parent is "voluntarily unemployed" or "voluntarily underemployed." The allegation that someone is voluntarily unemployed is made when there is a lack of employment, a positive earnings history in the past, and/or a measurable level of formal education, on-the-job training, or career advancement. The voluntarily underemployed shows up mostly in cases in which the secondary residential parent has a job, is showing income, but is earning less than might be expected based upon earnings history, education, training, career, or other factors.

Each of these allegations is easy to make but difficult to prove because the parent making the accusation has the burden of proof in the matter. The cases in this subtopic of child support are not simple; these are typically not situations of doctors leaving lucrative medical practices to work the take-out window at a hamburger hangout in an attempt to reduce income and thus child support.

One case on the issue of "voluntary unemployment" was about a father claiming a medical disability prevented him from having gainful employment. In *Lowery vs. Womble*,[40] the Tennessee Court of Appeals decided that the father was fit for employment only after lengthy proceedings and a detailed review of his medical record.

Lewis vs. Robinson, another case involving a father claiming a medical disability prevented him from having gainful employment, went through a "voluntary underemployment" analysis and defeated the father's claim after he was caught driving even though he had presented a physician's letter limiting his physical activity.[41]

---

40   No. M2010-01102-COA-R3-CV (Tenn. Ct. App. Jun. 28, 2011).

41   State of Tennessee, ex rel.; *Robinson vs. Robinson* was decided in 2009 by the Tennessee Court of Appeals, No. M2008-02275-COA-R3-CV (Tenn. Ct. App. Jul. 30, 2009).

You can compare the Lowery and the Lewis cases against the defeat suffered by the mother in her claim of voluntary underemployment in a case decided by the Tennessee Court of Appeals in 2007.[42] This case was initiated by the father when he sought a downward modification of child support due to a change in his income. This was countered by the mother's claim that the father was "voluntarily underemployed," as the father went from earning $80,000 per year at the time of the parents' divorce to earning $35,000 per year at the time of the modification case.

The father had been terminated from his employment after the divorce and was facing criminal charges. But the mother relied only on her testimony and that of the father, and the father was not willing to discuss what had happened at the job to result in his termination and the criminal investigation. On the advice of his attorney, the father pled the Fifth, and the courts allowed his change of jobs to result in a downward modification of child support because the mother had failed to establish that the father had done anything wrong.

In the event that a parent proves the other parent is either willfully or voluntarily underemployed or unemployed, the court then "imputes" income to that parent and completes the child support calculation using that imputed income. It is up to the discretion of the court how much income is imputed or attributed to a parent who is earning less than he or she should. The primary criteria under the Tennessee Child Support Guidelines for the determination of the imputed income are the parent's past and present employment and the parent's education and training. In cases in which there is no reliable way to impute income, the Tennessee Child Support Guidelines fix the reasonable earnings capacity of a male parent at $37,589 per year and a female parent at $29,300 per year (as of 2012). These income figures can be viewed as a minimum income threshold for a parent who can participate in gainful employment without limitations of lack of education, physical or mental impairment, or other attribute that would impair one's ability to work.

In cases in which upward modifications of child support are being requested and a parent fails to or refuses to produce evidence of income, the child support order can be increased by 10 percent a year for each year since the child support order was last computed.

---

42   *Wine vs. Wine,* No. M2006-00855-COA-R3-CV (Tenn. Ct. App. May 18, 2007).

Chapter 38:

RECEIVING CREDIT FOR SUPPORTING CHILDREN LIVING IN A PARENT'S HOME

As the very configuration of "family" changes, there is an important distinction to be highlighted under the Tennessee Child Support Guidelines in the treatment of children who are half-siblings. The difference of whether half-siblings live together in the same household or are split between two households can mean a difference in how a credit for supporting those children is determined and the proof required.

As with any "other" children outside of a pending child support case, there are three mandatory criteria to get the issue before the judge: a legal responsibility for children, proof of support payments, and children outside the pending case.[43]

To successfully make the argument of being legally responsible[44] for a child, an adult must establish a biological relationship, an adoptive relationship, a voluntary acknowledgment of being the biological parent, a determination by a court, birth during a marriage, or birth within 300 days of termination of a marriage.

One can be legally responsible for a child in the context of providing a primary residence for the child and having 50 percent or more of the parenting schedule. This can be established by presenting the court order. The Tennessee Child Support Guidelines also invite submission of school and medical records for the child, particularly showing the child's address.

Proof of legal responsibility can also include a birth certificate, DNA test results, or a written acknowledgment of paternity. The Tennessee Voluntary Acknowledgment of Paternity form is a sworn statement filed with the office of vital records and certified by the government. Similar acknowledgment of another state's paternity forms may also serve this purpose. More information about this process is in Tennessee Code Annotated Section 24-7-113.

Stepchildren don't qualify under this criterion. In Tennessee, a parent can't claim a credit against income or ask for a deviation from a child support order because he or she is supporting stepchildren who are living with the parent. Any financial help made by a stepparent is considered voluntary. The Tennessee rule is that a parent has legal responsibility only for his or her own children, not for any stepchildren.[45]

---

43 Tennessee Child Support Guidelines Rule 1240-02-04.04(5)(a): "Adjustments to Gross Income for Qualified Other Children."

44 The phrase "legally responsible for a child" is defined within the Tennessee Child Support Guidelines Rule 1240-02-04-.02(14).

45 Rule 1240-02-04-.04-5(b).

The second criterion addresses the math. When other children are part of a parent's current household, in almost all conceivable situations, there isn't going to be a payable child support order for the other child not the subject of the order.

According to the Tennessee Child Support Guidelines, a theoretical child support order should be calculated as if child support was owed for the child. The theoretical child support calculation is then multiplied by 75 percent, and the resulting number is the credit.

The amount of the credit is calculated separately on the Credit Worksheet, which is a subschedule that comes after the primary Child Support Worksheet. That amount then appears on the Child Support Worksheet at line "1d," which reads "Credit for in-home children." The credit amount is subtracted from the gross income of the parent paying child support, before the multiplication of the percentage of the parent's gross income for child support purposes.

Even if all three criteria are established, the judge is not required to make a downward adjustment of child support. He or she is required only to "consider" any other children but may or may not thus make adjustments to the child support computation.

One other provision contains discretionary language: Tennessee Child Support Guidelines Rule 1240-02-04-.01(3)(g) requires the judge to

> allocate a parent's financial child support responsibility from the parent's income among all of the parent's children for whom the parent is legally responsible in a manner that gives equitable consideration … to children for whom support is being set in the case before the tribunal and to other children for whom the parent is legally responsible and supporting.

While this it is no more predictable than the other section (see discussion in chapter 39), it speaks to all children of a parent across households with a goal of equitable financial treatment.

Chapter 39:

RECEIVING CREDIT FOR SUPPORTING CHILDREN NOT LIVING IN A PARENT'S HOME

Parents with children with more than one partner face a challenge when it comes to winning a reduction of their child support obligation based on the other children who are not the children of the pending case. The labyrinth of requirements confuses parents, family lawyers, and judges.

Tennessee Child Support Guidelines Rule 1240-02-04-.04(5)(a), "Adjustments to Gross Income for Qualified Other Children" deals with the criteria involved in requests for reducing the amount of child support when the parent paying has other children with other partners. The parent paying has to establish a legal responsibility for another child outside the pending case as well as prove that he or she is paying support for that child.

First, the adult parent must have a "legal responsibility" for children who are biologically related to the adult, legally adopted by the adult, voluntarily acknowledged as a biological child by the adult, determined by a court to be the parent of the child, or be born during a marriage or within 300 days of termination of a marriage. The phrase "legally responsible for a child" is defined within the Tennessee Child Support Guidelines Rule 1240-02-04-.02(14), a section of various definitions relating to child support.

To establish "legal responsibility for children," the parent could be required to submit a birth certificate and/or DNA test results. Another means to demonstrate paternity is the Tennessee "Voluntary Acknowledgment of Paternity" form, which is a sworn statement filed with the office of vital records, which is then certified by the government. A similar acknowledgment of paternity form, completed in another state, may also be admissible if it fulfilled the requirements in the foreign state at the time it was signed. Tennessee Code Annotated Section 24-7-113 contains more information about the acknowledgment of paternity process.

For example, if a parent has one child who is the subject of a pending proceeding and has another child by another parent who was the subject of a different child support proceeding, the biological parent of the two children could satisfy this first criterion. In this scenario, the two children are half-siblings, having just one parent in common. The key in this example is that the parent with two children by different partners already has a child support order directing support for another child.

No credit or deviation can be claimed on the basis of stepchildren. Under the rules, even if a parent is supporting a household in which there are stepchildren, the parent has no legal responsibility to do so and thus can't ask for a reduction based on his or her status as a stepparent.[46]

---

46   Tennessee Child Support Guidelines Rule 1240-02-04-.04-5(b).

To establish the second criteria, proof of support payments, a parent could produce a written court order along with proof of payment through canceled checks, wage garnishments, and bank statements. It isn't enough to offer a child support order; proof of payment is important here.

Next, there is a calculation of actual documented support of qualified other children living less than 50 percent of the time in the parent's home. There are three types of documented proof of payments made. First, the parent seeking credit can produce checks or money orders paid to the other parent. Second, the parent seeking credit can provide a payment history of support that can come from the state's Internet website. Finally, actual documented support can include proof of "in kind" payments of food, clothing, diapers, or formula as long as payments like this were approved by the court. Depending on the situation, that proof may be very difficult to obtain.

Once the documented proof of support has been determined, there are a couple of limitations. First, to be eligible for the credit, the support for the other child must have been provided for at least twelve months prior to the new support order. Second, the total of actual documented support of the qualified other children living less than 50 percent of the time in the parent's home proven to be paid over the previous twelve months cannot exceed 75 percent of a theoretical support order. This means that a hypothetical child support order must be computed for the total number of qualified other children living less than 50 percent of the time in the parent's home. No specific details or requirements for that calculation is provided, but it is recommended that the assumptions made for this theoretical support order be as consistent as possible with the child support order being determined.

Even if all three criteria are established and an amount for credit is determined, the judge is not required to make a downward adjustment of child support but simply to take into consideration this financial obligation to those other children. The judge can make no changes or as much a downward adjustment as seems sensible.

The judge gets discretion in another matter. Tennessee Child Support Guidelines[47] require the judge to

> allocate a parent's financial child support responsibility from the parent's income among all of the parent's children for whom the parent is legally responsible in a manner that gives equitable consideration … to children for whom support is being set in the case before the tribunal and to other children for whom the parent is legally responsible and supporting.

While it is no more predictable than the other section, the idea behind it is that all children of a parent even in different households should be treated equitably in terms of financial support.

This credit is calculated on the Credit Worksheet part of the primary Child Support Worksheet. The result of the Credit Worksheet appears in the child support calculation is on line "1e" of the first page of the Child Support Worksheets which reads "Credit for not-in-home children." The math for the credit is calculated on the subschedule, and that bottom-line amount is then pulled up to the first page of the child support worksheet to reduce the gross income of the parent who provides support for the additional child or children.

---

47   Rule 1240-02-04-.01(3)(g).

Chapter 40:

TRAVEL EXPENSES FOR LONG-DISTANCE PARENTING

In the global economy, more and more parents have to travel farther and farther to find good-paying jobs, and that can mean second families are being started in other states, even abroad.

If an alternative residential parent has children living with a primary residential parent in Tennessee, the visiting parent has to factor into his or her relocation decision whether the costs of long-distance visitation exceed the financial gain of long-distance employment. There is no requirement for the parent in Tennessee to make any financial contribution to long-distance visitation expenses. As well, long-distance visitation expenses might not result in a reduction of the departing parent's child support obligations. Under Tennessee's parental relocation laws,

> The court shall assess the costs of transporting the child for visitation and determine whether a deviation from the child support guidelines should be considered in light of all factors including, but not limited to, additional costs incurred for transporting the child for visitation.[48]

An additional sentence also enters into this topic:

> If parenting time-related travel expenses are substantial due to the distance between the parents, the tribunal may order the allocation of such costs by deviation from the [presumptive child support obligation], taking into consideration the circumstances of the respective parents as well as which parent moved and the reason that the move was made.[49]

These provisions merely require the judge to "consider" whether a reduction in child support should occur as a result of visitation transportation costs. There is no mandatory reduction in child support for travel related to visitation. There is also no formula to tell a judge how to calculate an adjustment to a parent's child support obligation such as allocating costs between the parents or cost-offset ratio against a strict computation of the child support obligation.

Because the travel expenses reduction is fraught with judicial discretion, the long-distance parent should be ready to argue for a specific, quantified reduction in child support and to demonstrate the reduction relative to the actual costs of long-distance visitation. The relocating parent might also want

---

48   Tennessee Code Annotated Section 36-6-108.
49   Tennessee Child Support Guidelines at Rule 1240-2-4-.07(2)(c).

to demonstrate a solid history of taking part in all local visitation opportunities to help bolster the claim that visitation, even if expensive, will continue.

Another common proof problem in these types of cases is that the application will be quickly filed before any pattern of expenses has been incurred. Perhaps there was only one round-trip ticket and the local parent argues that cheaper flights are available. Perhaps the relocating parent also has a modification application pending for the parenting schedule, leaving the amount of travel for the child as yet undetermined. Or perhaps a long-distance schedule was agreed upon as well as a downward modification of child support but the schedule isn't being followed.

The Tennessee Court of Appeals in the 2008 case of *Long vs. Long* attempted to deal with long-distance visitation expenses. The father lost his request for a reduction of child support due to long-distance visitation expenses. The Longs had three minor children when they divorced. The family had moved several times over the years—indeed, one child was born in Virginia, another in Florida, and the third in Tennessee. The parents separated while both lived in Tennessee, but during their separation, the father moved to Maryland. If the facts had stopped there and remained focused on employment as the basis of relocation, the case might have had a different outcome.

However, the Court of Appeals did not consider the father as a sympathetic parent and concluded that the father's move to Maryland was to be closer to his girlfriend. Unfortunately for the father, the trial court and the Court of Appeals repeatedly focused on the father's trips with his girlfriend, gifts to her, secret bank accounts, cashing of work checks, gambling debts, and his claims he couldn't meet the temporary child support and alimony awards of the trial court. Between these judicial findings and the father's greater income, there was no adjustment to his child support obligation to account for long-distance visitation expenses.

If anything is certain about the long-distance visitation case, it is that it will be fact-intensive and that the motivation of the parent who is moving will be crucial to asserting a winning case for a child support adjustment based on travel expenses.

Chapter 41:

SPECIAL-NEEDS CHILDREN

Child support is generally payable in Tennessee until a child turns eighteen or graduates from high school, whichever is later. But when a child is disabled, child support can be ordered until the child turns twenty-one, and, in specific circumstances, even longer. Children with disabilities are exceptions to the general rule that a parent's duty to financial support a child ends at the age of majority.

Under Tennessee Child Support Guidelines,[50] a disabled child is defined (in line with the Americans with Disabilities Act language) someone with a physical or mental impairment that substantially limits one or more major life activities, when a person has a history or record of such an impairment, or when a person is perceived by others as having such an impairment.[51]

The phrase "major life activities" is also explained in the ADA section to include caring for oneself, performing manual tasks, seeing, hearing, eating, sleeping, walking, standing, lifting, bending, speaking, breathing, learning, reading, concentrating, thinking, communicating, or working. The stated timeframe is a substantial limitation of a major life activity lasting six months or longer.

When a child over twenty-one is "severely disabled" and continues to live under the care and supervision of a parent, the court can determine it to be in the child's best interests to remain at home with the parent and to order continuing support if the other parent is financially able. The child must have been severely disabled before reaching age eighteen. When all factors of Tenn. Code Ann. section 36-5-101(k)(2) are met, the court may use the Child Support Guidelines to set the amount of support to be paid.

Although there are various laws involved that can sound quite technical, the reality is that in cases involving children with disabilities and special needs, the courts normally craft very practical and individualized solutions. Judges may want evidence from various witnesses such as doctors, therapists, teachers, and other professionals providing services to the child. The testimony about the child's needs can be as technically complex as the laws, but with that information, judges have the legal authority to design and implement a ruling suited to each child.

---

50   Tennessee Code Annotated Section 36-5-101(k).
51   42 United States Code Section 12102.

Chapter 42:

PRIVATE SCHOOL TUITION

Any discussion of financial support for children, including a conversation about private school tuition, must begin with child support essentials. One must begin with the formula computation of each parent's child support obligation, including the capture of each parent's total income. Until this mandatory base child support calculation has been performed, one cannot move on to consider anything else.

In the Tennessee Child Support Guidelines, private school tuition comes under the heading of an "extraordinary educational expense" that can trigger a greater child support award. The standard child support computation takes into consideration that a child will attend public schools, so when a parent requests a private school contribution from the other parent, that's a request for money in addition to the base child support computation.

According to the Tennessee Child Support Guidelines, "extraordinary education expenses" include, for example, tuition, room and board, fees, books, and other expenses associated with private elementary or secondary schooling and/or associated with special-needs education. Such costs are reduced by any scholarships, grants, stipends, or other cost-reducing programs award to or received by the child to offset costs of attendance.

A primary residential parent can have the authority to make educational decisions on behalf of the child and even to enroll a child in a private school without seeking or obtaining the other parent's consent and turn to the court to obligate the other parent to contribute to those expenses. When a child lives at a private school at any point through grade twelve, the child is deemed to be living in the primary residential parent's household for child support purposes.

The equation is not all within the control of the primary residential parent, however, as the courts will determine the private school tuition contribution of the other parent based on each parent's income. The courts will look also to the primary residential parent's income when considering the upward deviation to the child support obligation of the other parent.

The ability of the courts to consider the income of the primary residential parent when setting the contribution of the alternate residential parent to private school tuition was created by *Barnett vs. Barnett* in 2000.[52] The alternate residential parent was a doctor who was paying $3,700 per month in child support based on $209,206 in gross income. Already $700 per month of that child support award was to go into a trust fund for the child's college education.

In a thorough discussion of the authority of the court to require a parent to pay "extraordinary" sums toward private school tuition in addition to the mandatory child support award, the Supreme Court concluded that consideration of both parents' incomes would best achieve the equity intended by the Child Support Guidelines.

---

52   27 S.W.3d 904, decided by the Supreme Court of Tennessee (Tenn. 2000).

A central goal of the guidelines and court decisions such as Barnett is to achieve the economic benefits for children that they would have enjoyed if the parents were living together. The Barnett decision cautioned against the wholesale imposition of a private school tuition on the noncustodial parent, however, lest it be "unjust or inappropriate" to balancing the economics of the household of each parent.

While it is not a requirement for the primary residential parent to consult with or justify the selection of a private school with the other parent, the Tennessee courts have commented at times in favor of private school enrollment. One situation is a child with special educational needs or the need for special classroom and support structures to meet emotional and behavioral needs.

One case that well illustrates all these principles is *Richardson vs. Spanos*,[53] a 2005 Tennessee Court of Appeals case. The parents had an eleven-year-old who had developmental challenges and learning disabilities. He had attended private schools from kindergarten on. He was moved through several different private schools and additional testing until enrolling at a Nashville school that offered individualized programs for students.

His father was a physician who was paying $1,314 per month in child support. The court noted that the combined annual income of the parents was $160,000 and that the father's income was $135,000 per year, so it required the father to pay 55 percent of the private school tuition.

The Richardson decision and others tell us that private school tuition court decisions are determined on a case-by-case basis and are fact-intensive. Each parent can expect to present information about income, earnings history, education, and assets. The principles of these and other court decisions have become part of the Tennessee Child Support Guidelines and are now the required analysis in all cases involving applications for contribution to private or special-needs education.

---

53   No. M2003-01139-COA-R3-CV (Tenn. Ct. App. Oct. 5, 2005).

Chapter 43:

COLLEGE TUITION AND COSTS

A court can't order a parent to pay college expenses and tuition, but it can order more-affluent parents to contribute to a college trust fund. Tennessee Child Support Guidelines in 2013 state that a child support obligor who earns more than $10,000 a month net may be required to have money "be placed in an educational or other trust fund for the benefit of the child."[54]

The pillar of the Tennessee child support system is the "base child support" paid by the alternative residential parent to the primary residential parent for the support of a child until age eighteen or graduation from high school, whichever occurs later. The Tennessee Child Support Guidelines don't provide for college or other postsecondary education. This limitation on court authority is a bright line that even restricts a court from ordering a parent to produce financial information for college financial support applications.

So when we talk about college tuition child support cases, we are talking only about cases in which parents have entered into a written, signed contract that meets all requirements to be enforceable by the courts. These clauses are typically found in a Marital Dissolution Agreement that the parents sign to settle all legal matters between them in divorce cases. The agreement can also appear as part of a Permanent Parenting Plan.

Once the college expenses of a child are part of a legally binding contract, the courts have authority to interpret these terms just as with any other contract. This is true even when the contract is part of a final decree of divorce.

Taken with this important caveat, what we see in our discussion of this topic are contracts entered into by parents before children enter college that are litigated in courtrooms some years after they were signed.

It is not uncommon for parents to enter into a written contract with a provision for contribution to "college costs." The first question that arises is to define those costs, whether tuition, room and board, college-sponsored health insurance, or books and supplies. Contract language can and should be negotiated and written with care to define the term "college costs" from these and other related examples.

The second—and more significant—question is to define "college costs" to specify any limits. Consider, for example, the difference in cost of in-state tuition for the 2012–2013 academic year at the public college Columbia State Community College of $2,605 compared to Vanderbilt University, a private college whose tuition is $35,278. These tuition-only figures do not reflect all the additional charges that can be incurred. Before signing a contract to contribute to college costs, parents should consider their incomes, career trajectories, and anticipated assets.

---

54 Rule of Tenn. Dept. of Human Services 1240-2-4-.07(2)(g)(2)(iii).

This suggested analysis is not unlike that which is performed by the courts as they evaluate parents' current income, income at the time of signing the contract, career history, career prospects, and anticipated financial assets. The courts frequently get involved in this analysis because of the common use of the phrase, "reasonable college costs." When this phrase appears in a contract, the courts have no choice but to determine reasonable to whom? Courts will use a parent's income, employment, and assets at the time of signing the contract as a benchmark to piece together what a parent might have had in mind when approving that contract language.

One interesting case on this very matter of "reasonableness" of tuition is *Hathaway vs. Hathaway.*[55] The parents' contract included the sentence, "The husband shall pay all customary and reasonable tuition expenses for the parties' minor children in obtaining a bachelor's degree or its equivalent." The question before the court was whether the $19,800 tuition for the 1999–2000 academic year at the Maryland Institute of Art was "reasonable," particularly in consideration of the father's nineteen years' employment with the state and his annual income of $50,000.

The Court of Appeals determined that "reasonable" college costs must be evaluated on the facts and circumstances of each particular family: "Courts must consider the practical results of their decisions, and not inflexibly apply a rule with no thought to the consequences."

With the father's income and employment history in mind, the Court of Appeals fashioned guidelines for the trial court to recalculate the father's required college tuition contribution, limited to 50 percent of in-state tuition at Tennessee or Florida state universities, whichever was higher (Tennessee being the father's home state, Florida being the residential state of the mother and daughter).

Finally, it is interesting to note that in families with sufficient financial resources, the Tennessee courts have extended their authority to include the ability to order a portion of child support during a child's minority be set aside in a trust fund to be established to pay for future college expenses. This can be true even in the absence of a contract binding the child support paying parent to contribute to college expenses, as was found in the case *Nash vs. Mulle.*[56]

---

55   No. E2002-00659-COA-R3-CV (Tenn. Ct. App. Nov. 26, 2002).
56   846 S.W.2d 803 (Tenn. 1993).

Chapter 44:

EQUAL PARENTING TIME

Questions about the calculation of child support can arise when parents share parenting time with their children. The phrase "shared time" in Tennessee is a very strict calculation of the days the children spend with each parent. The Child Support Guidelines in Rule 1240-2-4-.02(12) defines "Fifty-Fifty Parenting" synonymous to "equal parenting," as each parent having precisely 182.5 days with the children.

One might think that in such a mathematically equal parenting situation there would be no "primary residential parent" and "alternative residential parent" designation. However, the Child Support Guidelines dictates that "the Father is deemed the [Alternative Residential Parent]"[57] and "the Mother assumes the role of the [Primary Residential Parent] for all children."[58] The Tennessee Child Support Guidelines very strictly reinforce traditional divorce parenting roles even in the circumstances of a true, shared custodial relationship.

The mandatory designations of the mother as the Primary Residential Parent means that child support will be calculated against the father as if it were a typical, or less than fifty-fifty shared custodial schedule. Any adjustment to the child support obligation as a direct result of engaging in 50/50 parenting occurs as an adjustment to the father's strict child support obligation to the mother.[59]

Every child support case in Tennessee begins with a strict computation of the primary residential parent's "basic child support obligation." This strictly calculated basic child support obligation is "presumed" to be correct.[60] Then and only then can the court consider any "adjustments" to be made for parenting time and/or additional expenses. An "adjusted support obligation" is one that is changed to reflect parenting time, health care insurance, work-related child care expenses, and recurring uninsured medical expenses.[61] The rationale for this formulaic approach can be found deep into Rule 1240-2-4-.04(7), which states that in cases of equal parenting time, the parent with the higher income is expected to contribute to the expenses at the other household even if the parent with the higher income is the primary residential parent. So, Tennessee primary residential parents can owe child support to the alternate residential parents.

---

57 Rule 1240-2-4-.04(7)(b)(2).
58 Rule 1240-2-4-.08(2)(c)(1)(iii)(I).
59 Rule 1240-2-4-.08(2)(c)(4)(iii).
60 Rule 1240-2-4-.02(5) and (20), along with Rule 1240-2-4-.04(6)(a).
61 This is as defined in Rule 1240-2-4-.02(2) and (18), as well as Rule 1240-2-4-.03(6)(d)(2) and 1240-2-4.04(7).

Chapter 45:

CAPS ON CHILD SUPPORT FOR
HIGH-INCOME PARENTS

When it comes to computation of child support, one hears repeatedly the critical importance of starting the analysis with a strict computation in accordance with the Tennessee Child Support Guidelines before considering any variation or special circumstances. However, there is a caveat to put on this rule: the strict computation applies only to the first $10,000 of monthly net income after taxes, above which the primary residential parent must demonstrate additional needs of the child that would justify a higher award.

The cap plays out as follows. The strict computation is made on all income from all sources, just as in every other Tennessee child support case. Likewise, certain deductions to incomes and various credits will be applied. However, the net income is capped at $10,000 per month, to which the child support percentages are applied. The top line calculation of child support becomes to the following dollar amounts:

- $2,100 per month for one child
- $3,200 per month for two children
- $4,100 per month for three children
- $4,600 per month for four children
- $5,000 per month for five or more children

The primary residential parent has the option to argue that child support should be awarded above the cap to meet the reasonably necessary needs of the child or children. The burden of proof on the primary residential parent is a "preponderance of the evidence," which simply translates into roughly more than half in favor of the argument. The primary residential parent must establish that it is more reasonable than not for the child to receive a higher amount of child support than provided under the cap.

The primary residential parent can build the argument for additional support in many ways because the goal is to provide the child of wealthy parents with the advantages the child would have enjoyed if the parents were cohabiting. Arguments have successfully been made for additional child support for purposes such as investment in an educational trust, athletic skills, extra amenities, and opportunities to begin lucrative careers. Other available additions can include study abroad, traveling with sports teams, or private lessons.

Part of what the primary residential parent seeks to establish in these cases is that the child support will actually be spent on or invested into a trust for the benefit of the child. A detailed budget of current expenditures along with documentation of proposed expenditures combined will help the court understand what is being proposed to benefit the child. Safe housing, nutritious food, private school, lessons, cultural and recreational activities, memberships, travel, and such other things as are directly involving the child should be the focus of the presentation.

Detailed arguments along these lines can help rebut the idea that additional child support will end up benefiting the primary residential parent or other household members. While it might be true that a primary custodial parent who moves with a child into a safer neighborhood also receives a benefit, the emphasis should be placed on how it benefits the child in terms of the child's safety, opportunities for friendships, and progressive independence of movement between home and school.

An often cited case on this topic is the Supreme Court of Tennessee case *Nash vs. Mulle*.[62] The father's earning history started at approximately $30,000 per year and climbed as high as $292,000. The decision empowered the primary residential parent to put $1,780 per month of a child support order of $3,092 per month in a trust fund for the child's college education.

The court crafted the decision with great care, reaching back through more than a hundred years of Tennessee child support cases to extract the consistent, guiding principles that supported its decision. The court emphasized the goal of supporting a child in a manner reflective of both parents' financial circumstances as a goal "consistent with our long-established common law rule, which requires that a parent must provide support in a manner commensurate with his means and station in life." The court also very plainly stated that "the child of a well-to-do parent [should] share in that very high standard of living."

It is worth considering an approach to these cases that highlights the lifestyle of the parent paying child support, particularly if he or she has other children who receive lifestyle benefits not otherwise available to the child. In one case on this topic, the court commented on a father's multimillion dollar assets, $1,700 house payment, $1,550 car payments, and $750 boat payment. It also cited an $18,000 in-ground swimming pool recently installed at the father's house. The case of *Norton vs. Norton*, decided in the Madison County Chancery Court in 2000, remains an interesting illustration on the persuasive value of lifestyle information.

Also interesting to note in high-income cases is that the benefits of the child support payments may be given to the child even after the child support order has concluded. For example, a child support order might conclude at age eighteen, while the child continues to receive the benefits of an educational trust accumulated during the child's minority to pay for college after age eighteen. In such cases, caution should be taken that a failure to actually use the accumulated funds for the intended purpose may create an argument for the parent who paid the child support to obtain a refund of that money. The court order and trust document should clearly state what must happen with leftover funds.

---

62   846 S.W.2d 803 (Tenn. 1993).

Chapter 46:

ENDING CHILD SUPPORT

ENDING CHILD SUPPORT WITH ONE CHILD

If you are obligated to pay child support in Tennessee, eighteen is the magic age for ending it. Under the Tennessee Child Support Guidelines,[63] a "child" is defined to be someone under eighteen or still in high school, whichever occurs later. In Tennessee, we generally refer to the age of majority as eighteen, the legal age established by state law after which an individual is no longer an unemancipated minor.

There are variations to this general rule that eighteen is the age of emancipation from the child support obligation in Tennessee. First, there is a separate Tennessee guideline for a disabled child who may be entitled to the benefit of child support until age twenty-one. For severely disabled children, child support may continue for the life of the child. Also, parents can enter into a consensual, written agreement to continue child support until college graduation.

Additional circumstances under which a child support order may be terminated are the marriage of the child, the death of the child, or if the whereabouts of the child and the other parent are unknown.[64]

Just as the child support obligation tends to begin with a court proceeding, parents who pay child support are prudent to file a court action to seek a court order at the end of their child support obligation. This move to declare an end date for child support payments can also be used to memorialize that there is no child support owing or to quantify any arrears and establish a repayment schedule.

A parent who believes his or her child support obligation is about to or has ended can file a petition to terminate that obligation. The basic allegations made in this petition are that the child is emancipated by virtue of age and that the parent has fully discharged the child support obligation or has otherwise met the requirements of the case. The relief requested is the termination of child support.

A parent filing a petition to terminate child support should be given a hearing date within thirty days of the filing of the petition.[65] If both parents appear and agree their child is emancipated, the court can approve such an agreement. If there is a conflict over whether the child is emancipated, the court can hear testimony to reach its decision.

As part of the proceeding, any arrears due at the time an order for child support would otherwise terminate are then reduced to a judgment. The monthly payment or such amount set by the court will then continue, including by an income withholding arrangement, until the arrears and any costs are satisfied.[66] Child support arrears remain enforceable through court-ordered contempt, even after a child is emancipated, and courts cannot forgive child support arrears.[67]

---

63 Rule 1240-2-4-.02(7).
64 Tennessee Code Annotated Section 36-5-503.
65 Tennessee Code Annotated § 36-5-405.
66 Tennessee Code Annotated § 36-5-101(f)(3).
67 Tennessee Code Annotated § 36-5-101(f)(1).

Some judges have ruled that a parent remains obligated to continue child support payments until the court enters the order terminating the support obligation, so parents are strongly advised to take care of this in a timely fashion and not risk this potential legal nightmare.

Whatever the basis for the claim of emancipation of a child, the child support payor should file with the court in a timely manner to terminate his or her obligation to pay that support. The court proceeding can determine the validity of the claimed emancipation event, order the termination of child support, and quantify any arrears due and the terms of payment.

PRORATING CHILD SUPPORT WITH MORE THAN ONE CHILD AS AGE OF MAJORITY IS REACHED

When parents have more than one child in common who are the subject of a child support order, as each child is emancipated, the parent paying child support is entitled to request a downward modification of child support. Specifically, the child support paying parent can request the child support obligation be prorated to reflect the lesser obligation to fewer children. The new calculation of the child support obligation will take into consideration each parent's current income and the numbers of nights the remaining children are with each parent.

The most common basis for declaring a child emancipated is the child's eighteenth birthday or graduation from high school, whichever is later. As stated by the Tennessee Supreme Court, "Proration is simply a rule of law which derives from the legal principle that parents generally owe no duty to support children who have attained the age of majority."

As each child is emancipated, the parent paying child support is entitled to request a downward modification of the existing child support order. The parent can simultaneously request confirmation that no child support arrears are owed or a statement that quantifies the arrears owed and the terms of repayment. The court proceeding to terminate child support for one or more children is an opportunity to "set the record straight" and helps to reduce ongoing conflict or confusion over what is owed and for which children.

A parent remains obligated to continue paying child support as per the current court order even if it appears a child has become emancipated. Only the court—not a parent—has the authority to modify or terminate a child support order. When it reaches its decision, the court can make its final decision retroactive to the date of the termination event if that's appropriate. If excess child support is paid while the court is determining the case, the court can order that excess to be a credit toward future child support for the remaining children.

It is not enough to rely on a verbal agreement with the custodial parent to modify child support in the case of emancipation or any other circumstance. Until and unless the governing child support order of the court is modified by a judge, the court order remains fully enforceable by the parent collecting child support.

The gravity of the problem that can befall a child support payor who relies solely on a verbal agreement with the primary residential parent is illustrated by *Clinard (Brown) vs. Clinard.*[68] The mother, who was the primary residential parent, accepted $25 per week instead of the court-ordered $60 per week for fifteen years only to sue the father for child support arrears, plus interest, plus contempt a full eight years after the youngest child was emancipated. The court prorated the father's child support obligation as each one of three children became emancipated and calculated the arrears owed by the father at $15,235 plus interest be paid at the rate of 12 percent per year.

A court isn't required to reduce the total amount of child support payable for multiple children even when one or more children become emancipated. The court will be obligated to make a fresh child support computation as per the Tennessee Child Support Guidelines, but the court can decide that an upward deviation from the strict computation is appropriate to the facts and circumstances of the case. In other words, the court is empowered to continue the same amount of child support even if it will benefit fewer children.

Parents who believe a child has or is about to become emancipated should consult with an attorney about filing a petition with the court to prorate the child support obligation. It is important to utilize current income information to calculate a comparison between the current order and the prospective order for the remaining children. Also, a review of the current child support order is an opportunity to quantify any arrears, reduce them to a judgment, and set payment terms, but there is no substitute for good bookkeeping that will avoid misunderstandings and mistakes that can costs thousands of dollars.

---

68   No. 01-S-01-9502-CV-00021 (Tenn. Ct. App. Sept. 25, 1995).

Chapter 47:

MODIFYING CHILD SUPPORT

Tennessee, like many other states, has established methods or models the court will use to calculate the amount of a support obligation. Previously, Tennessee courts determined support orders using a Flat Percentage model, which calculated support based only on the income of the alternative residential parent, and the courts presumed that the residential parent would provide an equal amount of support. But the Flat Percentage model failed to take into account the incomes of both parents and failed to consider the actual expenses of child rearing such as health insurance, work-related child care, and the number of nights the child spent with each parent.

The change in legislation from the Flat Percentage model to the Income Shares model has an important effect on how a court will examine a parent's modification request. This manner is dependent on the date that a current support order was established as well as the model was used to calculate it. Specific criteria must be met prior to requesting a modification, and this can vary depending on whether a current support order was established under the Flat Percentage model or the Income Shares model.

Both models utilize what is called a "significant variance" standard, the minimum level of change required to seek modification. Depending on the situation, this minimum change may consider factors such as changes in income, changes in support amounts based on application of the new model, and other factors that would permit an exception to the significant variance rule or deviation from the guidelines.

ORDERS ISSUED AFTER JANUARY 18, 2005, TO BE MODIFIED

If the child support order to be modified was established after January 18, 2005, under the Income Shares model, there is a more simplified "significant variance" standard to be met. Here, the only condition required to establish a significant variance is the 15 percent change requirement for support orders of $100 or more or a 7.5 percent change for low-income providers.

In sum, both models determine whether a significant variance exists based upon a comparison of the percentage of change between the current and proposed order. The main difference is that orders established before January 18, 2005, require additional circumstances to be present to determine whether there is a significant variance.

In either case, deviations, whether previously ordered or proposed, should not be used to calculate a percentage in change for purposes of determining whether a significant variance exists. A deviation is when the court permits an adjustment in the amount of support that would have been ordered under support guidelines when certain circumstances exist that would make the application of the guidelines unjust or inappropriate. When circumstances that permitted the deviation have not changed, a modification may not be requested unless other independent circumstances have occurred and have created a significant variance.

There are exceptions to modification requests regardless of when or which model a current support order was established under. First, when there has been a change in the health care needs of the children, a modification may be requested even if there is no significant variance. Second, when a significant variance exists numerically in terms of percentage of change but a request for a decrease in support is made by a willfully or voluntarily underemployed parent, that request will be denied. Third, where the person making the modification request has failed to pay previous support obligations as a result of deliberate actions, that request will be denied. However, if the failure to pay previous support obligations resulted through no fault of the parent supposed to pay that support, a modification request is permitted.

Two additional exceptions to the general rule for significant variance exist with regard to a fifty-fifty split in parenting time based on a court order established between January 18, 2005 and April 1, 2005. Under the Income Shares model, modification may be requested to correct a calculation error even if there is no significant variance. Also, when the parents split parenting fifty-fifty and support is owed, this past-due amount may be recalculated to reflect the change in support established in the modification order. However, this recalculation considers only those amounts owed subsequent to the date the request was filed with the court and the other parent was provided proper notice. This effective-date timing rule applies to all requests for modification, so when circumstances cause a significant variance, a modification should be sought as soon as possible.

ORDERS ISSUED PRIOR TO JANUARY 18, 2005 TO BE MODIFIED

Support orders established or modified before to January 18, 2005, under the Flat Percentage Model are modifiable under the Income Shares model. However, prior to qualifying for a modification, two conditions must be present to establish the presence of a significant variance.

The first condition required to modify a support order established under the Flat Percentage model prior to January 18, 2005, requires the occurrence of one or more of the following circumstances since the entry of the current support order:

1. a 15 percent increase or decrease in the gross income of the alternative residential parent
2. the alternative residential parent becomes legally obligated for the support of additional children
3. the child becomes disabled
4. the parents have supplied the court with a written agreement to modify support

The second condition required to modify a support order established under the Flat Percentage model prior to January 18, 2005 requires the existence of a 15 percent increase or decrease between a current support order amount and the amount of support sought in the modification request. However, the 15 percent change requirement applies only to modifications sought on current orders of support for

$100 per month or more. Where modification is sought on a support obligation under $100, the court must first determine that the parent is a low-income provider.

Under Tennessee Law, two standards must be met for a parent to be defined as a low-income provider. First the provider must not be "willfully and voluntarily unemployed or underemployed when working at his or her full capacity according to his or her education and experience."[69] This means that through no fault of his or her own, the parent is not working or is working for less money or for less time than he or she is capable of. The second requirement for establishing a low-income provider is an income at or below the federal poverty level. As of 2013, the federal poverty level for a single adult was $11,700. Upon the court's determination that a parent is a low-income provider, the 15 percent change requirement is reduced to a 7.5 percent change requirement.

HARDSHIP EXCEPTION

Additional exceptions take into account the effects caused by the change from the previous model to the Income Shares model. Where the change in legislation creates a substantial reduction in the children's support, or alternatively, a substantial increase in the amount the amount a parent is required to pay, a hardship deviation may be granted on the court's written finding that an upward deviation is in the children's best interest.

In making a hardship deviation determination, the court will consider several factors, including whether the application of the new model has resulted in the significant variance or whether the variance also includes a significant change in income.

The second factor the court will take into account in its consideration of a deviation hardship is whether fixed expenses were acquired as a result of a parent's reliance on a previously ordered obligation amount. If a parent became responsible for additional debts such as a mortgage or auto payments and the obligations arose because the parent expected to continue paying a previously established support amount, the court will take these expenses into consideration.

The third factor the court will consider in a hardship deviation determination is the standard of living enjoyed by the children under the existing order. In doing so, a comparison will be made of the children's presumed living expenses as stated in the current order with the actual amounts put forth for the children's basic living expenses.

The fourth factor taken into consideration for purposes of determining a hardship request occurs when the current guidelines don't adequately account for extraordinary education expenses or special expenses. Extraordinary educational expenses are decided on a case-by-case basis, but in general, they include items such as tuition, room and board, lab fees, books, fees, special-needs education, and private education. Special expenses include things such as summer camp, music lessons, art lessons, athletics, participation in clubs, or the like. When the amount of Special expenses can be calculated, these expenses may be included in the support obligation amount for deviation purposes.

Last, a hardship deviation determination requires the court to consider the current order's division, if any, of medical and/or dental insurance and uninsured medical expenses.

---

69   Rule 1240-2-4-.05(2)(d)(1).

The considerations listed here are not the only factors the court can take into consideration for purposes of a hardship deviation. If there are excessive parenting-related travel expenses, the court will consider such expenses, but the court will not permit a deviation if it would substantially affect the residential parent's ability to provide basic necessities to the children. Consequently, where application of support guidelines would result in unjust or inappropriate results, the court is permitted to deviate from the guidelines. However, when a deviation is granted by the court, this deviation shall not later be used for purposes of establishing a significant variance.

Chapter 48:

COLLECTING CHILD SUPPORT

Obtaining an order for support payments is often just the initial step in the child support process. The parties to a support proceeding include the children and the parents responsible for the children. The Child Support Guidelines define the parent obligated to pay support as the alternate residential parent (ARP). The parent who lives with the children and receives the support payments is the primary residential parent (PRP). When an ARP fails to make support payments, those payments are in arrears, and a PRP shouldn't wait long before getting help enforcing the support order.

If the ARP is considerably past due in support payments, the amount must first be reduced to a judgment that you can then ask to be enforced. Child support obligations are not dischargeable in bankruptcy and also are not subject to the same statutory time limitations as other judgments.

The state in which your support order was established matters. As long as Tennessee remains the residence of the children and both parents, Tennessee courts will continue to oversee the matter until specific steps are taken to grant another court authority over your matter. However, even if Tennessee courts lose jurisdiction, it might still be possible to enforce your order in Tennessee for support amounts that became due while your case was still being handled by a Tennessee court.

In the case of Tennessee orders of support, you can generally seek enforcement in the court of the county that issued the order. However, you may have the option of requesting a transfer of your matter to another county in Tennessee. A request for transfer can be made when the PRP, the ARP, and the children no longer live in the county that issued the support order.

Federal law requires states to recognize other state's orders when parents move. There are additional considerations and specific procedural steps that you should take to enforce child support orders across state lines. Tennessee courts require registration of out-of-state orders prior to seeking enforcement; this involves filing a certified copy of the out-of-state order and certain supporting documents as part of a petition to enroll a foreign child support order and serve that on the ARP. If no objection is made by the ARP, the support order will be registered and can then be enforced. The procedures governing these matters can be very complicated; therefore, you should consult with a lawyer to determine the appropriate procedures for enforcement.

Tennessee has an expedited process for support that can be achieved through filing a petition for enforcement. Upon filing of such petition, the clerk will assign a hearing date, which, according to Tennessee law, shall be no more than forty-five days for certain cases or thirty days for all other cases from the date of filing such petition. If the ARP fails to appear, the court can enter an order of default. This determination may be dependent on the service of process method used. Service of process is the manner in which copies of the documents, and therefore notice, were provided to the ARP.

Prior to seeking enforcement, parents must consider all options. There are many remedies available for which the PRP may achieve payment under a legally valid support order. If the ARP is employed, the PRP could seek a wage assignment, often referred to as garnishment of wages. In some cases, a lien could be placed on property owned by the ARP. Additionally, Tennessee may intercept federal income tax refunds due the ARP.

In the event the ARP doesn't have identifiable income or assets, other collection methods can be tried. One is to seek an order to deny, revoke, or suspend the alternative residential parent's Tennessee driver's license or business, trade, or even hunting and fishing licenses if the ARP doesn't comply with an order of support.

Another way to collect child support is by seeking criminal sanctions, which courts may order in extreme cases to force compliance. A parent can request of a court that the obligated parent be held in contempt, or the court can do it on its own. Available remedies include court-ordered community service or imprisonment.

If the ARP is ordered to perform community service, this may include removal of litter from public roadways or property or work in Tennessee recycling centers. However, orders requiring community service usually will not interfere with the ARP's normal work hours.

Jail time can be imprisonment for up to ten days per missed payment. However, sentences are typically less harsh unless the ARP has persistently failed to make payments.

Consult with a lawyer when seeking collection or enforcement of a Tennessee child support order because it is often difficult to determine the appropriate steps to take to enforce support payments.

Chapter 49:

STRATEGIC ADVICE ABOUT CHILD SUPPORT

Do you want to consider learning the child support worksheets? The calculations the spreadsheet does are complicated, but inputting the data and calculating a child support amount due is not impossible. You might want to start on MemphisDivorce.com's Child Support Resources page or read the instructions from the State of Tennessee: www.state.tn.us/humanserv/is/isdownloads.html. With the downloaded software, your computer is ready to interact with the state's computer to calculate child support.

For all child support situations, there is no substitute for running different scenarios with an experienced family lawyer. Using the child support calculator, run different sets of worksheets inputting each parents' known or estimated income and parenting time at the high and low ends of the possible ranges. See how each variable impacts the resulting child support amounts. You may be surprised. Focus your efforts primarily on those variables that impact the results the most.

Don't be intimidated by the complexity of the Tennessee's Child Support Guidelines. Study them patiently. Details matter. Links to the guidelines and calculator are available MemphisDivorce.com's Child Support Resources page.

Write down questions you have. Ask your family lawyer how a particular legal provision may apply to your situation. Don't be surprised if your lawyer looks up the guidelines and does some legal research before answering your question! That's what family lawyers do to give the best answers. There are so many possible permutations and situations that it can be years in between facing really unique factual and legal situations.

A FEW TIPS

Maximize the amount used for the other parent's income. Ask to review the other parent's tax returns, W-2s, 1099s, and supporting schedules. Make sure all earned income and passive income is included. The definition of gross income is very broad and can include income not taxed under federal law.

Maximize your parenting time with the children when negotiating the Permanent Parenting Plan. There is no adjustment to child support for an alternative residential parent (ARP) enjoying from sixty-eight to ninety-two parenting days a year. If there are fewer than sixty-eight, child support will be adjusted higher according to a formula spelled out in the guidelines. If the ARP enjoys more than ninety-two parenting days, the child support will be decreased. While both parents will want to spend as much time as possible with their children, keep in mind what is in the best interests of the children. A parent can't always spend as much time with the children as he or she wants. It's better to have a parenting plan that makes practical sense for both parents and the children than a parenting plan engineered to reduce child support.

Make sure the costs for certain categories of your children's expenses such as health insurance premiums and child care are accurate. If you don't know the amount, find out from the source. Obtain documentation. Anticipate future cost increases. Deal with likely contingencies. Knowing what is most likely to be incurred will prevent you from agreeing to something that is unlikely to occur.

Finally, think about all the extra expenses your children may need such as tutoring, sports, and educational travel—now and in the future. Share those expenses with your lawyer and discuss specific strategies.

Section III

EXAMPLES OF PERMANENT PARENTING PLANS AND CHILD SUPPORT WORKSHEETS

INTRODUCTION

Divorcing parents rarely know where to start when faced with the parenting plan requirement. The most difficult question a family lawyer may ask a divorcing parent is "What do you want?" One of the most important goals of parenting plans is to avoid disputes by providing a detailed framework for the future.

This collection of parenting plans is presented to provide a spectrum of examples. Many divorcing parents have found reading through these examples very helpful as a jumping-off point to hand-crafting a solution for future parenting.

These are actual parenting plans with names, dates, and specific facts changed. The level of detail included in these plans reflects the result, not the process, of negotiations. For example, a mother may have sought to include a postdivorce parenting restriction preventing a future girlfriend from spending the night when the children are visiting the father. If the father did not agree to the proposed provision, it would not be included in the final parenting plan. All of these examples were the result of negotiations, not trial.

The parenting plan form itself evolves over time, as does Tennessee law. Originally, most of the parenting plans presented here appeared on a prior generation of the form but have been copied onto the most current version of the parenting plan form as of the writing of this book. To find the most current version of the parenting plan form, child support worksheets and updates to this book, visit MemphisDivorce.com.

None of the parenting plans are presented as perfect examples of solutions to any particular problem. Not every sentence is absolutely clear, and if a sentence is not absolutely clear to you, it won't be clear to the other parent either. As you prepare your parenting plan, take your time. Be patient. Make sure what you want and agree to is clear and as well written as possible.

As time and society progresses, more fathers are designated as the primary residential parents as a result of negotiation and trial. In this book, all of the parenting plans presented have the mother as primary residential parent. These plans were selected merely as examples. For all Permanent Parenting Plans with fathers as primary residential parent, the forms would reflect the same details.

The chapters that follow are examples of Permanent Parenting Plans.

- Alpha Family—80 Days per Year Parenting Time
- Bravo Family—118 Days per Year Parenting Time
- Charlie Family—141 Days per Year Parenting Time
- Delta Family—170 Days per Year Parenting Time
- Echo Family—182.5 Days per Year Equal Parenting Time

- Foxtrot Family—182.5 Days per Year Equal Parenting Time
- Golf Family—93 Days per Year Parenting Time: Out-of-Town Schedule
- Hotel Family—113 Days per Year Parenting Time: Out-of-Town Schedule

After the permanent parenting plans, two examples of child support worksheets are provided.

Chapter 50:

ALPHA FAMILY
80 DAYS PER YEAR PARENTING TIME

Eighty days with father. Mr. and Mrs. Alpha were married twelve years and have two children, a boy and a girl, ages six and seven. The mother was a well-paid kindergarten teacher. The father worked with an insurance company and was often required to travel during the week. He expected to be able to have eighty nights per year. The mother is the primary residential parent and shared joint decision-making authority for major decisions. The parents agreed to a "right of first refusal" provision. Eighty days per year is considered by many to be "standard visitation," although there is no strict definition for that term in Tennessee law.

STATE OF TENNESSEE	CHANCERY COURT *(Must be completed)*	SHELBY COUNTY*(Must be completed)*
PERMANENT PARENTING PLAN ORDER ☐ **PROPOSED** X **AGREED** ☐ **ORDERED BY THE COURT**	FILE No. CH-09-ABCD-E *(Must be completed)* **PART II**	
PLAINTIFF *(Name: First, Middle, Last)* **JAMES JOYCE ALPHA** ☐ Mother X Father	**DEFENDANT** *(Name: First, Middle, Last)* **SAVANNAH SMITH ALPHA** X Mother ☐ Father	

The mother and father will behave with each other and each child so as to provide a loving, stable, consistent and nurturing relationship with the child even though they are divorced. They will not speak badly of each other or the members of the family of the other parent. They will encourage each child to continue to love the other parent and be comfortable in both families.

This plan   X   is a new plan.

    ☐ modifies an existing Parenting Plan dated _____.

    ☐ modifies an existing Order dated _____.

Child's Name	Date of Birth
Charles Joyce Alpha	09/03/2006
Charlene Ann Alpha	08/15/2007

I.   RESIDENTIAL PARENTING SCHEDULE

A.   RESIDENTIAL TIME WITH EACH PARENT

The Primary Residential Parent is <u>Mother</u>

Under the schedule set forth below, each parent will spend the following number of days with the children:

Mother <u>285</u> days   Father <u>80</u> days

B.   DAY-TO-DAY SCHEDULE

The X mother ☐ father shall have responsibility for the care of the child or children except at the following times when the other parent shall have responsibility:

From <u>Saturday at 8:00 a.m.</u> to <u>Sunday at 2:00 p.m.</u>
Day and Time   *Day and Time*

    ☐ every week X every other week ☐ other: _____.

The other parent shall also have responsibility for the care of the child or children at the additional parenting times specified below:

From   Wednesday afternoon after school to Thursday morning when Father delivers
the children to school   *Day and Time*
    Day and Time
    X   every week   ☐   every other week   ☐ other: _____.

This parenting schedule begins ☐ _____ **or** X date of the Court's Order.
                                        Day and Time

C.   HOLIDAY SCHEDULE AND OTHER SCHOOL FREE DAYS

Indicate if child or children will be with parent in ODD or EVEN numbered years or EVERY year:

	MOTHER	FATHER
New Year's Day	Day-to-Day Schedule shall apply	
Martin Luther King Day	Day-to-Day Schedule shall apply	
Presidents' Day	Day-to-Day Schedule shall apply	
Easter Day (unless otherwise coinciding with Spring Vacation)	Shared	Shared
Passover Day (unless otherwise coinciding with Spring Vacation)	N/A	N/A
Mother's Day	Every	None
Memorial Day (if no school)	Day-to-Day Schedule shall apply	
Father's Day	None	Every
July 4th	Shared	Shared
Labor Day	Day-to-Day Schedule shall apply	
Halloween	Day-to-Day Schedule shall apply	
Thanksgiving Day & Friday	Shared*	Shared*
Children's Birthdays	Day-to-Day Schedule shall apply	
Other School-Free Days	Day-to-Day Schedule shall apply	
Mother's Birthday	Every	None
Father's Birthday	None	Every
Other: _____		_____

*The Thanksgiving Day holiday will be shared between the parents as follows: Father shall have the option to exercise parenting time with the children beginning at 8:00 a.m. until 12:00 p.m. on Thanksgiving Day and Mother shall have parenting time with the children beginning at 12:00 p.m. on Thanksgiving Day.

Holiday parenting time supersedes regularly scheduled residential time.

A holiday shall begin at 6:00 p.m. on the night preceding the holiday and end at 6:00 p.m. the night of the holiday, unless otherwise noted here_____.

D.   FALL VACATION (*If applicable*)

The day to day schedule shall apply except as follows: Mother and Father shall alternate the Fall Vacation. Mother shall exercise parenting time with the children in odd numbered years and Father shall exercise parenting time with the children in even numbered years.

E.   WINTER (CHRISTMAS) VACATION

The ☐ mother ☐ father shall have the child or children for the first period from the day and time school is dismissed until December _____ at _____ a.m./p.m. ☐ in odd-numbered years ☐ in even-numbered years ☐ every year. The other parent will have the child or children for the second period from the day and time indicated above until 6:00 p.m. on the evening before school resumes. The parties shall alternate the first and second periods each year.

Other agreement of the parents: The day-to-day schedule shall apply except as follows: Mother shall have the children every year from December 24th at 3:00 p.m. until December 25th at 3:00 p.m. and Father shall have the children from December 25th at 3:00 p.m. to December 26th at 3:00 p.m. every year.

F.   SPRING VACATION (*If applicable*)

The day-to-day schedule shall apply except as follows: Mother and Father shall alternate the Spring Vacation. Mother shall exercise parenting time with the children in even numbered years and Father shall exercise parenting time with the children in odd numbered years.

G.   SUMMER VACATION

The day-to-day schedule shall apply except as follows: A) Father and Mother shall each have two (2) consecutive or nonconsecutive weeks, at their choosing, beginning June 1, 2014. A week shall consist of seven (7) days; B) If Father's work schedule allows, the parties shall make a reasonable effort to allow Father additional parenting time with the children during Summer Vacation. Father shall provide Mother reasonable notice of the dates and times that he would like to exercise additional parenting time. Mother shall not unreasonably withhold additional parenting time from Father.

Is written notice required?   X ☐ Yes ☐ No.   If so, 60 number of days. Written notice only applies to provision "A".

Father has the first choice of dates in even numbered years and Mother has the first choice of dates in odd numbered years.

Both parties shall give the other parent the first right of refusal for baby-sitting purposes.

H.   TRANSPORTATION ARRANGEMENTS

The place of meeting for the exchange of the child or children shall be: Mother's residence.

Payment of long distance transportation costs *(if applicable):* ☐ mother ☐ father X both equally.
Other arrangements: _____.

If a parent does not possess a valid driver's license, he or she must make reasonable transportation arrangements to protect the child or children while in the care of that parent.

I.   SUPERVISION OF PARENTING TIME (*If applicable*)
☐ **Check if applicable**

Supervised parenting time shall apply during the day-to-day schedule as follows:

▢ Place: _____.

▢ Person or organization supervising: _____.

▢ Responsibility for cost, if any: ▢ mother ▢ father ▢ both equally.

J.   OTHER

The following special provisions apply :

1.   When the parties' children are with Mother, and Mother cannot watch the child, Father shall have first right of refusal for baby-sitting purposes. When the parties' children are with Father, and Father cannot watch the children, Mother shall have the first right of refusal for baby-sitting purposes.

2.   Both parties agree to a mutual consent injunction to the effect that neither party will allow adult members of the opposite sex who are not family members or to whom he or she is not married spend the night in the presence of, or in the same residence of, the minor children.

3.   The parties will equally divide the cost of all agreed upon extracurricular activities for the children.

4.   The parties will equally divide the cost of mutually agreed upon summer camps for the children. The parties contemplate that the children will attend summer camp two weeks prior to the school year beginning and two weeks prior to the school year ending.

5.   The parties contemplate that Father will obtain employment with a regular work schedule. In the even he does so, Father shall have additional parenting time with the children.

II.   DECISION-MAKING

A.   DAY-TO-DAY DECISIONS

Each parent shall make decisions regarding the day-to-day care of a child while the child is residing with that parent, including any emergency decisions affecting the health or safety of a child.

B.   MAJOR DECISIONS

Major decisions regarding each child shall be made as follows:

Educational decisions	▢ mother	▢ father	**x** joint
Non-emergency health care	▢ mother	▢ father	**x** joint
Religious upbringing	▢ mother	▢ father	**x** joint
Extracurricular activities	▢ mother	▢ father	**x** joint
_____	▢ mother	▢ father	▢ joint

Given the parties financial circumstances, the parties agree that the children will not participate in more than one extracurricular activity at a time unless otherwise agreed. Additionally, the parties agree to mutually discuss and agree upon the cost of each activity prior to enrolling the children in each activity.

The parties agree to communicate with each other concerning all major decisions. In the event the parties cannot agree, then Mother shall have final decision making authority.

III.   FINANCIAL SUPPORT

A.   CHILD SUPPORT

Father's gross monthly income is $ 2,059.00
Mother's gross monthly income is $ 3,909.00

1. The final child support order is as follows:
    a. The ☐ mother **X** father shall pay to the other parent as regular child support the sum of $507.00 ☐ weekly **X** monthly ☐ twice per month
    ☐ every two weeks. **The Child Support Worksheet shall be attached to this Order as an Exhibit.***

    If this is a deviation from the Child Support Guidelines, explain why:
    The parties agree that Father's current gross monthly income as listed in the Child Support Worksheet is an agreed upon number given Father's past earning history and his current temporary job situation.

2. Retroactive Support: A judgment is hereby awarded in the amount of $_____ to ☐ mother ☐ father against the child support payor representing retroactive support required under Section 1240-2-4.06 of the D.H.S. Income Shares Child Support Guidelines dating from _____ which shall be paid (including pre/post judgment interest) at the rate of $_____ per ☐ week ☐ month ☐ twice per month ☐ every two weeks until the judgment is paid in full.

3. Payments shall begin on the 1st day of the month following Mother vacating the marital residence, but no earlier than January 1, 2014. Mother shall provide Father with two weeks notice of the date she intends to vacate the residence.

This support shall be paid:

X directly to the other parent.

☐ to the Central Child Support Receipting Unit, P. O. Box 305200, Nashville, Tennessee 37229, and sent from there to the other parent at: _____.

☐ A Wage Assignment Order is attached to this Parenting Plan.

☐ by direct deposit to the other parent at _____ Bank for deposit in account no. _____.

☐ income assignment not required; Explanation:_____.

☐ other:_____.

The parents acknowledge that court approval must be obtained before child support can be reduced or modified.

*Child Support Worksheet can be found on DHS website at http://www.state.tn.us/humanserv/is/isdocuments.html or at your local child support offices.

B.   FEDERAL INCOME TAX EXEMPTION[*]

The X mother ☐ father is the parent receiving child support.

The Mother shall claim the following children: <u>Charles Joyce Alpha and Charlene Ann Alpha</u>

The Father shall claim the following children: _____

The X mother ☐ father may claim the exemptions for the child or children so long as child support payments are current by the claiming parent on January 15 of the year when the return is due. The exemptions may be claimed in: ☐ alternate years starting _____
X each year ☐ other: _____.

The ☐ mother X father will furnish IRS Form 8332 to the parent entitled to the exemption by February 15 of the year the tax return is due.

C.   PROOF OF INCOME AND WORK-RELATED CHILD CARE EXPENSES

Each parent shall send proof of income to the other parent for the prior calendar year as follows:

- IRS Forms W-2 and 1099 shall be sent to the other parent on or before   February 15.
- A copy of his or her federal income tax return shall be sent to the other parent on or before April 15 or any later date when it is due because of an extension of time for filing.
- The completed form required by the Department of Human Services shall be sent to the Department on or before the date the federal income tax return is due by the parent paying child support. *This requirement applies only if a parent is receiving benefits from the Department for a child.*

The parent paying work-related child care expenses shall send proof of expenses to the other parent for the prior calendar year and an estimate for the next calendar year, on or before February 15.

D.   HEALTH AND DENTAL INSURANCE

Reasonable health insurance on the child or children will be:
     X   maintained by the mother
     ☐   maintained by the father
     ☐   maintained by both

Proof of continuing coverage shall be furnished to the other parent annually or as coverage changes. The parent maintaining coverage shall authorize the other parent to consult with the insurance carrier regarding the coverage in effect.

Uncovered reasonable and necessary medical expenses, which may include but is not limited to, deductibles or co-payments, eyeglasses, contact lens, routine annual physicals,

---

[*] NOTE: The child support schedule assumptions in the guidelines (1240-2-4-.03 (6)(b)) assume that the parent receiving the child support will get the tax exemptions for the child.

and counseling will be paid by ☐ mother ☐ father X pro rata in accordance with their incomes. After insurance has paid its portion, the parent receiving the bill will send it to the other parent within ten days. The other parent will pay his or her share within 30 days of receipt of the bill.

If available through work, the ☐ mother X father shall maintain dental, orthodontic, and optical insurance on the minor child or children.

E.   LIFE INSURANCE

If agreed upon by the parties, the X mother ☐ father ☐ both shall insure her own life in the minimum amount of $250,000.00 by whole life or term insurance.   Until the child support obligation has been completed, each policy shall name the child/children as sole irrevocable primary beneficiary, with the X other parent ☐ other _____, as trustee for the benefit of the child(ren), to serve without bond or accounting.

Father shall insure his own life in the minimum amount of $500,000.00 by whole life or term insurance.   Until the child support obligation has been completed, Father's policy shall name the children as sole irrevocable primary beneficiary, with the other parent, as trustee for the benefit of the children, to serve without bond or accounting.

IV. PRIMARY RESIDENTIAL PARENT (CUSTODIAN) FOR OTHER LEGAL PURPOSES

The child or children are scheduled to reside the majority of the time with the X mother   ☐ father. This parent is designated as the primary residential parent also known as the custodian, **SOLELY** for purposes of any other applicable state and federal laws. If the parents are listed in Section II as joint decision-makers, then, for purposes of obtaining health or other insurance, they shall be considered to be joint custodians. THIS DESIGNATION DOES NOT AFFECT EITHER PARENT'S RIGHTS OR RESPONSIBILITIES UNDER THIS PARENTING PLAN.

V. DISAGREEMENTS OR MODIFICATION OF PLAN

Should the parents disagree about this Parenting Plan or wish to modify it, they must make a good faith effort to resolve the issue by the process selected below before returning to Court. *Except for financial support issues including child support, health and dental insurance, uncovered medical and dental expenses, and life insurance*, disputes must be submitted to:

> X Mediation by a neutral party chosen by the parents or the Court.
> ☐ Arbitration by a neutral party selected by parents or the Court.
> ☐ The Court DUE TO ORDER OF PROTECTION OR RESTRICTIONS.

The costs of this process may be determined by the alternative dispute process or may be assessed by the Court based upon the incomes of the parents. It must be commenced by notifying the other parent and the Court by X written request ☐ certified mail ☐ other: _____.

In the dispute resolution process:

> A. Preference shall be given to carrying out this Parenting Plan.
> B. The parents shall use the process to resolve disputes relating to implementation of the Plan.

C. A written record shall be prepared of any agreement reached, and it shall be provided to each parent.

D. If the Court finds that a parent willfully failed to appear without good reason, the Court, upon motion, may award attorney fees and financial sanctions to the prevailing parent.

VI.   RIGHTS OF PARENTS

Under T.C.A. § 36-6-101 of Tennessee law, both parents are entitled to the following rights:

(1) The right to unimpeded telephone conversations with the child at least twice a week at reasonable times and for reasonable durations;

(2) The right to send mail to the child which the other parent shall not open or censor;

(3) The right to receive notice and relevant information as soon as practicable but within twenty-four (24) hours of any event of hospitalization, major illness or death of the child;

(4) The right to receive directly from the child's school any school records customarily made available to parents. (The school may require a written request which includes a current mailing address and upon payment of reasonable costs of duplicating.) These include copies of the child's report cards, attendance records, names of teachers, class schedules, and standardized test scores;

(5) Unless otherwise provided by law, the right to receive copies of the child's medical health or other treatment records directly from the physician or health care provider who provided treatment or health care. (The keeper of the records may require a written request which contains a current mailing address and the payment of reasonable costs of duplication.) No person who receives the mailing address of a parent as a result of this requirement shall provide such address to the other parent or a third person;

(6) The right to be free of unwarranted derogatory remarks made about the parent or his or her family by the other parent to the child or in the presence of the child;

(7) The right to be given at least forty-eight (48) hours notice, whenever possible, of all extra-curricular activities, and the opportunity to participate or observe them. These include the following: school activities, athletic activities, church activities and other activities where parental participation or observation would be appropriate;

(8) The right to receive from the other parent, in the event the other parent leaves the state with the minor child or children for more than two (2) days, an itinerary including telephone numbers for use in the event of an emergency;

(9) The right to access and participation in education on the same basis that is provided to all parents. This includes the right of access to the child for lunch and other activities. However participation or access must be reasonable and not interfere with day-to-day operations or with the child's educational performance.

VII.   NOTICE REGARDING PARENTAL RELOCATION

The Tennessee statute (T.C.A. § 36-6-108) which governs the notice to be given in connection with the relocation of a parent reads in pertinent part as follows:

If a parent who is spending intervals of time with a child desires to relocate outside the state or more than fifty (50) miles from the other parent within the state, the relocating parent shall send a notice to the other parent at the other parent's last known address by registered or certified mail. Unless excused by the court for exigent circumstances, the notice shall be mailed not later than sixty (60) days prior to the move. The notice shall contain the following:

(1) Statement of intent to move;

(2) Location of proposed new residence;

(3) Reasons for proposed relocation; and

(4) Statement that the other parent may file a petition in opposition to the move within thirty (30) days of receipt of the notice.

VIII.   PARENT EDUCATION CLASS

This requirement has been fulfilled by X both parents ☐ mother ☐ father ☐ neither. Failure to attend the parent education class within 60 days of this order is punishable by contempt.

Under penalty of perjury, we declare that this plan has been proposed in good faith and is in the best interest of each minor child and that the statements herein and on the attached child support worksheets are true and correct. *(A notary public is required if this is a proposed plan by one parent rather than one agreed by both parents.)*

_____   _____
Mother   Date and Place Signed

Sworn to and subscribed before me this _____ day of _____, 20_____.

My commission expires:_____   _____
                                                                                         Notary Public

_____   _____
Father   Date and Place Signed

Sworn to and subscribed before me this _____ day of _____, 20_____.

My commission expires:_____   _____
                                                                                         Notary Public

APPROVED FOR ENTRY:

_____   _____
Attorney for Mother   *Attorney for Father*

_____   _____
Address   *Address*

_____   _____
Address   *Address*

_____   _____
Phone and BPR Number   *Phone and BPR Number*

Note: The judge or chancellor may sign below or, instead, sign a Final Decree or a separate Order incorporating this plan.

COURT COSTS (If applicable)

Court costs, if any, are taxed as follows:

_____.

It is so ORDERED this the _____ day of _____, _____.

_____
Judge or Chancellor

Chapter 51:

BRAVO FAMILY—118 DAYS PER YEAR PARENTING TIME

The father received 118 days per year. Mr. and Mrs. Bravo have a three-year-old. The mother was employed at a hospital, and the father worked for a liquor distributor. The mother is the primary residential parent and has final decision-making authority over nonemergency health care decisions, but she shares decision-making authority with the father for the balance of major decisions. This plan was entered postdivorce following the father exercising more parenting time and a modest reduction in income, warranting a reduction in child support.

STATE OF TENNESSEE	CIRCUIT **COURT** *(Must be completed)*	SHELBY **COUNTY***(Must be completed)*
PERMANENT PARENTING PLAN ORDER ☐ **PROPOSED** X **AGREED** ☐ **ORDERED BY THE COURT**	FILE **No.** CT-ABCDEF-06 *(Must be completed)* **DIVISION 5**	
PLAINTIFF *(Name: First, Middle, Last)* **ROBERTA J. BRAVO** X Mother ☐ Father	**DEFENDANT** *(Name: First, Middle, Last)* **HENRY J. BRAVO** ☐ Mother X Father	

The mother and father will behave with each other and each child so as to provide a loving, stable, consistent and nurturing relationship with the child even though they are divorced. They will not speak badly of each other or the members of the family of the other parent. They will encourage each child to continue to love the other parent and be comfortable in both families.

This plan   X   is a new plan.

☐   modifies an existing Parenting Plan dated _____.

☐   modifies an existing Order dated _____.

Child's Name	Date of Birth
Andrea Jones Bravo	2/11/2009

I.   RESIDENTIAL PARENTING SCHEDULE

A.   RESIDENTIAL TIME WITH EACH PARENT

The Primary Residential Parent is Mother

Under the schedule set forth below, each parent will spend the following number of days with the children:

Mother 247 days   Father 118 days

B.   DAY-TO-DAY SCHEDULE

The X mother ☐ father shall have responsibility for the care of the child or children except at the following times when the other parent shall have responsibility:

From Friday @ 6:00 p.m. to Sunday @ 6:00 p.m.
Day and Time   *Day and Time*

☐ every week X every other week ☐ other: _____.

The other parent shall also have responsibility for the care of the child or children at the additional parenting times specified below:

From <u>Wednesday @ 5:00 p.m.</u> to <u>Thursday @ 9:00 a.m.</u>
           Day and Time   *Day and Time*

X   every week   ☐   every other week   ☐ other: _____ .

This parenting schedule begins ☐ _____ **or** X   date of the Court's Order.
                                  Day and Time

C.   HOLIDAY SCHEDULE AND OTHER SCHOOL FREE DAYS

Indicate if child or children will be with parent in ODD or EVEN numbered years or EVERY year:

	MOTHER	FATHER
New Year's Day	Odd	Even
Martin Luther King Day	N/A	N/A
Presidents' Day	N/A	N/A
Easter Day (unless otherwise coinciding with Spring Vacation)	Odd	Even
Passover Day (unless otherwise coinciding with Spring Vacation)	N/A	N/A
Mother's Day	Always	Never
Memorial Day (if no school)	Always	Never
Father's Day	Never	Always
July 4th	Even	Odd
Labor Day	Odd	Even
Halloween	Odd	Even
Thanksgiving Day & Friday	Odd	Even
Children's Birthdays	Odd	Even
Other School-Free Days	_____	_____
Mother's Birthday	Always	Never
Father's Birthday	_____	Always – if a school day, 3
hours after school		
Other: _____		_____

A holiday shall begin at 6:00 p.m. on the night preceding the holiday and end at 6:00 p.m. the night of the holiday, unless otherwise noted here_____ .

D.   FALL VACATION (*If applicable*)

The day to day schedule shall apply except as follows: <u>Mother has odd years, Father has even years.</u>

E.   WINTER (CHRISTMAS) VACATION

The X mother ☐ father shall have the child or children for the first period from the day and time school is dismissed until <u>December 24th at 6:00 p.m.</u> ☐ in odd-numbered years   ☐ in even-numbered years   X   every year. The other parent will have the child or children for the second period from the day and time indicated above until 6:00 p.m. on the evening before school resumes. The parties shall alternate the first and second periods each year.

Other agreement of the parents: _____

F.   SPRING VACATION (*If applicable*)

The day-to-day schedule shall apply except as follows: _____
_____
_____beginning _____.

G.   SUMMER VACATION

The day-to-day schedule shall apply except as follows: <u>The Father shall have 2 continuous</u>
<u>weeks during the summer. The dates and times are to be arranged between the parties</u>
<u>when the Father provides his written notice to the Mother.</u>

Is written notice required?   x Yes   ☐ No.   If so, <u>60</u> number of days.

H.   TRANSPORTATION ARRANGEMENTS

The place of meeting for the exchange of the child or children shall be: _____
_____.
Payment of long distance transportation costs *(if applicable):* ☐ mother   x father ☐ both
equally.
Other arrangements: <u>In the event either party moves further than 30 miles from Memphis,</u>
<u>Tennessee this provision shall be revised.</u>
If a parent does not possess a valid driver's license, he or she must make reasonable
transportation arrangements to protect the child or children while in the care of that parent.

I.   SUPERVISION OF PARENTING TIME (*If applicable*)
☐ **Check if applicable**

Supervised parenting time shall apply during the day-to-day schedule as follows:
☐ Place: _____.
☐ Person or organization supervising: _____.
☐ Responsibility for cost, if any: ☐ mother ☐ father ☐ both equally.

J.   OTHER

The following special provisions apply :
<u>Their one child of preschool age will reside with the Mother. Upon the child's enrollment in</u>
<u>school the Mother will continue to have custody. The parties agree that if, within one (1)</u>
<u>year of the child's graduation from high school if the child is enrolled as a full time student</u>
<u>in a fully accredited college, university or vocational education facility, then the parties will</u>
<u>divide the cost of tuition, room, board, book expenses and all other normal and reasonable</u>
<u>expenses related directly to the child's education equal to the and not to exceed the</u>
<u>customary cost, then prevailing for the State Institution within the State of Tennessee. This</u>
<u>will continue for period not to exceed 4 ½ years or until the child graduates whichever</u>
<u>happens first.</u>

II.   DECISION-MAKING

A.   DAY-TO-DAY DECISIONS

Each parent shall make decisions regarding the day-to-day care of a child while the child is residing with that parent, including any emergency decisions affecting the health or safety of a child.

B.   MAJOR DECISIONS

Major decisions regarding each child shall be made as follows:

Educational decisions	☐ mother	☐ father	**X** joint
Non-emergency health care	**X** mother	☐ father	☐ joint
Religious upbringing	☐ mother	☐ father	**X** joint
Extracurricular activities	☐ mother	☐ father	**X** joint
_____	☐ mother	☐ father	☐ joint

III.   FINANCIAL SUPPORT

A.   CHILD SUPPORT

Father's gross monthly income is $ <u>3,400.00</u>
Mother's gross monthly income is $ <u>1,040.00</u>

1. The final child support order is as follows:
   a. The ☐ mother **X** father shall pay to the other parent as regular child support the sum of $<u>831.00</u> ☐ weekly **X** monthly ☐ twice per month ☐ every two weeks. **The Child Support Worksheet shall be attached to this Order as an Exhibit.***

   If this is a deviation from the Child Support Guidelines, explain why:
   _____

2. Retroactive Support: A judgment is hereby awarded in the amount of $_____ to ☐ mother ☐ father against the child support payor representing retroactive support required under Section 1240-2-4.06 of the D.H.S. Income Shares Child Support Guidelines dating from _____ which shall be paid (including pre/post judgment interest) at the rate of $_____ per ☐ week ☐ month ☐ twice per month ☐ every two weeks until the judgment is paid in full.

3. Payments shall begin on the <u>1st day of June, 2013</u>.

This support shall be paid:

☐ directly to the other parent.
X to the Central Child Support Receipting Unit, P. O. Box 305200, Nashville, Tennessee 37229, and sent from there to the other parent at: _____.
☐ A Wage Assignment Order is attached to this Parenting Plan.
☐ by direct deposit to the other parent at _____ Bank for deposit in account no. _____.
☐ income assignment not required; Explanation:_____.

☐ other:_____.

The parents acknowledge that court approval must be obtained before child support can be reduced or modified.

*Child Support Worksheet can be found on DHS website at http://www.state.tn.us/humanserv/is/isdocuments.html or at your local child support offices.

B.   FEDERAL INCOME TAX EXEMPTION*

The X mother ☐ father is the parent receiving child support.

The Mother shall claim the following children: <u>Andrea Jones Bravo</u>

The Father shall claim the following children: _____

The ☐ mother ☐ father may claim the exemptions for the child or children so long as child support payments are current by the claiming parent on January 15 of the year when the return is due. The exemptions may be claimed in: ☐ alternate years starting _____
☐ each year ☐ other: _____.

The ☐ mother ☐ father will furnish IRS Form 8332 to the parent entitled to the exemption by February 15 of the year the tax return is due.

C.   PROOF OF INCOME AND WORK-RELATED CHILD CARE EXPENSES

Each parent shall send proof of income to the other parent for the prior calendar year as follows:

- IRS Forms W-2 and 1099 shall be sent to the other parent on or before   February 15.
- A copy of his or her federal income tax return shall be sent to the other parent on or before April 15 or any later date when it is due because of an extension of time for filing.
- The completed form required by the Department of Human Services shall be sent to the Department on or before the date the federal income tax return is due by the parent paying child support. *This requirement applies only if a parent is receiving benefits from the Department for a child.*

The parent paying work-related child care expenses shall send proof of expenses to the other parent for the prior calendar year and an estimate for the next calendar year, on or before February 15.

D.   HEALTH AND DENTAL INSURANCE

Reasonable health insurance on the child or children will be:
        ☐ maintained by the mother
        X maintained by the father
        ☐ maintained by both

Proof of continuing coverage shall be furnished to the other parent annually or as coverage changes. The parent maintaining coverage shall authorize the other parent to consult with the insurance carrier regarding the coverage in effect.

Uncovered reasonable and necessary medical expenses, which may include but is not limited to, deductibles or co-payments, eyeglasses, contact lens, routine annual physicals,

---

* NOTE: The child support schedule assumptions in the guidelines (1240-2-4-.03 (6)(b)) assume that the parent receiving the child support will get the tax exemptions for the child.

and counseling will be paid by ☐ mother ☐ father x pro rata in accordance with their incomes. After insurance has paid its portion, the parent receiving the bill will send it to the other parent within ten days. The other parent will pay his or her share within 30 days of receipt of the bill.

If available through work, the ☐ mother x father shall maintain dental, orthodontic, and optical insurance on the minor child or children.

E.   LIFE INSURANCE

If agreed upon by the parties, the ☐ mother x father ☐ both shall insure his/her own life in the minimum amount of $100,000.00 by whole life or term insurance.   Until the child support obligation has been completed, each policy shall name the child/children as sole irrevocable primary beneficiary, with the x other parent ☐ other _____, as trustee for the benefit of the child(ren), to serve without bond or accounting.

IV. PRIMARY RESIDENTIAL PARENT (CUSTODIAN) FOR OTHER LEGAL PURPOSES

The child or children are scheduled to reside the majority of the time with the x mother   ☐ father. This parent is designated as the primary residential parent also known as the custodian, **SOLELY** for purposes of any other applicable state and federal laws. If the parents are listed in Section II as joint decision-makers, then, for purposes of obtaining health or other insurance, they shall be considered to be joint custodians. THIS DESIGNATION DOES NOT AFFECT EITHER PARENT'S RIGHTS OR RESPONSIBILITIES UNDER THIS PARENTING PLAN.

V. DISAGREEMENTS OR MODIFICATION OF PLAN

Should the parents disagree about this Parenting Plan or wish to modify it, they must make a good faith effort to resolve the issue by the process selected below before returning to Court. *Except for financial support issues including child support, health and dental insurance, uncovered medical and dental expenses, and life insurance*, disputes must be submitted to:

  x Mediation by a neutral party chosen by the parents or the Court.
  ☐ Arbitration by a neutral party selected by parents or the Court.
  ☐ The Court DUE TO ORDER OF PROTECTION OR RESTRICTIONS.

The costs of this process may be determined by the alternative dispute process or may be assessed by the Court based upon the incomes of the parents. It must be commenced by notifying the other parent and the Court by ☐ written request x certified mail
☐ other: _____.

In the dispute resolution process:
  A. Preference shall be given to carrying out this Parenting Plan.
  B. The parents shall use the process to resolve disputes relating to implementation of the Plan.
  C. A written record shall be prepared of any agreement reached, and it shall be provided to each parent.
  D. If the Court finds that a parent willfully failed to appear without good reason, the Court, upon motion, may award attorney fees and financial sanctions to the prevailing parent.

VI.   RIGHTS OF PARENTS

Under T.C.A. § 36-6-101 of Tennessee law, both parents are entitled to the following rights:

(1) The right to unimpeded telephone conversations with the child at least twice a week at reasonable times and for reasonable durations;

(2) The right to send mail to the child which the other parent shall not open or censor;

(3) The right to receive notice and relevant information as soon as practicable but within twenty-four (24) hours of any event of hospitalization, major illness or death of the child;

(4) The right to receive directly from the child's school any school records customarily made available to parents. (The school may require a written request which includes a current mailing address and upon payment of reasonable costs of duplicating.) These include copies of the child's report cards, attendance records, names of teachers, class schedules, and standardized test scores;

(5) Unless otherwise provided by law, the right to receive copies of the child's medical health or other treatment records directly from the physician or health care provider who provided treatment or health care. (The keeper of the records may require a written request which contains a current mailing address and the payment of reasonable costs of duplication.) No person who receives the mailing address of a parent as a result of this requirement shall provide such address to the other parent or a third person;

(6) The right to be free of unwarranted derogatory remarks made about the parent or his or her family by the other parent to the child or in the presence of the child;

(7) The right to be given at least forty-eight (48) hours notice, whenever possible, of all extra-curricular activities, and the opportunity to participate or observe them. These include the following: school activities, athletic activities, church activities and other activities where parental participation or observation would be appropriate;

(8) The right to receive from the other parent, in the event the other parent leaves the state with the minor child or children for more than two (2) days, an itinerary including telephone numbers for use in the event of an emergency;

(9) The right to access and participation in education on the same basis that is provided to all parents. This includes the right of access to the child for lunch and other activities. However participation or access must be reasonable and not interfere with day-to-day operations or with the child's educational performance.

VII.   NOTICE REGARDING PARENTAL RELOCATION

The Tennessee statute (T.C.A. § 36-6-108) which governs the notice to be given in connection with the relocation of a parent reads in pertinent part as follows:

If a parent who is spending intervals of time with a child desires to relocate outside the state or more than fifty(50) miles from the other parent within the state, the relocating parent shall send a notice to the other parent at the other parent's last known address by registered or certified mail. Unless excused by the court for exigent circumstances, the notice shall be mailed not later than sixty (60) days prior to the move. The notice shall contain the following:

(1) Statement of intent to move;

(2) Location of proposed new residence;

(3) Reasons for proposed relocation; and

(4) Statement that the other parent may file a petition in opposition to the move within thirty (30) days of receipt of the notice.

VIII. PARENT EDUCATION CLASS

This requirement has been fulfilled by ☐ both parents ☐ mother ☐ father X neither.
Failure to attend the parent education class within 60 days of this order is punishable by contempt.

Under penalty of perjury, we declare that this plan has been proposed in good faith and is in the best interest of each minor child and that the statements herein and on the attached child support worksheets are true and correct. *(A notary public is required if this is a proposed plan by one parent rather than one agreed by both parents.)*

_____   _____
Mother   Date and Place Signed

Sworn to and subscribed before me this _____ day of _____, 20_____.

My commission expires:_____   _____
                                                                                    Notary Public

_____   _____
Father   Date and Place Signed

Sworn to and subscribed before me this _____ day of _____, 20_____.

My commission expires:_____   _____
                                                                                    Notary Public

APPROVED FOR ENTRY:

_____   _____
Attorney for Mother   *Attorney for Father*
_____   _____
Address   *Address*
_____   _____
Address   *Address*
_____   _____
Phone and BPR Number   *Phone and BPR Number*

Note: The judge or chancellor may sign below or, instead, sign a Final Decree or a separate Order incorporating this plan.

COURT COSTS (If applicable)

Court costs, if any, are taxed as follows:

_____.

It is so ORDERED this the _____ day of _____, _____.

                                                _____
                                                             Judge or Chancellor

Chapter 52:
CHARLIE FAMILY—141 DAYS PER YEAR PARENTING TIME

The father received 141 days with the children. Mr. and Mrs. Charlie were married eight years and have two sons, ages four and one. The father enjoys parenting time every Wednesday evening through Friday evening. The mother is the primary residential parent, and the parents share joint decision-making authority on all major decisions. The mother planned on returning to school. The father had a very highly paid position in the medical profession. Although both parents desperately wanted a divorce (and were ready to date openly), they trusted the other on parenting time.

STATE OF TENNESSEE	CHANCERY **COURT** *(Must be completed)*	SHELBY **COUNTY***(Must be completed)*
PERMANENT PARENTING PLAN ORDER X **PROPOSED** ☐ **AGREED** ☐ **ORDERED BY THE COURT**	**FILE No.** CH-09-ABCD-E *(Must be completed)* **PART II**	
PLAINTIFF *(Name: First, Middle, Last)* **MICHAEL JACKSON CHARLIE** ☐ Mother X Father	**DEFENDANT** *(Name: First, Middle, Last)* **PRISCILLA PRESLEY CHARLIE** X Mother ☐ Father	

The mother and father will behave with each other and each child so as to provide a loving, stable, consistent and nurturing relationship with the child even though they are divorced. They will not speak badly of each other or the members of the family of the other parent. They will encourage each child to continue to love the other parent and be comfortable in both families.

This plan   X is a new plan.

☐ modifies an existing Parenting Plan dated _____.

☐ modifies an existing Order dated _____.

Child's Name	Date of Birth
Garrett Boyd Charlie	9/15/08
Harold James Charlie	8/14/11

I.   RESIDENTIAL PARENTING SCHEDULE

A.   RESIDENTIAL TIME WITH EACH PARENT

The Primary Residential Parent is Mother

Under the schedule set forth below, each parent will spend the following number of days with the children:

Mother 224 days   Father 141 days

B.   DAY-TO-DAY SCHEDULE

The X mother ☐ father shall have responsibility for the care of the child or children except at the following times when the other parent shall have responsibility:

From Friday at 6:00 p.m. to Sunday at 6:00 p.m.
Day and Time   *Day and Time*

☐ every week X every other week ☐ other: _____.

The other parent shall also have responsibility for the care of the child or children at the additional parenting times specified below:

From <u>Wednesday at 6:00 p.m.</u> to <u>Friday at 6:00 p.m.</u>
          Day and Time   *Day and Time*

X every week ☐ every other week X other: <u>Mother shall be allowed to collect the children from school or daycare during Father's parenting time on occasions that Father is working and Mother is not, and Mother shall care for the children until their collection by Father. In the Summer, if Father is working on Thursday or Friday, Mother will have first option to care for the children while Father works.</u>

This parenting schedule begins X <u>July 1, 2013</u> **or** ☐ date of the Court's Order.
                                                    Day and Time

C.   HOLIDAY SCHEDULE AND OTHER SCHOOL FREE DAYS

Indicate if child or children will be with parent in ODD or EVEN numbered years or EVERY year:

	MOTHER	**FATHER**
New Year's Day	N/A	N/A
Martin Luther King Day	N/A	N/A
Presidents' Day	N/A	N/A
Easter Day (unless otherwise coinciding with Spring Vacation)		
Mardi Gras Holiday	Odd	Even
Mother's Day	Every	None
Memorial Day (if no school)	N/A	N/A
Father's Day	None	Every
July 4th	N/A	N/A
Labor Day	N/A	N/A
Halloween	N/A	N/A
Thanksgiving Day & Friday		
Children's Birthdays	Shared	Shared
Other School-Free Days	N/A	N/A
Mother's Birthday	Every	None
Father's Birthday	None	Every
Other:		

A holiday shall begin at 6:00 p.m. on the night preceding the holiday and end at 6:00 p.m. the night of the holiday, unless otherwise noted here: <u>Any and all children's Monday holidays from school (including a school Monday holiday) shall be the parent's that has the preceding weekend. This includes Memorial Day. The holiday ends at 6:00 p.m. on Monday. All holiday and special occasion parenting time shall supersede the day-to-day parenting time.</u>

D.   THANKSGIVING BREAK

The day to day schedule shall apply except as follows: <u>The Father shall have the children the Monday before Thanksgiving at 12:00 noon until Sunday at 6:00 p.m. in even-numbered years. Mother shall have the children the Monday before Thanksgiving at 12:00 noon until Sunday at 6:00 p.m. in odd-numbered years.</u>

E.   WINTER (CHRISTMAS) VACATION

The ☐ mother x father shall have the child or children for the first period from the day and time school is dismissed until <u>December 25th at 2:00p.m.</u> ☐ in odd-numbered years ☐ in even-numbered years   ☐ every year. The other parent will have the child or children for the second period from the day and time indicated above until 6:00 p.m. on the evening before school resumes. The parties shall alternate the first and second periods each year.

Other agreement of the parents: _____

F.   EASTER & SPRING VACATION (*If applicable*)

The day-to-day schedule shall apply except as follows: <u>Father shall have the children from 6:00 p.m. the day school is dismissed until Easter Sunday at 6:00 p.m. in odd-numbered years. Mother shall have the children from 6:00 p.m. the day school is dismissed until Easter Sunday at 6:00 p.m. in even-numbered years. For Spring Break in odd-numbered years, Father shall have the children from 6:00 p.m. Sunday before Spring Break until Sunday at 6:00 p.m. following Spring Break unless Spring Break is the week immediately following Easter and then there shall be no break in parenting time. For Spring Break in even numbered years, Mother shall have the children from 6:00 p.m. Sunday before Spring Break until Sunday at 6:00 p.m. following Spring Break unless Spring Break is the week immediately following Easter and then there shall be no break in parenting time.</u>

G.   SUMMER VACATION

The day-to-day schedule shall apply except as follows: <u>Each parent shall choose two (2) nonconsecutive weeks by April 1st of each year. Mother shall select her weeks first in even-numbered years and Father shall select his weeks first in odd-numbered years. The parents will not select any week that interferes with the other parent's scheduled holiday parenting time.</u>

Is written notice required? x Yes ☐ No.   If so, _____ number of days.

H.   TRANSPORTATION ARRANGEMENTS

The place of meeting for the exchange of the child or children shall be: <u>Father shall be responsible for picking up the children at Mother's residence when his parenting time commences and for returning the children to Mother's residence at the conclusion of his parenting time.</u>
Payment of long distance transportation costs *(if applicable):* ☐ mother   ☐ father ☐ both equally.
Other arrangements: _____.
If a parent does not possess a valid driver's license, he or she must make reasonable transportation arrangements to protect the child or children while in the care of that parent.

I.   SUPERVISION OF PARENTING TIME (*If applicable*)
☐ **Check if applicable**

Supervised parenting time shall apply during the day-to-day schedule as follows:
☐ Place: _____.
☐ Person or organization supervising: _____.

⬜ Responsibility for cost, if any: ⬜ mother ⬜ father ⬜ both equally.

J.   OTHER

The following special provisions apply :
(a) The parties agree to follow the Temporary Parenting Plan until July 1, 2013.

(b) Both Mother and Father shall be allowed to take the children on vacations or trips, including trips outside the state, on reasonable terms and conditions with the other party's knowledge, permission and consent, which approval shall not be unreasonably withheld.

(c) **College Education Expenses.** Father hereby agrees to pay, when due, the reasonable and necessary expense of providing a college education to the children of the parties, the majority of such child not withstanding, so long as said child shall be continuously enrolled, summer and other regular vacations and absence due to physical illness excepted, in a college or university by the American Association of Colleges and Schools as a full-time student, in good standing, according to the standard therefore established by said college or university, in the curriculum calculated to result in the award of a baccalaureate degree within four (4) calendar years, or eight regular semesters, after said child shall graduate from high school, whichever is more. The obligation of Husband created herein shall include the following expenses, to-wit: tuition denominated as such; other mandatory fees and charges incident to enrollment and assessed directly by the college or university; the cost of room and board in an amount no greater than the charge for private accommodations in institutional dormitories and the charge for a meal plan, meal ticket, or similar program entitling students to no more than fourteen (14) meals per week in institutional dining facilities; the cost of private telephone service, long-distance charges, or cellular phone service; the cost of an internet connection charged by the college or university; the cost of textbooks and other assigned reading materials; lab fees, activity fees and other fees charged directly by the college or university. The obligation of Husband created herein shall be further limited in amount to the expenses identified hereinabove prevailing at the time of the child's matriculation in a college or university at Tulane University in New Orleans, Louisiana. The obligation of Husband created herein shall terminate upon said child's marriage, upon said child's withdrawal from said college or university during any regular term, upon said child's failure to register timely in every consecutive regular term, that is excluding summer terms, for the minimum course load required for completion of work necessary to award of a degree within the time provided for herein, upon said child's failure to attend more than fifty percent (50%) of regular scheduled classes in courses in which he is enrolled; and, once terminated according to this provision, the obligation of Husband created herein, however shall be deemed to preclude either party from any expenditure on behalf or for the benefit of the child on such terms and conditions as such party shall deem appropriate in his or her sole discretion.

(d) **Private School Tuition**. Father shall pay private school tuition, books, fees and uniforms for both minor children until they each graduate from high school. In the event Mother teaches or is otherwise employed by a private school and the children attend that school, and Mother receives a credit or discount on the children's private school tuition, Father shall pay directly to Mother as child support the difference between the regular price of tuition for the children and the actual price paid for the children's tuition due to the discount Mother receives in incremental payments as tuition is paid by Father.

(e) **Sports**. Father shall pay all registration fees, dues, uniforms and equipment for both minor children to participate in sports, if Father agrees to the children's participation in that activity. Father's agreement for a child to participate in a particular activity shall not be unreasonably withheld.

(f) The parties are also to advise each other concerning any medications or other "at home" medical treatment that many be needed by their children.

(g) **Address and phone**. Both parties shall keep the other party informed of his or her address and telephone number so that either parent may call the children when the children are visiting or residing with the other party, at reasonable intervals and at reasonable times, and if either parent takes the minor children out of town, he or she will notify the other parent as to where the minor children may be reached.

(h) **Definition of "Telephone Number."** For all portions of this Permanent Parenting Plan, the definition of "Telephone Number" shall include, but is not limited to the following: land based (traditional) telephone number, cellular telephone number, child's cellular telephone number (whether permanent or temporary), or any other voice communication method. For vacations or temporary residences for any reason, said numbers shall include contact numbers such as vacation rental homes.

(i) Neither parent shall deny the child reasonable use of the telephone to place and receive phone calls with the other parent and relatives.

(j) In the event a parent changes his or her address in town, the moving parent will notify the other parent in writing prior to the move, providing the new address and telephone number, unless an order has been obtained from the Court specifically exempting this requirement.

(k) Neither parent shall enroll or encourage a child of the parties to enroll, participate or engage in any extracurricular, social, recreational, or educational activity, including optional tutoring or study sessions related to school work but which are not required as a condition to continued enrollment in school, which activities take place during the parenting time of the other without the express consent of the other. Each parent shall, during his or her parenting time, transport a child of the parties to facilitate the child's participation in any such extracurricular, social, recreational, or educational activity in which said child is engaged by consent of both parties shall be paid, when due, by Father.

(l) Neither parent will allow materials with adult content or of a sexually-explicit nature appealing to prurient interest where such is any way accessible by the children. Should a parent possess such materials, they will be locked up at any time the children are in the home of or under the supervision of that parent.

(m) Both parents shall, at all times, take all action necessary to promote the safety and well being of the children, provide all adequate care and supervision, mandate the use of seatbelts, and otherwise make the children's well being and safety a paramount consideration at all times.

(n) The parent who receives a schedule of children's activities or other information regarding children's events will fax, mail, or e-mail this information to the other parent in a timely manner so that the other parent has the opportunity to plan for and attend those activities or events.

(o) **Canceling Visitation**. Except in emergency situations, the alternate residential parent must give at least 24 hours' advance notice when canceling a visitation period.

(p) **Opportunity for Additional Parenting Time**. When it becomes necessary that a child be cared for by a person other than a parent or family member exceeding twelve (12) consecutive hours, the parent needing the child care shall first offer the other parent the opportunity for additional parenting time. The other parent is under no obligation to provide the child care. If the other parent elects to provide this care, it shall be done at no cost.

(q) The parties will thoroughly discuss and consult with each other in regard to, and will be kept advised of, all decisions to be made concerning the education, medical and dental treatment, religious training, and dating of the children. The parties will also discuss and be advised of a child's participation in driving, sports, or other dangerous activities.

(r) The alternate residential parent will be notified in advance of any prearranged medical or dental treatment, and in the event of an emergency, both parents are to be notified as soon as possible.

(s) Father and Mother hereby stipulate that it is in the children's best interest that the children reside in Lake Charles, Louisiana, or its environs, due to the presence of extended family, including both the maternal and paternal grandparents, and agree, therefore, that, in the event either parents shall make their primary residence with the parent remaining in Lake Charles, Louisiana, or its environs, subject to visitation or parenting time by or for the other on such terms and conditions as the parties may subsequently agree, or as a court of competent jurisdiction may determine. If Father moves further that 60 miles away from Lake Charles, Louisiana, this paragraph is null and void.

(t) Father and Mother hereby stipulate that it is not in the best interest of the minor children of the parties that they have contact with Bryan Spears, and they agree that the minor children of the parties shall have no contact whatsoever with Bryan Spears. Accidental or unintentional contact is excluded, and any such contact will be momentary.

(u) Father and Mother agree that, in the event Mother anticipates any contact between the minor children and Nick Ordoyne, said contact shall be conditioned on Mother providing Father, in advance of such contact, a report of a comprehensive drug screen of the said Nicki Ordoyne rendered by a reputable drug testing laboratory. Further, Mother and the said Nick Ordoyne shall not cohabitate in any residence in which the minor children of the parties are present for a period of thirty-six (36) months following approval of the Permanent Parenting Plan.

II.   DECISION-MAKING

A.   DAY-TO-DAY DECISIONS

Each parent shall make decisions regarding the day-to-day care of a child while the child is residing with that parent, including any emergency decisions affecting the health or safety of a child.

B.   MAJOR DECISIONS

Major decisions regarding each child shall be made as follows:

Educational decisions	☐ mother	☐ father	**x** joint
Non-emergency health care	☐ mother	☐ father	**x** joint
Religious upbringing	☐ mother	☐ father	**x** joint
Extracurricular activities	☐ mother	☐ father	**x** joint
_____	☐ mother	☐ father	☐ joint

III.   FINANCIAL SUPPORT

A.   CHILD SUPPORT

Father's gross monthly income is $ 43,416.00*
Mother's gross monthly income is $ 0.00

   *The parents will be moving to Louisiana within the next several months, and it is impossible to predict what their exact incomes will be in their new situations. For that reason, on the child support worksheet attached to this Permanent Parenting Plan the parents have used possible projected income figures for themselves. The parents agree that in the event of any future court proceedings these projected income figures shall not be used by either parent against the other as an admission of fact that the figures used in the child support guideline worksheet represent the income actually received during the projected time. Each party shall remain free to present evidence of actual income. Furthermore, the use of these figures shall not constitute a waiver by either parent of the right to produce evidence that actual income turned out to be different from the incomes projected in the child support worksheet.

   1. The final child support order is as follows:
   a.   The   ☐ mother   **x**   father   shall pay to the other parent as regular child support the sum of $3,200.00 ☐ weekly   **x** monthly ☐ twice per month
   ☐ every two weeks. **The Child Support Worksheet shall be attached to this Order as an Exhibit.***

   If this is a deviation from the Child Support Guidelines, explain why:

2. Retroactive Support: A judgment is hereby awarded in the amount of $\$$_____ to ☐ mother ☐ father against the child support payor representing retroactive support required under Section 1240-2-4.06 of the D.H.S. Income Shares Child Support Guidelines dating from _____ which shall be paid (including pre/post judgment interest) at the rate of $\$$_____ per ☐ week ☐ month ☐ twice per month ☐ every two weeks until the judgment is paid in full.

3. Payments shall begin on the <u>1st day of September, 2013, and due on the first (1st)</u> <u>day of each month thereafter. Until that time, Father shall pay to Mother the sum of</u> <u>$2,039.00 per month, as temporary support, commencing on February 1, 2013, with</u> <u>$500.00 due on the first (1st) day of each month and $1,539.00, due on the tenth (10th) day</u> <u>of each month.</u>

This support shall be paid:

x directly to the other parent.

☐ to the Central Child Support Receipting Unit, P. O. Box 305200, Nashville, Tennessee 37229, and sent from there to the other parent at: _____.

☐ A Wage Assignment Order is attached to this Parenting Plan.

☐ by direct deposit to the other parent at _____ Bank for deposit in account no. _____.

☐ income assignment not required; Explanation:_____.

☐ other:_____.

The parents acknowledge that court approval must be obtained before child support can be reduced or modified.

*Child Support Worksheet can be found on DHS website at http://www.state.tn.us/humanserv/is/isdocuments.html or at your local child support offices.

B.   FEDERAL INCOME TAX EXEMPTION*

The X mother ☐ father is the parent receiving child support.

The Mother shall claim the following children: <u>Garrett Boyd Charlie and Harold James Charlie</u>

The Father shall claim the following children: _____

The X mother ☐ father may claim the exemptions for the child or children so long as child support payments are current by the claiming parent on January 15 of the year when the return is due. The exemptions may be claimed in: ☐ alternate years starting _____ ☐ each year ☐ other: _____.

The X mother ☐ father will furnish IRS Form 8332 to the parent entitled to the exemption by February 15 of the year the tax return is due.

C.   PROOF OF INCOME AND WORK-RELATED CHILD CARE EXPENSES

Each parent shall send proof of income to the other parent for the prior calendar year as follows:

- IRS Forms W-2 and 1099 shall be sent to the other parent on or before   February 15.
- A copy of his or her federal income tax return shall be sent to the other parent on or before April 15 or any later date when it is due because of an extension of time for filing.
- The completed form required by the Department of Human Services shall be sent to the Department on or before the date the federal income tax return is due by the parent paying child support. *This requirement applies only if a parent is receiving benefits from the Department for a child.*

The parent paying work-related child care expenses shall send proof of expenses to the other parent for the prior calendar year and an estimate for the next calendar year, on or before February 15.

D.   HEALTH AND DENTAL INSURANCE

Reasonable health insurance on the child or children will be:
   ☐ maintained by the mother
   X maintained by the father
   ☐ maintained by both

Proof of continuing coverage shall be furnished to the other parent annually or as coverage changes. The parent maintaining coverage shall authorize the other parent to consult with the insurance carrier regarding the coverage in effect.

Uncovered reasonable and necessary medical expenses, which may include but is not limited to, deductibles or co-payments, eyeglasses, contact lens, routine annual physicals, and counseling will be paid by ☐ mother X father ☐ pro rata in accordance with their incomes. After insurance has paid its portion, the parent receiving the bill will send it to the other parent within ten days. The other parent will pay his or her share within 30 days of receipt of the bill.

---

* NOTE: The child support schedule assumptions in the guidelines (1240-2-4-.03 (6)(b)) assume that the parent receiving the child support will get the tax exemptions for the child.

If available through work, the ☐ mother X father shall maintain dental, orthodontic, and optical insurance on the minor child or children.

E.   LIFE INSURANCE

If agreed upon by the parties, the ☐ mother X father ☐ both shall insure his/her own life in the minimum amount of $2,000,000.00 by whole life or term insurance.   Until the child support obligation has been completed, each policy shall name the child/children as sole irrevocable primary beneficiary, with the X other parent ☐ other _____, as trustee for the benefit of the children, to serve without bond or accounting.

IV. PRIMARY RESIDENTIAL PARENT (CUSTODIAN) FOR OTHER LEGAL PURPOSES

The child or children are scheduled to reside the majority of the time with the X mother   ☐ father. This parent is designated as the primary residential parent also known as the custodian, **SOLELY** for purposes of any other applicable state and federal laws. If the parents are listed in Section II as joint decision-makers, then, for purposes of obtaining health or other insurance, they shall be considered to be joint custodians. THIS DESIGNATION DOES NOT AFFECT EITHER PARENT'S RIGHTS OR RESPONSIBILITIES UNDER THIS PARENTING PLAN.

V. DISAGREEMENTS OR MODIFICATION OF PLAN

Should the parents disagree about this Parenting Plan or wish to modify it, they must make a good faith effort to resolve the issue by the process selected below before returning to Court. *Except for financial support issues including child support, health and dental insurance, uncovered medical and dental expenses, and life insurance*, disputes must be submitted to:

> X   Mediation by a neutral party chosen by the parents or the Court.
> ☐   Arbitration by a neutral party selected by parents or the Court.
> ☐   The Court DUE TO ORDER OF PROTECTION OR RESTRICTIONS.

The costs of this process may be determined by the alternative dispute process or may be assessed by the Court based upon the incomes of the parents. It must be commenced by notifying the other parent and the Court by ☐ written request ☐ certified mail
☐ other: _____.

In the dispute resolution process:
> A. Preference shall be given to carrying out this Parenting Plan.
> B. The parents shall use the process to resolve disputes relating to implementation of the Plan.
> C. A written record shall be prepared of any agreement reached, and it shall be provided to each parent.
> D. If the Court finds that a parent willfully failed to appear without good reason, the Court, upon motion, may award attorney fees and financial sanctions to the prevailing parent.

VI.   RIGHTS OF PARENTS

Under T.C.A. § 36-6-101 of Tennessee law, both parents are entitled to the following rights:

> (1) The right to unimpeded telephone conversations with the child at least twice a week at reasonable times and for reasonable durations;

(2) The right to send mail to the child which the other parent shall not open or censor;

(3) The right to receive notice and relevant information as soon as practicable but within twenty-four (24) hours of any event of hospitalization, major illness or death of the child;

(4) The right to receive directly from the child's school any school records customarily made available to parents. (The school may require a written request which includes a current mailing address and upon payment of reasonable costs of duplicating.) These include copies of the child's report cards, attendance records, names of teachers, class schedules, and standardized test scores;

(5) Unless otherwise provided by law, the right to receive copies of the child's medical health or other treatment records directly from the physician or health care provider who provided treatment or health care. (The keeper of the records may require a written request which contains a current mailing address and the payment of reasonable costs of duplication.) No person who receives the mailing address of a parent as a result of this requirement shall provide such address to the other parent or a third person;

(6) The right to be free of unwarranted derogatory remarks made about the parent or his or her family by the other parent to the child or in the presence of the child;

(7) The right to be given at least forty-eight (48) hours notice, whenever possible, of all extra-curricular activities, and the opportunity to participate or observe them. These include the following: school activities, athletic activities, church activities and other activities where parental participation or observation would be appropriate;

(8) The right to receive from the other parent, in the event the other parent leaves the state with the minor child or children for more than two (2) days, an itinerary including telephone numbers for use in the event of an emergency;

(9) The right to access and participation in education on the same basis that is provided to all parents. This includes the right of access to the child for lunch and other activities. However participation or access must be reasonable and not interfere with day-to-day operations or with the child's educational performance.

VII.   NOTICE REGARDING PARENTAL RELOCATION

The Tennessee statute (T.C.A. § 36-6-108) which governs the notice to be given in connection with the relocation of a parent reads in pertinent part as follows:

If a parent who is spending intervals of time with a child desires to relocate outside the state or more than fifty (50) miles from the other parent within the state, the relocating parent shall send a notice to the other parent at the other parent's last known address by registered or certified mail. Unless excused by the court for exigent circumstances, the notice shall be mailed not later than sixty (60) days prior to the move. The notice shall contain the following:

(1) Statement of intent to move;

(2) Location of proposed new residence;

(3) Reasons for proposed relocation; and

(4) Statement that the other parent may file a petition in opposition to the move within thirty (30) days of receipt of the notice.

VIII.   PARENT EDUCATION CLASS

This requirement has been fulfilled by ☐ both parents X mother ☐ father   ☐ neither. Failure to attend the parent education class within 60 days of this order is punishable by contempt.

Under penalty of perjury, we declare that this plan has been proposed in good faith and is in the best interest of each minor child and that the statements herein and on the attached child support worksheets are true and correct. *(A notary public is required if this is a proposed plan by one parent rather than one agreed by both parents.)*

_____   _____
Mother   Date and Place Signed

Sworn to and subscribed before me this _____ day of _____, 20_____.

My commission expires:_____   _____
                                                                             Notary Public

_____   _____
Father   Date and Place Signed

Sworn to and subscribed before me this _____ day of _____, 20_____.

My commission expires:_____   _____
                                                                             Notary Public

APPROVED FOR ENTRY:

_____   _____
Attorney for Mother   *Attorney for Father*
_____   _____
Address   *Address*
_____   _____
Address   *Address*
_____   _____
Phone and BPR Number   *Phone and BPR Number*

Note: The judge or chancellor may sign below or, instead, sign a Final Decree or a separate Order incorporating this plan.

COURT COSTS (If applicable)

Court costs, if any, are taxed as follows:

_____.

It is so ORDERED this the _____ day of _____, _____.

_____
Judge or Chancellor

Chapter 53:

DELTA FAMILY—170 DAYS PER YEAR PARENTING TIME

Father has the children for 170 days a year. Mr. and Mrs. Delta were married for seventeen years and have a son, age eleven, and a daughter, age ten. The father is a pilot (not for Delta), and the mother worked part time in sales. By the time the divorce was filed, both parents had new exclusive relationships. Because the father flies only around fifteen days a month, the parents sought a very flexible parenting plan. The mother was designated the primary residential parent, but the parties share final decision-making on all major decisions. This is an example of roughly equal time.

STATE OF TENNESSEE	COURT *(Must be completed)* CIRCUIT	COUNTY*(Must be completed)* SHELBY COUNTY
PERMANENT PARENTING PLAN ORDER ☐ **PROPOSED** X **AGREED** ☐ **ORDERED BY THE COURT**		**FILE No.** <u>CT-ABCDEF-11</u> *(Must be completed)* **DIVISION** <u>II</u>
PLAINTIFF *(Name: First, Middle, Last)* <u>CHERIE LYNN DELTA</u> <u>X</u> Mother ☐ Father	**DEFENDANT** *(Name: First, Middle, Last)* <u>DAVID ALLEN DELTA</u> ☐ Mother X Father	

> *The mother and father will behave with each other and each child so as to provide a loving, stable, consistent and nurturing relationship with the child even though they are divorced. They will not speak badly of each other or the members of the family of the other parent. They will encourage each child to continue to love the other parent and be comfortable in both families.*

This plan   <u>X</u> is a new plan.

                  ☐ modifies an existing Parenting Plan dated _____.

                  ☐ modifies an existing Order dated _____.

Child's Name	Date of Birth
Raymond Delta	June 20, 2001
Kylie Delta	November 2, 2002

I.   RESIDENTIAL PARENTING SCHEDULE

A.   RESIDENTIAL TIME WITH EACH PARENT

The Primary Residential Parent is <u>Mother</u>.

Under the schedule set forth below, each parent will spend the following number of days with the children:

       Mother <u>195</u> days   Father <u>170</u> days

B.   DAY-TO-DAY SCHEDULE

The <u>X</u> Mother __ Father shall have responsibility for the care of the child or children except at the following times when the <u>Father</u> shall have responsibility:

<u>11 days per month based on Father's work schedule. For purposes of this parenting schedule, "month" shall be construed as the FedEx pilots' "bid" month, which does not coincide with a calendar month.</u>

In December, Father will have the children 7 days instead of 11 days; these 7 days shall not coincide with Father's Winter Vacation parenting time.

On the years Father has the children for Fall Vacation he will have the children 7 days instead of 11 days the month of Fall Vacation; these 7 days shall not coincide with Father's Fall Vacation parenting time.

On the years Father has the children for Spring Vacation, he will have the children 7 days instead of 11 days for the month of Spring Vacation; these 7 days shall not coincide with Father's Spring Vacation parenting time.

During Summer Vacation, Father's 15 days per month of Summer Vacation parenting time shall replace Father's 11 days per month of the Day-to-Day Schedule.

The parties acknowledge that Father's job as a FedEx pilot offers him much time off work; however, this schedule changes from month to month. In order to ensure that Father receives at least 11 days per month with the children, Father shall deliver a copy of his work schedule within 24 hours of receiving it, along with his proposed schedule of parenting time for that month. The parties agree to be flexible and cooperate in creating a monthly schedule. Nothing in this paragraph shall prohibit Father from making up parenting time in later months in the event Father in unable to enjoy his allowable parenting time in a given month.

The other parent shall also have responsibility for the care of the child or children at the additional parenting times specified below:

From _____ to _____
       Day and Time   *Day and Time*

☐ every week ☐ every other week ☐ other: _____.

This parenting schedule begins ☐ _____ **or** X date of the Court's Order.
                         Day and Time

C. HOLIDAY SCHEDULE AND OTHER SCHOOL FREE DAYS

Indicate if child or children will be with parent in ODD or EVEN numbered years or EVERY year:

	MOTHER	FATHER
New Year's Day	see Winter Vacation	see Winter Vacation
Martin Luther King Day	odd	even
Presidents' Day	even	odd
Easter Day (unless otherwise coinciding with Spring Vacation)	odd	even
Passover Day (unless otherwise coinciding with Spring Vacation)	N/A	N/A
Mother's Day	every	none
Memorial Day (if no school)	odd	even
Father's Day	none	every
July 4th	even	odd
Labor Day	even	odd
Halloween	Day-to-Day Schedule	Day-to-Day Schedule

Thanksgiving Day & Friday	odd	even
Children's Birthdays	shared	shared
Other School-Free Days	Day-to-Day Schedule	Day-to-Day Schedule
Mother's Birthday	every	none
Father's Birthday	none	every

A holiday shall begin at 4:00 p.m. on the night preceding the holiday and end at 4:00 p.m. the night of the holiday, unless otherwise noted here: For holidays that fall on a weekend or Monday, the holiday shall begin after school on Friday until the evening before school resumes at 4:00 p.m. For Thanksgiving, the holiday begins after school on Wednesday and ends Sunday at 4:00 p.m.

D. FALL VACATION (*If applicable*)

The day to day schedule shall apply except as follows: Mother shall have the children in odd-numbered years and Father shall have the children in even-numbered years, beginning after school lets out on Friday until the evening before school resumes at 4:00 p.m.

E. WINTER (CHRISTMAS) VACATION

The X mother ☐ father shall have the child or children for the first period from the day and time school is dismissed until December 25 at 4:00 p.m. X in odd-numbered years ☐ in even-numbered years ☐ every year. The Father will have the child or children for the second period from the day and time indicated above until 4:00 p.m. on the evening before school resumes. The parties shall alternate the first and second periods each year.

Other agreement of the parents: None.

F. SPRING VACATION (*If applicable*)

The day-to-day schedule shall apply except as follows: Mother shall have the children in even-numbered years and Father shall have the children in odd-numbered years, beginning after school lets out on Friday until the evening before school resumes at 4:00 p.m.

G. SUMMER VACATION

The day-to-day schedule shall apply except as follows: Father shall have the children 13

days in May, 15 days in June, 15 days in July and 13 days in August beginning May 2014.

Is written notice required?   X Yes ☐ No.   If so, 45 number of days. Written notice shall be by e-mail.

H. TRANSPORTATION ARRANGEMENTS

The place of meeting for the exchange of the child or children shall be: Mother shall bring the children to Father's residence at the end of her parenting time and Father shall bring the children to Mother's residence at the end of his parenting time,

Payment of long distance transportation costs *(if applicable):* ☐ mother ☐ father X both equally.

Other arrangements: None.

If a parent does not possess a valid driver's license, he or she must make reasonable transportation arrangements to protect the child or children while in the care of that parent.

I.   SUPERVISION OF PARENTING TIME *(If applicable)*
☐ **Check if applicable**

Supervised parenting time shall apply during the day-to-day schedule as follows:
☐ Place: _____.
☐ Person or organization supervising: _____.
☐ Responsibility for cost, if any: ☐ mother ☐ father ☐ both equally.

J.   OTHER

The following special provisions apply: Prior to arranging for child care or babysitting of the children, the other parent shall be consulted and the other parent will have the right of refusal to perform such child care or babysitting services. The other parent is under no obligation to provide the child care and if the other parent elects to do so, it shall be done at no cost.

In the event Father misses scheduled parenting time as a result of an unanticipated work schedule or training, Father may make up that time within 6 months to a time mutually agreeable to both parties.

If a parent will be away from the children for more than two (2) hours or if a parent plans to arrange for child care or babysitting of the children for more than two (2) hours, the other parent shall be consulted and the other parent will have the right of first refusal to care for the children. The other parent is under no obligation to provide child care and if the other parent elects to do so, it shall be done at no cost.

The parents realize the key to co-parenting is flexibility and the parents will do their best to be flexible month in and month out.

Father will ensure Mother gets his FedEx schedule no later than the day following the day of Father receiving it.

II.   DECISION-MAKING

A.   DAY-TO-DAY DECISIONS

Each parent shall make decisions regarding the day-to-day care of a child while the child is residing with that parent, including any emergency decisions affecting the health or safety of a child.

B.   MAJOR DECISIONS

Major decisions regarding each child shall be made as follows:

Educational decisions	☐ mother	☐ father	X joint
Non-emergency health care	☐ mother	☐ father	X joint
Religious upbringing	☐ mother	☐ father	X joint
Extracurricular activities	☐ mother	☐ father	X joint
_____	☐ mother	☐ father	☐ joint

III.   FINANCIAL SUPPORT

A.   CHILD SUPPORT

Father's gross monthly income is $12,062.00
Mother's gross monthly income is $2,441.66

1. The final child support order is as follows:
   a.   The ☐ mother X father shall pay to the other parent as regular child support the sum of $1,272.00 ☐ weekly X monthly ☐ twice per month ☐ every two weeks. **The Child Support Worksheet shall be attached to this Order as an Exhibit.***

   If this is a deviation from the Child Support Guidelines, explain why:
   Father's income from U.S. Air Force Reserves is not included. Said income varies depending on his assignments. In addition, Father will retire from the Reserves in November 2013 and will no longer have this source of income. The parents agree that this deviation is reasonable and in the best interests of the children.

2. Retroactive Support: A judgment is hereby awarded in the amount of $_____ to ☐ mother ☐ father against the child support payor representing retroactive support required under Section 1240-2-4.06 of the D.H.S. Income Shares Child Support Guidelines dating from _____ which shall be paid (including pre/post judgment interest) at the rate of $_____ per ☐ week ☐ month ☐ twice per month ☐ every two weeks until the judgment is paid in full.

3. Payments shall begin on September 15, 2013 and shall be payable to Mother by the 15th of each month.

This support shall be paid by direct deposit to Mother at SunTrust Bank for deposit in account no. 1234567890.

The parents acknowledge that court approval must be obtained before child support can be reduced or modified.

*Child Support Worksheet can be found on DHS website at http://www.state.tn.us/humanserv/is/isdocuments.html or at your local child support offices.

B.   FEDERAL INCOME TAX EXEMPTION*

The X mother ☐ father is the parent receiving child support.

The Mother shall claim the following children: Raymond Delta every year.

The Father shall claim the following children: Kylie Delta every year.

The ☐ mother X father may claim the exemptions for the child or children so long as child support payments are current by the claiming parent on January 15 of the year when the return is due. The exemptions may be claimed in: ☐ alternate years starting _____ ☐ each year ☐ other: _____.

---

* NOTE: The child support schedule assumptions in the guidelines (1240-2-4-.03 (6)(b)) assume that the parent receiving the child support will get the tax exemptions for the child.

The X̲ mother ☐ father will furnish IRS Form 8332 to the parent entitled to the exemption by February 15 of the year the tax return is due.

C.   PROOF OF INCOME AND WORK-RELATED CHILD CARE EXPENSES

Each parent shall send proof of income to the other parent for the prior calendar year as follows:

- IRS Forms W-2 and 1099 shall be sent to the other parent on or before   February 15.
- A copy of his or her federal income tax return shall be sent to the other parent on or before April 15 or any later date when it is due because of an extension of time for filing.
- The completed form required by the Department of Human Services shall be sent to the Department on or before the date the federal income tax return is due by the parent paying child support. *This requirement applies only if a parent is receiving benefits from the Department for a child.*

The parent paying work-related child care expenses shall send proof of expenses to the other parent for the prior calendar year and an estimate for the next calendar year, on or before February 15.

D.   HEALTH AND DENTAL INSURANCE

Reasonable health insurance on the child or children will be:
      ☐   maintained by the mother
      X̲   maintained by the father
      ☐   maintained by both

Proof of continuing coverage shall be furnished to the other parent annually or as coverage changes. The parent maintaining coverage shall authorize the other parent to consult with the insurance carrier regarding the coverage in effect.

Uncovered reasonable and necessary medical expenses, which may include but is not limited to, deductibles or co-payments, eyeglasses, contact lens, routine annual physicals, and counseling will be paid by ☐ mother ☐ father X̲ pro rata in accordance with their incomes on any expense agreed upon by the parties. After insurance has paid its portion, the parent receiving the bill will send it to the other parent within ten days. The other parent will pay his or her share within 30 days of receipt of the bill. Any medical expense incurred by a party not agreed to by the other party shall be paid 100% by the party who incurred the expense.

All medical, dental and vision care will be with an in-network provider unless otherwise agreed by the parties.

If available through work, the ☐ mother X̲ father shall maintain dental, orthodontic, and optical insurance on the minor child or children.

E.   LIFE INSURANCE

If agreed upon by the parties, ☐ the mother ☐ father X̲ both shall insure his/her own life in the minimum amount of $200,000.00 by whole life or term insurance. Until the child support obligation has been completed, each policy shall name the child/children as sole irrevocable primary beneficiary, with the X̲ other parent ☐ other _____, as trustee for the benefit of the child(ren), to serve without bond or accounting.

IV. PRIMARY RESIDENTIAL PARENT (CUSTODIAN) FOR OTHER LEGAL PURPOSES

The child or children are scheduled to reside the majority of the time with the X mother ☐ father. This parent is designated as the primary residential parent also known as the custodian, **SOLELY** for purposes of any other applicable state and federal laws. If the parents are listed in Section II as joint decision-makers, then, for purposes of obtaining health or other insurance, they shall be considered to be joint custodians. THIS DESIGNATION DOES NOT AFFECT EITHER PARENT'S RIGHTS OR RESPONSIBILITIES UNDER THIS PARENTING PLAN.

V. DISAGREEMENTS OR MODIFICATION OF PLAN

Should the parents disagree about this Parenting Plan or wish to modify it, they must make a good faith effort to resolve the issue by the process selected below before returning to Court. *Except for financial support issues including child support, health and dental insurance, uncovered medical and dental expenses, and life insurance*, disputes must be submitted to:

  X   Mediation by a neutral party chosen by the parents or the Court.
  ☐   Arbitration by a neutral party selected by parents or the Court.
  ☐   The Court DUE TO ORDER OF PROTECTION OR RESTRICTIONS.

The costs of this process may be determined by the alternative dispute process or may be assessed by the Court based upon the incomes of the parents. It must be commenced by notifying the other parent and the Court by X written request ☐ certified mail ☐ other: _____.

In the dispute resolution process:

  A. Preference shall be given to carrying out this Parenting Plan.
  B. The parents shall use the process to resolve disputes relating to implementation of the Plan.
  C. A written record shall be prepared of any agreement reached, and it shall be provided to each parent.
  D. If the Court finds that a parent willfully failed to appear without good reason, the Court, upon motion, may award attorney fees and financial sanctions to the prevailing parent.
  E.

VI.   RIGHTS OF PARENTS

Under T.C.A. § 36-6-101 of Tennessee law, both parents are entitled to the following rights:

  (1) The right to unimpeded telephone conversations with the child at least twice a week at reasonable times and for reasonable durations;
  (2) The right to send mail to the child which the other parent shall not open or censor;
  (3) The right to receive notice and relevant information as soon as practicable but within twenty-four (24) hours of any event of hospitalization, major illness or death of the child;
  (4) The right to receive directly from the child's school any school records customarily made available to parents. (The school may require a written request which includes a current mailing address and upon payment of reasonable costs

of duplicating.) These include copies of the child's report cards, attendance records, names of teachers, class schedules, and standardized test scores;

(5) Unless otherwise provided by law, the right to receive copies of the child's medical health or other treatment records directly from the physician or health care provider who provided treatment or health care. (The keeper of the records may require a written request which contains a current mailing address and the payment of reasonable costs of duplication.) No person who receives the mailing address of a parent as a result of this requirement shall provide such address to the other parent or a third person;

(6) The right to be free of unwarranted derogatory remarks made about the parent or his or her family by the other parent to the child or in the presence of the child;

(7) The right to be given at least forty-eight (48) hours notice, whenever possible, of all extra-curricular activities, and the opportunity to participate or observe them. These include the following: school activities, athletic activities, church activities and other activities where parental participation or observation would be appropriate;

(8) The right to receive from the other parent, in the event the other parent leaves the state with the minor child or children for more than two (2) days, an itinerary including telephone numbers for use in the event of an emergency;

(9) The right to access and participation in education on the same basis that is provided to all parents. This includes the right of access to the child for lunch and other activities. However participation or access must be reasonable and not interfere with day-to-day operations or with the child's educational performance.

VII. NOTICE REGARDING PARENTAL RELOCATION

The Tennessee statute (T.C.A. § 36-6-108) which governs the notice to be given in connection with the relocation of a parent reads in pertinent part as follows:

If a parent who is spending intervals of time with a child desires to relocate outside the state or more than fifty (50) miles from the other parent within the state, the relocating parent shall send a notice to the other parent at the other parent's last known address by registered or certified mail. Unless excused by the court for exigent circumstances, the notice shall be mailed not later than sixty (60) days prior to the move. The notice shall contain the following:

(1) Statement of intent to move;

(2) Location of proposed new residence;

(3) Reasons for proposed relocation; and

(4) Statement that the other parent may file a petition in opposition to the move within thirty (30) days of receipt of the notice.

VIII. PARENT EDUCATION CLASS

This requirement has been fulfilled by X both parents ☐ mother ☐ father ☐ neither.
Failure to attend the parent education class within 60 days of this order is punishable by contempt.

Under penalty of perjury, we declare that this plan has been proposed in good faith and is in the best interest of each minor child and that the statements herein and on the attached child support worksheets are true and correct. *(A notary public is*

Chapter 54:

ECHO FAMILY—182.5 DAYS PER YEAR EQUAL PARENTING TIME

The father has 182.5 days with the children. Mr. and Mrs. Echo were married twenty-two years and have a son, age sixteen, and a daughter, age fourteen. The father is a CPA and CFO of a large business, and the mother is a registered nurse. The mother was designated as the primary residential parent, but the parents share joint decision-making authority over all major decisions. With older children, especially ones who drive, logistics tend to become less important. This an example of an "alternating weeks" schedule.

STATE OF TENNESSEE	CIRCUIT **COURT** *(Must be completed)*	SHELBY **COUNTY** *(Must be completed)*
PERMANENT PARENTING PLAN ORDER ☐ **PROPOSED** ☐ **AGREED** ☐ **ORDERED BY THE COURT**	**FILE No.** CT-ABCDEF-08_____ *(Must be completed)* DIVISION ___III___	
PLAINTIFF *(Name: First, Middle, Last)* **DEBORAH JULIE ECHO** X Mother ☐ Father	**DEFENDANT** *(Name: First, Middle, Last)* **GRANT LEE ECHO** ☐ Mother X Father	

The mother and father will behave with each other and each child so as to provide a loving, stable, consistent and nurturing relationship with the child even though they are divorced. They will not speak badly of each other or the members of the family of the other parent. They will encourage each child to continue to love the other parent and be comfortable in both families.

This plan   X is a new plan.

                   ☐ modifies an existing Parenting Plan dated _____.

                   ☐ modifies an existing Order dated _____.

Child's Name	Date of Birth
Donald Echo	12/20/96
Delinda Echo	6/15/98

I.   RESIDENTIAL PARENTING SCHEDULE

A.   RESIDENTIAL TIME WITH EACH PARENT

The Primary Residential Parent is Mother

Under the schedule set forth below, each parent will spend the following number of days with the children:

        Mother <u>182.5</u> days   Father <u>182.5</u> days

B.   DAY-TO-DAY SCHEDULE

The X mother ☐ father shall have responsibility for the care of the child or children except at the following times when the other parent shall have responsibility:

        From <u>Monday at 8:00 a.m.</u> to <u>Monday at 8:00 a.m.</u>
        Day and Time   *Day and Time*

        ☐ every week X every other week ☐ other: _____.

The other parent shall also have responsibility for the care of the child or children at the additional parenting times specified below:

From   <u>Monday at 8:00 a.m.</u> to <u>Monday at 8:00 a.m.</u>
            Day and Time   *Day and Time*
☐ every week   X every other week ☐ other: _____.

This parenting schedule begins X <u>Immediately</u> **or** ☐ date of the Court's Order.
                                         Day and Time

C.   HOLIDAY SCHEDULE AND OTHER SCHOOL FREE DAYS

Indicate if child or children will be with parent in ODD or EVEN numbered years or EVERY year:

	MOTHER	FATHER
New Year's Day	Odd	Even
Martin Luther King Day	Even	Odd
Presidents' Day	Odd	Even
Easter Day (unless otherwise coinciding with Spring Vacation)	Even	Odd
Passover Day (unless otherwise coinciding with Spring Vacation)	N/A	N/A
Mother's Day	Every	None
Memorial Day (if no school)	Odd	Even
Father's Day	None	Every
July 4th	Even	Odd
Labor Day	Odd	Even
Halloween	N/A	N/A
Thanksgiving Day & Friday	Even	Odd
Children's Birthdays	Shared	Shared
Other School-Free Days	N/A	N/A
Mother's Birthday	Every	None
Father's Birthday	None	Every
Other: _____	N/A	N/A

A holiday shall begin at 6:00 p.m. on the night preceding the holiday and end at 6:00 p.m. the night of the holiday, unless otherwise noted here<u> If the parent having the holiday overnight also has residential time for the remainder of the weekend adjacent to the holiday, parenting time will end at the regular time on that weekend. Each parent shall have a minimum of four (4) hours of parenting time with the children on each child's birthday.</u>

D.   FALL VACATION (*If applicable*)

The day to day schedule shall apply except as follows: <u>Fall Break, if any, shall be from the day and time school is dismissed until the day before school resumes at 6:00 p.m. Father shall have Fall Break in odd years and Mother shall have Fall Break in even years.</u>

E.   WINTER (CHRISTMAS) VACATION

The x mother ☐ father shall have the child or children for the first period from the day and time school is dismissed until December <u>25th</u> at <u>12:00p.m.</u> x in odd-numbered years ☐ in even-numbered years ☐ every year. The other parent will have the child or children for the second period from the day and time indicated above until 6:00 p.m. on the evening before school resumes. The parties shall alternate the first and second periods each year.

Other agreement of the parents: _____

F.   SPRING VACATION *(If applicable)*

The day-to-day schedule shall apply except as follows: <u>Spring Break, if any, shall be from the day and time school is dismissed until the day before school resumes at 6:00 p.m. Father shall have Spring Break in odd years and Mother shall have Spring Break in even years.</u>

G.   SUMMER VACATION

The day-to-day schedule shall apply except as follows: <u>Each parent shall choose (2) nonconsecutive weeks by April 1st of each year. Mother shall select her weeks first in even-numbered years, and Father shall select his weeks first in odd-numbered years. The parents will not select any week that interferes with the other parent's scheduled holiday parenting time.</u>

Is written notice required?   x Yes ☐ No.   If so, _____ number of days.

H.   TRANSPORTATION ARRANGEMENTS

The place of meeting for the exchange of the child or children shall be: <u>The Father will be responsible for picking up the children and returning them to Mother's residence, until the children begin driving.</u>

Payment of long distance transportation costs *(if applicable):* ☐ mother ☐ father ☐ both equally.
Other arrangements: _____.
If a parent does not possess a valid driver's license, he or she must make reasonable transportation arrangements to protect the child or children while in the care of that parent.

I.   SUPERVISION OF PARENTING TIME *(If applicable)*
☐ Check if applicable

Supervised parenting time shall apply during the day-to-day schedule as follows:
☐ Place: _____.
☐ Person or organization supervising: _____.
☐ Responsibility for cost, if any: ☐ mother ☐ father ☐ both equally.

J.   OTHER

The following special provisions apply :
<u>Neither party shall administer corporal punishment to the children.</u>

Visitation shall take place in a suitable environment.

Mutual Injunction. Both parties agree to a mutual consent injunction to the effect that neither party will allow adult members of the opposite sex who are not family members or to whom he or she is not married spend the night in the presence of, or in the same residence of, the minor children of the parties.

Address and phone. Both parties shall keep the other party informed of his or her address and telephone number so that either parent may each call the children, when the children are visiting or residing with the other party, at reasonable intervals and at reasonable times, and if either parent takes the minor children out of town, he or she will notify the other parent as to where the minor children may be reached.

If either party or child has plans which conflict with scheduled residential time and wish to adjust that residential time, the parties should make arrangements for an adjustment acceptable to the schedules of every one involved. Predetermined schedules are not written in stone and both parties should be flexible for the sake of the children.

The parent who receives a schedule of children's activities or other information regarding children's events will fax, mail, and e-mail this information to the other parent in a timely manner so that the other parent has the opportunity to plan for and attend those activities or events.

The parent who receives a child's report card will copy and fax, mail or e-mail it to the other parent within 24 hours of receipt of the report card.

The parties will thoroughly discuss and consult with each other in regard to, and will be kept advised of, all decisions to be made concerning the education, medical and dental treatment, religious training, and dating of their children. The parties will also discuss and be advised of a child's participation in driving, sports, or other dangerous activities.

Husband & Wife agree to pay their *pro rata* share of automobile insurance to insure their children.

II. DECISION-MAKING

A. DAY-TO-DAY DECISIONS

Each parent shall make decisions regarding the day-to-day care of a child while the child is residing with that parent, including any emergency decisions affecting the health or safety of a child.

B. MAJOR DECISIONS

Major decisions regarding each child shall be made as follows:

Educational decisions	☐ mother	☐ father	**X** joint
Non-emergency health care	☐ mother	☐ father	**X** joint
Religious upbringing	☐ mother	☐ father	**X** joint

Extracurricular activities	☐ mother	☐ father	**x** joint
_____	☐ mother	☐ father	☐ joint

III.   FINANCIAL SUPPORT

A.   CHILD SUPPORT

Father's gross monthly income is $ 18,750.00
Mother's gross monthly income is $ 4,333.00

1. The final child support order is as follows:
    a.   The ☐ mother **x** father shall pay to the other parent as regular child support the sum of $2,000.00 ☐ weekly **x** monthly ☐ twice per month ☐ every two weeks. **The Child Support Worksheet shall be attached to this Order as an Exhibit.***

    If this is a deviation from the Child Support Guidelines, explain why:
    The parties agree that the upward deviation from the presumptive amount of child support established by the guidelines is due to the fact that Father agrees to pay $1,000.00 per month, per minor child, until August, 2015 for the parties' son, Donald, and until August, 2016, for the parties' daughter, Delinda. This payment extends support through the summer following graduation from high school only.

2. Retroactive Support: A judgment is hereby awarded in the amount of $_____ to ☐ mother ☐ father against the child support payor representing retroactive support required under Section 1240-2-4.06 of the D.H.S. Income Shares Child Support Guidelines dating from _____ which shall be paid (including pre/post judgment interest) at the rate of $_____ per ☐ week ☐ month ☐ twice per month ☐ every two weeks until the judgment is paid in full.

3. Payments shall begin on the _____ day of _____, 20___.

This support shall be paid:

☐ directly to the other parent.
☐ to the Central Child Support Receipting Unit, P. O. Box 305200, Nashville, Tennessee 37229, and sent from there to the other parent at: _____.
☐ A Wage Assignment Order is attached to this Parenting Plan.
x by direct deposit to the other parent at Regions Bank for deposit in account no. 1234567890.
☐ income assignment not required; Explanation:_____.

☐ other:_____.
The parents acknowledge that court approval must be obtained before child support can be reduced or modified.

*Child Support Worksheet can be found on DHS website at http://www.state.tn.us/humanserv/is/isdocuments.html or at your local child support offices.

B.   FEDERAL INCOME TAX EXEMPTION*

_____

* NOTE: The child support schedule assumptions in the guidelines (1240-2-4-.03 (6)(b)) assume that the parent receiving the child support will get the tax exemptions for the child.

The x mother ☐ father is the parent receiving child support.

The Mother shall claim the following children: <u>Donald Echo; Delinda Echo</u>

The Father shall claim the following children: _____

The ☐ mother ☐ father may claim the exemptions for the child or children so long as child support payments are current by the claiming parent on January 15 of the year when the return is due. The exemptions may be claimed in: ☐ alternate years starting _____ ☐ each year ☐ other: _____.

The x mother ☐ father will furnish IRS Form 8332 to the parent entitled to the exemption by February 15 of the year the tax return is due.

C.   PROOF OF INCOME AND WORK-RELATED CHILD CARE EXPENSES

Each parent shall send proof of income to the other parent for the prior calendar year as follows:

- IRS Forms W-2 and 1099 shall be sent to the other parent on or before   February 15.
- A copy of his or her federal income tax return shall be sent to the other parent on or before April 15 or any later date when it is due because of an extension of time for filing.
- The completed form required by the Department of Human Services shall be sent to the Department on or before the date the federal income tax return is due by the parent paying child support. *This requirement applies only if a parent is receiving benefits from the Department for a child.*

The parent paying work-related child care expenses shall send proof of expenses to the other parent for the prior calendar year and an estimate for the next calendar year, on or before February 15.

D.   HEALTH AND DENTAL INSURANCE

Reasonable health insurance on the child or children will be:
>   ☐   maintained by the mother
>   x   maintained by the father
>   ☐   maintained by both

Proof of continuing coverage shall be furnished to the other parent annually or as coverage changes. The parent maintaining coverage shall authorize the other parent to consult with the insurance carrier regarding the coverage in effect.

Uncovered reasonable and necessary medical expenses, which may include but is not limited to, deductibles or co-payments, eyeglasses, contact lens, routine annual physicals, and counseling will be paid by ☐ mother ☐ father x pro rata in accordance with their incomes. After insurance has paid its portion, the parent receiving the bill will send it to the other parent within ten days. The other parent will pay his or her share within 30 days of receipt of the bill.

If available through work, the ☐ mother x father shall maintain dental, orthodontic, and optical insurance on the minor child or children.

E.   LIFE INSURANCE

If agreed upon by the parties, the ☐ mother X father ☐ both shall insure his/her own life in the minimum amount of $300,000.00 by whole life or term insurance.   Until the child support obligation has been completed, each policy shall name the child/children as sole irrevocable primary beneficiary, with the X other parent ☐ other _____, as trustee for the benefit of the children, to serve without bond or accounting.

IV. PRIMARY RESIDENTIAL PARENT (CUSTODIAN) FOR OTHER LEGAL PURPOSES

The child or children are scheduled to reside the majority of the time with the X mother   ☐ father. This parent is designated as the primary residential parent also known as the custodian, **SOLELY** for purposes of any other applicable state and federal laws. If the parents are listed in Section II as joint decision-makers, then, for purposes of obtaining health or other insurance, they shall be considered to be joint custodians. THIS DESIGNATION DOES NOT AFFECT EITHER PARENT'S RIGHTS OR RESPONSIBILITIES UNDER THIS PARENTING PLAN.

V. DISAGREEMENTS OR MODIFICATION OF PLAN

Should the parents disagree about this Parenting Plan or wish to modify it, they must make a good faith effort to resolve the issue by the process selected below before returning to Court. *Except for financial support issues including child support, health and dental insurance, uncovered medical and dental expenses, and life insurance*, disputes must be submitted to:

> X Mediation by a neutral party chosen by the parents or the Court.
> ☐ Arbitration by a neutral party selected by parents or the Court.
> ☐ The Court DUE TO ORDER OF PROTECTION OR RESTRICTIONS.

The costs of this process may be determined by the alternative dispute process or may be assessed by the Court based upon the incomes of the parents. It must be commenced by notifying the other parent and the Court by ☐ written request X certified mail ☐ other: _____.

In the dispute resolution process:

> A. Preference shall be given to carrying out this Parenting Plan.
> B. The parents shall use the process to resolve disputes relating to implementation of the Plan.
> C. A written record shall be prepared of any agreement reached, and it shall be provided to each parent.
> D. If the Court finds that a parent willfully failed to appear without good reason, the Court, upon motion, may award attorney fees and financial sanctions to the prevailing parent.

VI.   RIGHTS OF PARENTS

Under T.C.A. § 36-6-101 of Tennessee law, both parents are entitled to the following rights:

> (1) The right to unimpeded telephone conversations with the child at least twice a week at reasonable times and for reasonable durations;
> (2) The right to send mail to the child which the other parent shall not open or censor;

(3) The right to receive notice and relevant information as soon as practicable but within twenty-four (24) hours of any event of hospitalization, major illness or death of the child;

(4) The right to receive directly from the child's school any school records customarily made available to parents. (The school may require a written request which includes a current mailing address and upon payment of reasonable costs of duplicating.) These include copies of the child's report cards, attendance records, names of teachers, class schedules, and standardized test scores;

(5) Unless otherwise provided by law, the right to receive copies of the child's medical health or other treatment records directly from the physician or health care provider who provided treatment or health care. (The keeper of the records may require a written request which contains a current mailing address and the payment of reasonable costs of duplication.) No person who receives the mailing address of a parent as a result of this requirement shall provide such address to the other parent or a third person;

(6) The right to be free of derogatory remarks made about the parent or his or her family by the other parent to the child or in the presence of the child;

(7) The right to be given at least forty-eight (48) hours notice, whenever possible, of all extra-curricular activities, and the opportunity to participate or observe them. These include the following: school activities, athletic activities, church activities and other activities where parental participation or observation would be appropriate;

(8) The right to receive from the other parent, in the event the other parent leaves the state with the minor child or children for more than two (2) days, an itinerary including telephone numbers for use in the event of an emergency;

(9) The right to access and participation in education on the same basis that is provided to all parents. This includes the right of access to the child for lunch and other activities. However participation or access must be reasonable and not interfere with day-to-day operations or with the child's educational performance.

VII.   NOTICE REGARDING PARENTAL RELOCATION

The Tennessee statute (T.C.A. § 36-6-108) which governs the notice to be given in connection with the relocation of a parent reads in pertinent part as follows:

If a parent who is spending intervals of time with a child desires to relocate outside the state or more than fifty (50) miles from the other parent within the state, the relocating parent shall send a notice to the other parent at the other parent's last known address by registered or certified mail. Unless excused by the court for exigent circumstances, the notice shall be mailed not later than sixty (60) days prior to the move. The notice shall contain the following:

(1) Statement of intent to move;

(2) Location of proposed new residence;

(3) Reasons for proposed relocation; and

(4) Statement that the other parent may file a petition in opposition to the move within thirty (30) days of receipt of the notice.

VIII.   PARENT EDUCATION CLASS

This requirement has been fulfilled by X both parents ☐ mother ☐ father   ☐ neither.
Failure to attend the parent education class within 60 days of this order is punishable by contempt.

Under penalty of perjury, we declare that this plan has been proposed in good faith and is in the best interest of each minor child and that the statements herein and on the attached child support worksheets are true and correct. *(A notary public is required if this is a proposed plan by one parent rather than one agreed by both parents.)*

_____   _____
Mother   Date and Place Signed

Sworn to and subscribed before me this _____ day of _____, 20_____.

My commission expires:_____   _____
                                                                                          Notary Public

_____   _____
Father   Date and Place Signed

Sworn to and subscribed before me this _____ day of _____, 20_____.

My commission expires:_____   _____
                                                                                          Notary Public

APPROVED FOR ENTRY:

_____   _____
Attorney for Mother   *Attorney for Father*
_____   _____
Address   *Address*
_____   _____
Address   *Address*
_____   _____
Phone and BPR Number   *Phone and BPR Number*

Note: The judge or chancellor may sign below or, instead, sign a Final Decree or a separate Order incorporating this plan.

COURT COSTS (If applicable)

Court costs, if any, are taxed as follows:

_____.

It is so ORDERED this the _____ day of _____, _____.

                                                      _____
                                                      Judge or Chancellor

Chapter 55:

FOXTROT FAMILY—182.5 DAYS PER YEAR EQUAL PARENTING TIME

The father has 182.5 days with the children. Mr. and Mrs. Foxtrot were married six years and have two sons, ages three and two. The mother was designated as the primary residential parent, but the parents have joint decision-making authority over all major decisions except educational decisions, which are decided by the father. The father was on active duty with the navy, and the mother had had at least one clandestine affair. The parents chopped up weekdays and alternated weekends. This is an example of equal parenting time but not with an "alternative weeks" schedule.

STATE OF TENNESSEE	CIRCUIT COURT *(Must be completed)*	SHELBY COUNTY *(Must be completed)*

PERMANENT PARENTING PLAN ORDER ☐ PROPOSED X AGREED ☐ ORDERED BY THE COURT	FILE No. CT-ABCDEF-05 *(Must be completed)* DIVISION IV

PLAINTIFF *(Name: First, Middle, Last)* ELSIE MAE FOXTROT X Mother ☐ Father	DEFENDANT *(Name: First, Middle, Last)* TYRONE WILLIAM FOXTROT ☐ Mother X Father

The mother and father will behave with each other and each child so as to provide a loving, stable, consistent and nurturing relationship with the child even though they are divorced. They will not speak badly of each other or the members of the family of the other parent. They will encourage each child to continue to love the other parent and be comfortable in both families.

This plan   X   is a new plan.

☐ modifies an existing Parenting Plan dated _____.

☐ modifies an existing Order dated _____.

Child's Name	Date of Birth
James Alan Foxtrot	4/18/09
John Browning Foxtrot	8/5/10

I.   RESIDENTIAL PARENTING SCHEDULE

A.   RESIDENTIAL TIME WITH EACH PARENT

The Primary Residential Parent is <u>Mother</u>

Under the schedule set forth below, each parent will spend the following number of days with the children:

Mother <u>182.5</u> days   Father <u>182.5</u> days

B.   DAY-TO-DAY SCHEDULE

The ☐ mother ☐ father shall have responsibility for the care of the child or children except at the following times when the other parent shall have responsibility:

From _____ to _____

    Day and Time   *Day and Time*

☐ every week ☐ every other week ☐ other: _____.

The other parent shall also have responsibility for the care of the child or children at the additional parenting times specified below:

From _____ to _____
              Day and Time   *Day and Time*

   ☐ every week ☐ every other week ☐ other: _____.

The parties agree that Father shall have parenting time with the children beginning on Monday at 8:00 a.m. and ending on Wednesday at 8:00 a.m. every week. The parties agree that Mother shall have parenting time with the children beginning on Wednesday at 8:00 a.m. and ending on Friday at 8:00a.m. Then, the parties agree to alternate parenting time with the children every weekend beginning on Friday at 8:00 a.m. and ending on Monday at 8:00 a.m.

This parenting schedule begins X February 26, 2013 **or** ☐ date of the Court's Order. Father shall begin the schedule on that date. Until that date, the parenting schedule the parties have been exercising shall be in effect.

C.   HOLIDAY SCHEDULE AND OTHER SCHOOL FREE DAYS

Indicate if child or children will be with parent in ODD or EVEN numbered years or EVERY year:

	MOTHER	FATHER
New Year's Day	_____	_____
Martin Luther King Day	_____	_____
Presidents' Day	_____	_____
Easter Day (unless otherwise coinciding with Spring Vacation)	Odd	Even
Passover Day (unless otherwise coinciding with Spring Vacation)	N/A	N/A
Mother's Day	Every	None
Memorial Day (if no school)	Every	None
Father's Day	None	Every
July 4th**	Even	Odd
Labor Day	None	Every
Halloween**	Even	Odd
Thanksgiving Day & Friday	Even	Odd
Children's Birthdays	Shared	Shared
Other School-Free Days	_____	_____
Mother's Birthday	Every	None
Father's Birthday	None	Every
Other: Weekend	Even	Odd

(Wednesday, 6:00 p.m. To Sunday, 6:00 p.m.)

**Holidays marked with double asterisk end at 8:00 a.m. the morning after the holiday.

A holiday shall begin at 6:00 p.m. on the night preceding the holiday and end at 6:00 p.m. the night of the holiday, unless otherwise noted here_____.

D.   FALL VACATION (*If applicable*)

The day to day schedule shall apply except as follows:<u>Father will have Fall Break in odd years and Mother will have Fall Break in even years, beginning at 6:00 p.m. on Friday following the last day of school, and ending the following Sunday evening at 5:00 p.m.</u>

E. WINTER (CHRISTMAS) VACATION

The x mother ☐ father shall have the child or children for the first period from the day and time school is dismissed until December <u>27</u> at <u>12:00p.m.</u> x in odd-numbered years ☐ in even-numbered years   ☐ every year. The father will have the child or children for the second period from the day and time indicated above until 6:00 p.m. on the evening before school resumes. The parties shall alternate the first and second periods each year.

Other agreement of the parents: _____

F. SPRING VACATION (*If applicable*)

The day-to-day schedule shall apply except as follows: <u>Father shall have Spring Break in even years and Mother shall have Spring Break in odd years beginning at 6:00 p.m. on Friday following the last day of school and ending the following Sunday evening at 5:00 p.m.</u>

G. SUMMER VACATION

<u>The day-to-day schedule shall apply except as follows: By April 1st of each odd year, the Mother will choose two (2) non-consecutive fourteen (14) day periods of residential time with the children and provide notice to Father in writing. Father shall choose two (2) non-interfering non-consecutive fourteen day periods and provide to Mother by May 1st of each year. Father chooses first in even years.</u>

Is written notice required? x Yes ☐ No.   If so, <u>by April 1st of each year.</u>

H. TRANSPORTATION ARRANGEMENTS

The place of meeting for the exchange of the child or children shall be: _____
_____.
Payment of long distance transportation costs *(if applicable):* ☐ mother   ☐ father ☐ both equally.
Other arrangements: _____.
If a parent does not possess a valid driver's license, he or she must make reasonable transportation arrangements to protect the child or children while in the care of that parent.

I. SUPERVISION OF PARENTING TIME (*If applicable)*
☐ **Check if applicable**

Supervised parenting time shall apply during the day-to-day schedule as follows:
☐ Place: _____.
☐ Person or organization supervising: _____.
☐ Responsibility for cost, if any: ☐ mother ☐ father ☐ both equally.

J. OTHER

The following special provisions apply :

The terms "father" and "mother," or their equivalents, will be used by the children only to refer to the parties to this Agreement in their proper role and to no other person.

The children will be raised Roman Catholic. Every effort will be made to attend weekly Roman Catholic Mass and Holy Days of Obligation. The parent who has the children in his or her care will facilitate the children attending mass. The parties agree that they will arrange for their children to attend Roman Catholic Religious Education classes if the children do not attend a Roman Catholic grade school and high school.

Punishment. The parties are to discuss the discipline of their children and any corporal punishment is to be administered only by each party when the children are in his or her care and custody, and not by a step-parent, paramour, or other child-care person.

The parties are also to advise each other concerning any medications or other "at home" medical treatment that may be needed by their children.

When a parent is dating someone exclusively, the person who the parent is dating may spend the night with that parent when the children are in that parent's care, provided that discretion is exercised. Unless the parent is formally engaged to a person, the parent will not openly passionately kiss or otherwise act in a sexual manner with that person in the presence of the children. Further, that person shall not establish his or her primary residence with the parent until such time as that person is married to the parent.

Address and phone. Both parties shall keep the other party informed of his or her address and telephone number so that either parent may each call the children, when the children are visiting or residing with the other party, at reasonable intervals and at reasonable times, and if either parent takes the minor children out of town, he or she will notify the other parent as to where the minor children may be reached.

Neither parent shall deny the child reasonable use of the telephone to place and receive calls with the other parent and relatives.

Both parties will be allowed to speak to the minor children via telephone once (1) per day for a reasonable period of time.

Both parties shall allow and encourage the children to maintain reasonable phone contact with the other party. Neither party shall withhold church attendance or phone conversations with the other parent as a form of punishment.

If either party or child has plans which conflict with scheduled residential time and wish to adjust that residential time, the parties should make arrangements for an adjustment acceptable to the schedules of every one involved. Predetermined schedules are not written in stone and both parties should be flexible for the sake of the children.

Neither party will permit in his or her presence any conversation which explicitly or inferentially derides, ridicules, condemns, or in any manner derogates the other party, the other party's relatives, and the other party's friends.

Neither parent will directly or indirectly attack or criticize to the child the extended family of the other parent, to the other parent's career, the living and travel arrangements of the other parent, or lawful activities of the other parent or associates of the other parent.

Neither parent will use the child as a "middleman" by using the child to communicate with the other parent on inappropriate topics.

Neither parent will discuss child support issues with the child.

Under no circumstances shall the question of support or any other payments either as to amount, manner, or transmission or payment, be raised in the presence of the children.

Parents should always avoid speaking negatively about the other and should firmly discourage such conduct by relatives and friends. In fact, the parents should speak in positive terms about the other parent in the presence of the children. Each parent should encourage the children to respect each other.

Each parent will permit the child to display photographs of the other parent or both parents in the child's room.

Neither parent will use tobacco products in the presence of the children, nor allow others in their company to do so.

Each parent will permit the child to carry gifts, toys, clothing, and other items belonging to the child with him or her to the residence of the other parent or relatives or permit the child to take gifts, toys, clothing, and other items belonging to the child back to the residence of the other parent, as the case may be, to facilitate the child having with him or her objects, important to the child. The gifts, toys, clothing and other items belonging to the child referred to here mean items which are reasonable transportable and does not include pets (which the parents agree are impractical to move about).

Both parents shall not threaten to withhold parenting time from the non-primary residential parent. Both parents shall not threaten to prevent or delay the return of the children to the other parent after a period of parenting time. Both parents agree that if they are not going to be on time to exchange the children that they shall phone the other parent and let them know.

Both parents shall, at all times, take all action necessary to promote the safety and well being of the children, provide adequate care and supervision, mandate the use of seatbelts, and otherwise make the children's well being and safety a paramount consideration at all times.

Each party will inform any future spouse of the provisions of this agreement and expect that spouse to honor this agreement.

The parent who receives a schedule of children's activities or other information regarding children's events will fax, mail or e-mail this information to the other parent in a timely manner so that the other parent has the opportunity to plan for and attend those activities or events.

The parent who receives a child's report card will copy and fax, mail or e-mail it to the other parent within 24 hours of receipt of the report card.

Extracurricular Activities. Regardless of where the children are residing, their continued participation in extracurricular activities, school related or otherwise, should not be interrupted. The parent with whom the children are residing shall be responsible for providing transportation arrangements to activities scheduled during residential time with that parent. Each parent shall provide the other parent with notice of all extracurricular activities, complete with schedules and the name, address and telephone number of the activity leader, if available.

Prior to arranging for child care or baby sitting of the children, each parent will give the other opportunity to perform such child care or baby sitting services if the parent will be away from the child eight hours or more.

All schoolwork for each child shall be saved and mad available for review to the other parent at the time the children are exchanged.

Notification of Events. Each party agrees to notify the other at least one (1) week in advance of any special occasion or event for the minor children as to any religious, educational, or athletic event, which shall include, without limitation, graduation, demonstration of acquired skills, recitals, or award ceremonies. Each party shall have an equal right to attend these special occasions.

The parents will acknowledge to the children that the children have two homes although the children may spend more time at one home than the other.

The parents shall cooperate to the greatest extent practicable in sharing time with the children.

Each parent will respect the physical integrity of items possessed by the children which depict the other parent or remind the children of the other parent.

If a child becomes seriously ill or injured during the time that they are with either parent hereto, that parent shall notify the other as soon as possible. The other parent shall be given details of the illness or injury and the name and telephone number of the attending physicians, if any.

The parties agree, that if they agree in the future, to share the cost of a mid-range, new or used motor vehicle for the children to share when each child satisfactorily completes a driver safety course and further agrees to share the cost of insurance for the said vehicle. Both parties have an equal vote in choosing said vehicle.

All-Terrain Vehicles. At no time shall either minor child be permitted to ride or be a passenger on any motorized off-road recreational vehicle including but not limited to ATV's, four-wheelers, three-wheelers, dirt bikes, go-carts, mini-bikes or the like, unless both parents agree that sufficient safety precautions are being taken to mitigate the inherent dangers of operating or riding on these machines, and both parents give their express permission for either the minor child to ride or be a passenger of said vehicle.

Child Support Excess Payments. Any payments made by either party at any time for any obligation under this Agreement over and above the amounts required are not binding upon them. Any excess payments are not proof or nor an indication of ability to make increased payments or of need for them. Any excess payments shall receive full credit for them, even to the point of crediting them against money not yet due under this Agreement.

Private Schools. Father shall bear all expenses of private school tuition if Father elects to place the children in private school. Mother shall contribute to private school tuition if she chooses. Preference shall be given to schools affiliated with the Roman Catholic Church.

Personal Computer. The parties agree to share *pro rate* according to the ratio of their incomes the cost of a personal, portable computer for each child suitable for that child's academic needs upon the child entering the 9th grade or at such time when the school program in which the child is enrolled requires such. Parties agree to share *pro rata* according to the ratio of their incomes of an upgrade upon that child entering college.

II.   DECISION-MAKING

A.   DAY-TO-DAY DECISIONS

Each parent shall make decisions regarding the day-to-day care of a child while the child is residing with that parent, including any emergency decisions affecting the health or safety of a child.

B.   MAJOR DECISIONS

Major decisions regarding each child shall be made as follows:

Educational decisions	☐ mother	**X** father	☐ joint
Non-emergency health care	☐ mother	☐ father	**X** joint
Religious upbringing	☐ mother	☐ father	**X** joint
Extracurricular activities	☐ mother	☐ father	**X** joint
_____	☐ mother	☐ father	☐ joint

III.   FINANCIAL SUPPORT

A.   CHILD SUPPORT

Father's gross monthly income is $ 7,525.15
Mother's gross monthly income is $ 3,466.68

1. The final child support order is as follows:
   a.   The   ☐ mother   **X**   father   shall pay to the other parent as regular child support the sum of $1,214.01 ☐ weekly   **X** monthly ☐ twice per month
   ☐ every two weeks. **The Child Support Worksheet shall be attached to this Order as an Exhibit.* Child support shall be paid on the first (1) of each month. The parents agree that child support shall be automatically modifiable for both parents without a finding of a significant difference by the Court on the one occasion when Father obtains a new job in 2013.**

If this is a deviation from the Child Support Guidelines, explain why:

_____

2. Retroactive Support: A judgment is hereby awarded in the amount of $_____ to ☐ mother ☐ father against the child support payor representing retroactive support required under Section 1240-2-4.06 of the D.H.S. Income Shares Child Support Guidelines dating from _____ which shall be paid (including pre/post judgment interest) at the rate of $_____ per ☐ week ☐ month ☐ twice per month ☐ every two weeks until the judgment is paid in full.

3. Payments shall begin on the <u>1st day of the month following the entry of the Final Decree of Divorce and Permanent Parenting Plan.</u>

This support shall be paid:

☐ directly to the other parent.
☐ to the Central Child Support Receipting Unit, P. O. Box 305200, Nashville, Tennessee 37229, and sent from there to the other parent at: _____.
☐ A Wage Assignment Order is attached to this Parenting Plan.
X by direct deposit to the other parent at Bank of Bartlett for deposit in account no. 1234567890.
☐ income assignment not required; Explanation:_____.
☐ other:_____.
The parents acknowledge that court approval must be obtained before child support can be reduced or modified.

*Child Support Worksheet can be found on DHS website at http://www.state.tn.us/humanserv/is/isdocuments.html or at your local child support offices.

B.   FEDERAL INCOME TAX EXEMPTION[*]

The X mother ☐ father is the parent receiving child support.

The Mother shall claim the following children: <u>James Alan Foxtrot</u>

The Father shall claim the following children: <u>John Browning Foxtrot</u>

The ☐ mother X father may claim the exemptions for the child or children so long as child support payments are current by the claiming parent on January 15 of the year when the return is due. The exemptions may be claimed in: ☐ alternate years starting _____ X each year ☐ other: _____.

The X mother X father will furnish IRS Form 8332 to the parent entitled to the exemption by February 15 of the year the tax return is due.

C.   PROOF OF INCOME AND WORK-RELATED CHILD CARE EXPENSES

Each parent shall send proof of income to the other parent for the prior calendar year as follows:

_____

[*] NOTE: The child support schedule assumptions in the guidelines (1240-2-4-.03 (6)(b)) assume that the parent receiving the child support will get the tax exemptions for the child.

- IRS Forms W-2 and 1099 shall be sent to the other parent on or before   February 15.
- A copy of his or her federal income tax return shall be sent to the other parent on or before April 15 or any later date when it is due because of an extension of time for filing.
- The completed form required by the Department of Human Services shall be sent to the Department on or before the date the federal income tax return is due by the parent paying child support. *This requirement applies only if a parent is receiving benefits from the Department for a child.*

The parent paying work-related child care expenses shall send proof of expenses to the other parent for the prior calendar year and an estimate for the next calendar year, on or before February 15.

D.   HEALTH AND DENTAL INSURANCE

Reasonable health insurance on the child or children will be:

     ☐   maintained by the mother
     X   maintained by the father
     ☐   maintained by both

Proof of continuing coverage shall be furnished to the other parent annually or as coverage changes. The parent maintaining coverage shall authorize the other parent to consult with the insurance carrier regarding the coverage in effect. Father is currently on active duty with the United States Navy. The health and dental benefits for the parties' minor children is through Tri-Care at a minimal cost to Father. Should Father opt out of the United States Navy, the parties agree that they shall work together to choose a mutually agreed upon health insurance plan and shall share the costs pro rata according to the ratio of their incomes.

Uncovered reasonable and necessary medical expenses, which may include but is not limited to, deductibles or co-payments, eyeglasses, contact lens, routine annual physicals, and counseling will be paid by ☐ mother ☐ father X pro rata in accordance with their incomes. After insurance has paid its portion, the parent receiving the bill will send it to the other parent within ten days. The other parent will pay his or her share within 30 days of receipt of the bill. While the parties' minor children are covered by Tri-Care, both parents shall utilize physicians, dentists, orthodontists, optometrists and ophthalmologists within the Tri-Care network. If either party fails to utilize Tri-Care providers, that party shall be responsible for and pay the uncovered medical expenses. If the children are referred to a specialist by their Primary Care Manager, then both parents must ensure that all aspects of the referral are properly handled, including but not limited to billing, payment of fees and ensuring the referral authorization number is properly used or the party at fault shall pay all costs incurred, including penalties. Both parties shall also vigorously pursue correction of all billing related errors through the Tri-Care Service Center or other appropriate means.

If available through work, the ☐ mother X father shall maintain dental, orthodontic, and optical insurance on the minor child or children.

E.   LIFE INSURANCE

If agreed upon by the parties, the ☐ mother ☐ father X both shall insure his/her own life in the minimum amount of $175,000.00 by whole life or term insurance.   Until the child support obligation has been completed, each policy shall name the child/children as sole irrevocable primary beneficiary, with the X other parent ☐ other _____, as trustee for the benefit of the child(ren), to serve without bond or accounting.

IV. PRIMARY RESIDENTIAL PARENT (CUSTODIAN) FOR OTHER LEGAL PURPOSES

The child or children are scheduled to reside the majority of the time with the ☐ mother ☐ father. This parent is designated as the primary residential parent also known as the custodian, **SOLELY** for purposes of any other applicable state and federal laws. If the parents are listed in Section II as joint decision-makers, then, for purposes of obtaining health or other insurance, they shall be considered to be joint custodians. THIS DESIGNATION DOES NOT AFFECT EITHER PARENT'S RIGHTS OR RESPONSIBILITIES UNDER THIS PARENTING PLAN.

V. DISAGREEMENTS OR MODIFICATION OF PLAN

Should the parents disagree about this Parenting Plan or wish to modify it, they must make a good faith effort to resolve the issue by the process selected below before returning to Court. *Except for financial support issues including child support, health and dental insurance, uncovered medical and dental expenses, and life insurance*, disputes must be submitted to:

    X Mediation by a neutral party chosen by the parents or the Court.
    ☐ Arbitration by a neutral party selected by parents or the Court.
    ☐ The Court DUE TO ORDER OF PROTECTION OR RESTRICTIONS.

The costs of this process may be determined by the alternative dispute process or may be assessed by the Court based upon the incomes of the parents. It must be commenced by notifying the other parent and the Court by ☐ written request X certified mail ☐ other: _____.

In the dispute resolution process:

    A. Preference shall be given to carrying out this Parenting Plan.
    B. The parents shall use the process to resolve disputes relating to implementation of the Plan.
    C. A written record shall be prepared of any agreement reached, and it shall be provided to each parent.
    D. If the Court finds that a parent willfully failed to appear without good reason, the Court, upon motion, may award attorney fees and financial sanctions to the prevailing parent.

VI.   RIGHTS OF PARENTS

Under T.C.A. § 36-6-101 of Tennessee law, both parents are entitled to the following rights:

    (1) The right to unimpeded telephone conversations with the child at least twice a week at reasonable times and for reasonable durations;
    (2) The right to send mail to the child which the other parent shall not open or censor;
    (3) The right to receive notice and relevant information as soon as practicable but within twenty-four (24) hours of any event of hospitalization, major illness or death of the child;
    (4) The right to receive directly from the child's school any school records customarily made available to parents. (The school may require a written request which includes a current mailing address and upon payment of reasonable costs

of duplicating.) These include copies of the child's report cards, attendance records, names of teachers, class schedules, and standardized test scores;

(5) Unless otherwise provided by law, the right to receive copies of the child's medical health or other treatment records directly from the physician or health care provider who provided treatment or health care. (The keeper of the records may require a written request which contains a current mailing address and the payment of reasonable costs of duplication.) No person who receives the mailing address of a parent as a result of this requirement shall provide such address to the other parent or a third person;

(6) The right to be free of unwarranted derogatory remarks made about the parent or his or her family by the other parent to the child or in the presence of the child;

(7) The right to be given at least forty-eight (48) hours notice, whenever possible, of all extra-curricular activities, and the opportunity to participate or observe them. These include the following: school activities, athletic activities, church activities and other activities where parental participation or observation would be appropriate;

(8) The right to receive from the other parent, in the event the other parent leaves the state with the minor child or children for more than two (2) days, an itinerary including telephone numbers for use in the event of an emergency;

(9) The right to access and participation in education on the same basis that is provided to all parents. This includes the right of access to the child for lunch and other activities. However participation or access must be reasonable and not interfere with day-to-day operations or with the child's educational performance.

VII. NOTICE REGARDING PARENTAL RELOCATION

The Tennessee statute (T.C.A. § 36-6-108) which governs the notice to be given in connection with the relocation of a parent reads in pertinent part as follows:

If a parent who is spending intervals of time with a child desires to relocate outside the state or more than fifty (50) miles from the other parent within the state, the relocating parent shall send a notice to the other parent at the other parent's last known address by registered or certified mail. Unless excused by the court for exigent circumstances, the notice shall be mailed not later than sixty (60) days prior to the move. The notice shall contain the following:

(1) Statement of intent to move;

(2) Location of proposed new residence;

(3) Reasons for proposed relocation; and

(4) Statement that the other parent may file a petition in opposition to the move within thirty (30) days of receipt of the notice.

VIII. PARENT EDUCATION CLASS

This requirement has been fulfilled by X both parents ☐ mother ☐ father ☐ neither. Failure to attend the parent education class within 60 days of this order is punishable by contempt.

Under penalty of perjury, we declare that this plan has been proposed in good faith and is in the best interest of each minor child and that the statements herein and on the attached child support worksheets are true and correct. *(A notary public is*

required if this is a proposed plan by one parent rather than one agreed by both parents.)

_____   _____
Mother   Date and Place Signed

Sworn to and subscribed before me this _____ day of _____, 20_____.

My commission expires:_____   _____
                                                                              Notary Public

_____   _____
Father   Date and Place Signed

Sworn to and subscribed before me this _____ day of _____, 20_____.

My commission expires:_____   _____
                                                                              Notary Public

APPROVED FOR ENTRY:

_____   _____
Attorney for Mother   *Attorney for Father*
_____   _____
Address   *Address*
_____   _____
Address   *Address*
_____   _____
Phone and BPR Number   *Phone and BPR Number*

Note: The judge or chancellor may sign below or, instead, sign a Final Decree or a separate Order incorporating this plan.

COURT COSTS (If applicable)

Court costs, if any, are taxed as follows:
_____.

It is so ORDERED this the _____ day of _____, _____.

_____
Judge or Chancellor

Chapter 56:

GOLF FAMILY—93 DAYS PER YEAR PARENTING TIME: OUT-OF-TOWN SCHEDULE

The father, who is frequently out of town, has ninety-three days with his son. Mr. and Mrs. Golf were married eight years and have a seven-year-old son. The mother was designated primary residential parent and had final decision-making authority over nonemergency health care and extracurricular activities, but she shares decision making about educational and religious decisions. The father was active-duty military with several Middle East deployments and specialized assignments. The mother was finishing a master's degree. The mother wanted to encourage parenting time by making it as easy as possible because parenting time had never been consistent, which resulted in their son's frequent disappointment.

STATE OF TENNESSEE	COURT *(Must be completed)* CHANCERY	COUNTY*(Must be completed)* SHELBY
PERMANENT PARENTING PLAN ORDER ☐ PROPOSED X AGREED ☐ ORDERED BY THE COURT		FILE No. CH-09-ABCD-2 *(Must be completed)* DIVISION __II____
PLAINTIFF *(Name: First, Middle, Last)* **ELEANOR JOHNSON GOLF** x Mother ☐ Father	DEFENDANT *(Name: First, Middle, Last)* **JOEL DONOVAN GOLF** ☐ Mother x Father	

The mother and father will behave with each other and each child so as to provide a loving, stable, consistent and nurturing relationship with the child even though they are divorced. They will not speak badly of each other or the members of the family of the other parent. They will encourage each child to continue to love the other parent and be comfortable in both families.

This plan   x is a new plan.

☐ modifies an existing Parenting Plan dated _____.

☐ modifies an existing Order dated _____.

Child's Name	Date of Birth
JACOB ANTHONY GOLF	November 1, 2005

I.   RESIDENTIAL PARENTING SCHEDULE

A.   RESIDENTIAL TIME WITH EACH PARENT

The Primary Residential Parent is <u>Mother</u>

Under the schedule set forth below, each parent will spend the following number of days with the children:

Mother <u>272</u> days   Father <u>93</u> days

B.   DAY-TO-DAY SCHEDULE

The **X** <u>mother</u> ☐ father shall have responsibility for the care of the child or children except at the following times when the other parent shall have responsibility:

From   <u>6:00 p.m. on Friday</u> to <u>4:30 p.m. on Sunday</u>
Day and Time   *Day and Time*

☐ every week ☐ every other week **X** other: <u>Second and Fifth weekend of every month.</u>

The first weekend of the month is a weekend that includes both a Saturday and a Sunday in the same month. A weekend begins Friday night at 6:00 p.m. and ends Sunday afternoon at 4:30 p.m.

The other parent shall also have responsibility for the care of the child or children at the additional parenting times specified below:

From   6:00 p.m. on Friday   to 6:30 p.m. on Sunday

       Day and Time   *Day and Time*

☐ every week   ☐ every other week   **X** other: Third weekend of every month.

With seven (7) days notice, Father will travel to Memphis to exercise his parenting time on the third weekend of the month. The parties agree it is best for the child not to travel to Clarksville every weekend. The parties agree Father shall not exercise his parenting time at Mother's residence. The parties further agree Father shall not reside at Mother's residence during Father's parenting time.

The parties contemplate that Father will re-deploy to Afghanistan in May 2014. Until Father's deployment, the parties agree that Mother will provide reasonable, open access to Father on the fourth weekend of the month during Mother's parenting time. Father will travel to Memphis to exercise this parenting time and will pay for all costs associated with traveling and residing in Memphis. The parties agree Father will not reside at Mother's residence when he travels to Memphis to exercise parenting time.

If Father deploys overseas, the parties also agree that Mother will provide reasonable, open access to Father for unexpected visitation opportunities with the minor child in Memphis during any unexpected or extended leaves from the U.S. Army. If the minor child has any scheduled activities when Father is available, Mother will provide Father with the details of any such activity as well as invite Father to attend and participate. Father shall advise Mother of the dates of any unexpected or extended leaves in which he intends to exercise parenting time with the minor child as soon as Father is aware of any such leave, as well as his desired visitation schedule in Memphis.

This parenting schedule begins ☐ _____ **or** **X** date of the Court's Order.

                                        Day and Time

C.   HOLIDAY SCHEDULE AND OTHER SCHOOL FREE DAYS

Indicate if child or children will be with parent in ODD or EVEN numbered years or EVERY year:

	MOTHER	FATHER
New Year's Day	Even	Odd
Martin Luther King Day	Not Applicable	Not Applicable
Presidents' Day	Not Applicable	Not Applicable
Easter Day (unless otherwise coinciding with Spring Vacation)	Odd	Even
Passover Day (unless otherwise coinciding with Spring Vacation)	Not Applicable	Not Applicable
Mother's Day	Every	None
Memorial Day (if no school)	None	Every

Father's Day	None	Every
July 4th	Odd	Even
Labor Day	Even	Odd
Halloween	Odd	Even
Thanksgiving Day & Friday	Even	Odd
Children's Birthdays	Shared	Shared
Other School-Free Days	Not Applicable	Not Applicable
Mother's Birthday	Every	None
Father's Birthday	None	Every
Other:	None	None

A holiday shall begin at 6:00 p.m. on the night preceding the holiday and end at 6:00 p.m. the night of the holiday, unless otherwise noted here. July 4th, Labor Day and Memorial Day holidays will include overnight visitation and if the parent having the holiday overnight also has residential time for the remainder of the weekend adjacent to the holiday, there will be no exchange. Holiday parenting time supercedes regularly scheduled residential time.

D.   FALL VACATION (*If applicable*)

The day to day schedule shall apply except as follows: Beginning Monday morning at 8:00 a.m. following the last day of school and ends Friday at 6:30 p.m. although no parent will have a break in residential time if that parent has residential time with the children on an adjacent weekend. Mother shall have Fall Break in even years and Father shall have Fall Break in odd years.

E.   WINTER (CHRISTMAS) VACATION

The ☐ mother **x** father shall have the child or children for the first period from the day and time school is dismissed until December 25th at 3:00 p.m. **x** in odd-numbered years ☐ in even-numbered years ☐ every year. The other parent will have the child or children for the second period from the day and time indicated above until 6:00 p.m. on the evening before school resumes. The parties shall alternate the first and second periods each year.

Other agreement of the parents: _____

F.   SPRING VACATION (*If applicable*)

The day-to-day schedule shall apply except as follows: Beginning Monday morning at 8:00 a.m. following that last day of school and ends Friday at 6:30 p.m. although no parent will have a break in residential time if that parent has residential time with the children on an adjacent weekend. Father shall have Spring Breaks in even years and Mother shall have Spring Breaks in odd years.

G.   SUMMER VACATION

The day-to-day schedule shall apply except as follows: Father shall have residential time for four (4) nonconsecutive seven (7) day weeks. Father shall have two (2) consecutive weeks in June and two (2) consecutive weeks in July.

A summer visitation week begins Saturday morning at 8:00 a.m. and ends Saturday at 6:30 p.m. The child will reside with Mother for the first full week after school lets out in the summer. The child will reside with Mother for a full week prior to school resuming in the fall. The parties agree it is in the best interest of the minor child to spend this transition period in Mother's residence.

The parties agree it is in the child's best interest to enjoy summer parenting time with Father during Father's vacation from work. The parties agree it is in the child's best interest to avoid, to the extent possible, parenting time when Father must work during the day. In the past, Father has enjoyed four consecutive weeks of vacation in the summer. In the event Father continues to have four consecutive vacation weeks in the summer, the Mother agrees Father can exercise summer residential time with the parties' minor child for those four consecutive (4) weeks only.

Is written notice required?   **x** Yes ☐ No.   Notice of residential time weeks shall be provided by Father no later than April 15th of each year. Prior to April 1st of each year, Mother may choose two (2) non-consecutive weeks with the child with one (1) week in June and one (1) week in July, and notice shall be provided in writing to Father.

H.   TRANSPORTATION ARRANGEMENTS

The place of meeting for the exchange of the child or children shall be: at a pre-arranged location in Atwood, Carroll County, Tennessee.
Payment of long distance transportation costs *(if applicable):* ☐ mother **x** father ☐ both equally.
Other arrangements: Father shall come to Memphis to exercise parenting time with the minor child on the third weekend of every month. Transportation and all other expenses incurred during this weekend shall be paid for by the Father.

If a parent does not possess a valid driver's license, he or she must make reasonable transportation arrangements to protect the child or children while in the care of that parent.

I.   SUPERVISION OF PARENTING TIME *(If applicable)*
☐ **Check if applicable**

Supervised parenting time shall apply during the day-to-day schedule as follows:
☐ Place: _____.
☐ Person or organization supervising: _____.
☐ Responsibility for cost, if any: ☐ mother ☐ father ☐ both equally.

J.   OTHER

The following special provisions apply:

1. **Punishment**. The parents are to discuss the discipline of their child and any corporal punishment is to be administered only by each parent when the child is in his or her care and custody, and not by a step-parent, paramour, or other child-care person.

2. The parents are also to advise each other concerning any medications or other "at home" medical treatment that may be needed by their child.

3. **Mutual Injunction**. Both parents agree to a mutual consent injunction to the effect that neither party will allow adult members of the opposite sex who are not family members or to whom he or she is not married spend the night in the presence of, or in the same residence of, the minor child of the parents.

4. **Address and phone**. Both parents shall keep the other part informed of his or her address and telephone number so that either parent may each call the child, when the child is visiting or residing with the other parent, at reasonable intervals and at reasonable times, and if either parent takes the minor child out of town, he or she will notify the other parent as to where the minor child may be reached.

5. **Definition of "Telephone Number."** For all portions of this Permanent Parenting Plan, the definition of "Telephone Number" shall include, but is not limited to the following: land based (traditional) telephone number, cellular telephone number, child's cellular telephone number (whether permanent or temporary), or any other voice communication method. For vacations or temporary residences for any reason, said numbers shall include contact numbers such as vacation rental homes.

6. Neither parent shall deny the child reasonable use of the telephone to place and receive calls with the other parent and relatives.

7. Both parents shall allow and encourage the child to maintain reasonable phone contact with the other parent. Neither parent shall withhold phone conversations with the other parent as a form of punishment.

8. In the event a parent changes his or her addresses, the moving parent will notify the other parent in writing prior to the move, providing the new address and telephone number, unless an order has been obtained from the Court specifically exempting this requirement.

9. Neither parent shall permit the children to overhear arguments, negotiations, or other substantive discussions about legal or business dealings between the parents.

10. Neither parent will question the children as to the personal lives of the other parent except insofar as necessary to insure personal safety of the children. By this we mean that the children will not be used as spies on the other parent. It is harmful to a child to be put in the role of a "spy."

11. Neither parent will allow materials with adult content or of a sexually-explicit nature where such is any was accessible by the children. Should a parent possess such materials, they will be locked up at any time the children are in the home of or under the supervision of that parent.

12. Either parent may temporarily take the child to another state for vacation or for other good reason with reasonable notice to the other parent.

13. The parent who receives a schedule of children's activities or other information regarding children's events will fax, mail, and e-mail this information to the other

parent in a timely manner so that the other parent has the opportunity to plan for and attend those activities and events.

14. In addition to both parents equal right of access to report cards under Tennessee Code Section 36-6-101(4), unless otherwise available on the internet, the parent who receives a child's report card will copy and fax, mail or e-mail it to the other parent within 24 hours of receipt of the report card.

15. If a parent is unable to keep a regularly scheduled parenting time, that parent should give immediate notice to the other parent, so as to avoid subjecting the children to unnecessary apprehension and failure of expectations.

16. If Father is transferred to a duty station in excess of 250 miles from the child's residence with Mother, Father shall have the right to have his minor child with his as follows:
    a. Six (6) weeks during each summer at a time to be selected by the Father, provided, however, that Father shall provide Mother written notice via mail of the dates of the intended parenting time at least forty-five (45) days prior to such parenting time.
    b. Each Christmas, beginning on December 26 at 9:00 a.m. and ending New Year's Day at 3:00 p.m.
    c. During the odd years, A.E.A. (Spring Break) vacation from 9:00 am Saturday until the following Saturday at 6:00 p.m.
    d. During the even years, Thanksgiving vacation from 6:00 p.m. Wednesday until Sunday at 6:00 p.m.
    e. Any other reasonable times the Father is in the town in which the minor child resides. Father shall give 48 hours notice. The parenting time can be no longer than 48 hours in duration, unless otherwise agreed upon.
    f. During any periods of parenting time, after the child reaches the age of 15 years, the said child may travel by commercial airliner, provided:
        1. The Father shall pay all air fares for the transportation of said child.
        2. The flights shall be either non-stop or direct.
        3. All travel arrangements shall be made by the Father.
        4. The father shall notify the Mother not less than forty-five (45) days of the date of parenting time, of the date, time, airline, and flight number of the proposed carrier.
        5. The Father shall send to the Mother the round trip airline tickets or shall ensure that they will be at the air terminal ready for said child at time of departure.
        6. The Mother shall be required to deliver the child to the nearest commercial airport offering direct flight service to the airport at which the Father will receive the child unless over 300 miles away. The Mother shall also pick up the child at the termination of the periods of parenting time.
        7. The Father shall ensure that either he or the child notifies the Mother of the safe arrival of the child as soon as possible after the child is met by the Father.
        8. At the end of the period of parenting time, the Father shall notify the Mother of the dates, time, carrier, and flight number of the

child's return. The Father shall notify the Mother twenty-four (24) hours prior to the time of departure.

9. On the return of the children, the Mother shall ensure that either she of the child notify the Father of the child's safe return.

II.   DECISION-MAKING

A.   DAY-TO-DAY DECISIONS

Each parent shall make decisions regarding the day-to-day care of a child while the child is residing with that parent, including any emergency decisions affecting the health or safety of a child.

B.   MAJOR DECISIONS

Major decisions regarding each child shall be made as follows:

Educational decisions	☐ mother	☐ father	X joint
Non-emergency health care	X mother	☐ father	☐ joint
Religious upbringing	☐ mother	☐ father	X joint
Extracurricular activities	X mother	☐ father	☐ joint
_____	☐ mother	☐ father	☐ joint

Mother and Father agree to communicate with one other concerning all major decisions. In the event the parties cannot agree, Mother shall have final decision making authority.

III.   FINANCIAL SUPPORT

A.   CHILD SUPPORT

Father's gross monthly income is $ 4,528.29
Mother's gross monthly income is $ **252.75**

1. The final child support order is as follows:
a.   The   ☐ mother   X   father   shall pay to the other parent as regular child support the sum of $906.00 ☐ weekly   X monthly ☐ twice per month ☐ every two weeks. **The Child Support Worksheet shall be attached to this Order as an Exhibit.***

If this is a deviation from the Child Support Guidelines, explain why:
_____

2. Retroactive Support: A judgment is hereby awarded in the amount of $_____ to ☐ mother ☐ father against the child support payor representing retroactive support required under Section 1240-2-4.06 of the D.H.S. Income Shares Child Support Guidelines dating from _____ which shall be paid (including pre/post judgment interest) at the rate of $_____ per ☐ week ☐ month ☐ twice per month ☐ every two weeks until the judgment is paid in full.

3. Payments shall begin on the _____ day of _____, 20___.

This support shall be paid:

☐ directly to the other parent.
☐ to the Central Child Support Receipting Unit, P. O. Box 305200, Nashville, Tennessee 37229, and sent from there to the other parent at: _____.
☐ A Wage Assignment Order is attached to this Parenting Plan.
X by direct deposit to the other parent at <u>Bank of America</u> for deposit in account no. <u>1234567890</u>.
☐ income assignment not required; Explanation:_____.

☐ other:_____.

The parents acknowledge that court approval must be obtained before child support can be reduced or modified.

*Child Support Worksheet can be found on DHS website at <u>http://www.state.tn.us/humanserv/is/isdocuments.html</u> or at your local child support offices.

B.   FEDERAL INCOME TAX EXEMPTION[*]

The **x** mother ☐ father is the parent receiving child support.

The Mother shall claim the following children: <u>Jacob Anthony Golf</u>_____

The Father shall claim the following children: _____

The ☐ mother ☐ father may claim the exemptions for the child or children so long as child support payments are current by the claiming parent on January 15 of the year when the return is due. The exemptions may be claimed in: ☐ alternate years starting _____
☐ each year ☐ other: _____.

The ☐ mother ☐ father will furnish IRS Form 8332 to the parent entitled to the exemption by February 15 of the year the tax return is due.

C.   PROOF OF INCOME AND WORK-RELATED CHILD CARE EXPENSES

Each parent shall send proof of income to the other parent for the prior calendar year as follows:

- IRS Forms W-2 and 1099 shall be sent to the other parent on or before   February 15.
- A copy of his or her federal income tax return shall be sent to the other parent on or before April 15 or any later date when it is due because of an extension of time for filing.
- The completed form required by the Department of Human Services shall be sent to the Department on or before the date the federal income tax return is due by the parent paying child support. *This requirement applies only if a parent is receiving benefits from the Department for a child.*

---

[*] NOTE: The child support schedule assumptions in the guidelines (1240-2-4-.03 (6)(b)) assume that the parent receiving the child support will get the tax exemptions for the child.

The parent paying work-related child care expenses shall send proof of expenses to the other parent for the prior calendar year and an estimate for the next calendar year, on or before February 15.

D.   HEALTH AND DENTAL INSURANCE

Reasonable health insurance on the child or children will be:

      ☐ maintained by the mother
      x maintained by the father
      ☐ maintained by both

Proof of continuing coverage shall be furnished to the other parent annually or as coverage changes. The parent maintaining coverage shall authorize the other parent to consult with the insurance carrier regarding the coverage in effect.

Uncovered reasonable and necessary medical expenses, which may include but is not limited to, deductibles or co-payments, eyeglasses, contact lens, routine annual physicals, and counseling will be paid by ☐ mother **x** father ☐ pro rata in accordance with their incomes. After insurance has paid its portion, the parent receiving the bill will send it to the other parent within ten days. The other parent will pay his or her share within 30 days of receipt of the bill.

If available through work, the ☐ mother **x** father shall maintain dental, orthodontic, and optical insurance on the minor child or children.

E.   LIFE INSURANCE

If agreed upon by the parties, the ☐ mother **x** father ☐ both shall insure his/her own life in the minimum amount of $_250,000.00_ by whole life or term insurance.   Until the child support obligation has been completed, each policy shall name the child/children as sole irrevocable primary beneficiary, with the ☐ other parent ☐ other _____, as trustee for the benefit of the child(ren), to serve without bond or accounting.

IV. PRIMARY RESIDENTIAL PARENT (CUSTODIAN) FOR OTHER LEGAL PURPOSES

The child or children are scheduled to reside the majority of the time with the **x** mother ☐ father. This parent is designated as the primary residential parent also known as the custodian, **SOLELY** for purposes of any other applicable state and federal laws. If the parents are listed in Section II as joint decision-makers, then, for purposes of obtaining health or other insurance, they shall be considered to be joint custodians. THIS DESIGNATION DOES NOT AFFECT EITHER PARENT'S RIGHTS OR RESPONSIBILITIES UNDER THIS PARENTING PLAN.

V. DISAGREEMENTS OR MODIFICATION OF PLAN

Should the parents disagree about this Parenting Plan or wish to modify it, they must make a good faith effort to resolve the issue by the process selected below before returning to Court. *Except for financial support issues including child support, health and dental insurance, uncovered medical and dental expenses, and life insurance,* disputes must be submitted to:

      x Mediation by a neutral party chosen by the parents or the Court.
      ☐ Arbitration by a neutral party selected by parents or the Court.
      ☐ The Court DUE TO ORDER OF PROTECTION OR RESTRICTIONS.

The costs of this process may be determined by the alternative dispute process or may be assessed by the Court based upon the incomes of the parents. It must be commenced by notifying the other parent and the Court by ☐ written request **X** certified mail ☐ other: _____.

In the dispute resolution process:

A. Preference shall be given to carrying out this Parenting Plan.
B. The parents shall use the process to resolve disputes relating to implementation of the Plan.
C. A written record shall be prepared of any agreement reached, and it shall be provided to each parent.
D. If the Court finds that a parent willfully failed to appear without good reason, the Court, upon motion, may award attorney fees and financial sanctions to the prevailing parent.

VI.   RIGHTS OF PARENTS

Under T.C.A. § 36-6-101 of Tennessee law, both parents are entitled to the following rights:

(1) The right to unimpeded telephone conversations with the child at least twice a week at reasonable times and for reasonable durations;

(2) The right to send mail to the child which the other parent shall not open or censor;

(3) The right to receive notice and relevant information as soon as practicable but within twenty-four (24) hours of any event of hospitalization, major illness or death of the child;

(4) The right to receive directly from the child's school any school records customarily made available to parents. (The school may require a written request which includes a current mailing address and upon payment of reasonable costs of duplicating.) These include copies of the child's report cards, attendance records, names of teachers, class schedules, and standardized test scores;

(5) Unless otherwise provided by law, the right to receive copies of the child's medical health or other treatment records directly from the physician or health care provider who provided treatment or health care. (The keeper of the records may require a written request which contains a current mailing address and the payment of reasonable costs of duplication.) No person who receives the mailing address of a parent as a result of this requirement shall provide such address to the other parent or a third person;

(6) The right to be free of unwarranted derogatory remarks made about the parent or his or her family by the other parent to the child or in the presence of the child;

(7) The right to be given at least forty-eight (48) hours notice, whenever possible, of all extra-curricular activities, and the opportunity to participate or observe them. These include the following: school activities, athletic activities, church activities and other activities where parental participation or observation would be appropriate;

(8) The right to receive from the other parent, in the event the other parent leaves the state with the minor child or children for more than two (2) days, an itinerary including telephone numbers for use in the event of an emergency;

(9) The right to access and participation in education on the same basis that is provided to all parents. This includes the right of access to the child for lunch and other activities. However participation or access must be reasonable and not interfere with day-to-day operations or with the child's educational performance.

VII.   NOTICE REGARDING PARENTAL RELOCATION

The Tennessee statute (T.C.A. § 36-6-108) which governs the notice to be given in connection with the relocation of a parent reads in pertinent part as follows:

If a parent who is spending intervals of time with a child desires to relocate outside the state or more than fifty (50) miles from the other parent within the state, the relocating parent shall send a notice to the other parent at the other parent's last known address by registered or certified mail.   Unless excused by the court for exigent circumstances, the notice shall be mailed not later than sixty (60) days prior to the move.   The notice shall contain the following:

(1) Statement of intent to move;

(2) Location of proposed new residence;

(3) Reasons for proposed relocation; and

(4) Statement that the other parent may file a petition in opposition to the move within thirty (30) days of receipt of the notice.

VIII.   PARENT EDUCATION CLASS

This requirement has been fulfilled by ☐ both parents ☐ mother ☐ father ☐ neither.
Failure to attend the parent education class within 60 days of this order is punishable by contempt.

Under penalty of perjury, we declare that this plan has been proposed in good faith and is in the best interest of each minor child and that the statements herein and on the attached child support worksheets are true and correct. *(A notary public is required if this is a proposed plan by one parent rather than one agreed by both parents.)*

_____   _____
Mother   Date and Place Signed

Sworn to and subscribed before me this _____ day of _____, 20_____.

My commission expires:_____   _____
                                                                             Notary Public

_____   _____
Father   Date and Place Signed

Sworn to and subscribed before me this _____ day of _____, 20_____.

My commission expires:_____   _____
                                                                             Notary Public

APPROVED FOR ENTRY:

_____   _____
Attorney for Mother   *Attorney for Father*
_____   _____
Address   *Address*
_____   _____
Address   *Address*
_____   _____
Phone and BPR Number   *Phone and BPR Number*

Note: The judge or chancellor may sign below or, instead, sign a Final Decree or a separate Order incorporating this plan.

COURT COSTS (If applicable)

Court costs, if any, are taxed as follows:

_____.

    It is so ORDERED this the _____ day of _____, _____.

_____
Judge or Chancellor

Chapter 57:

HOTEL FAMILY—113 DAYS PER YEAR PARENTING TIME: OUT-OF-TOWN SCHEDULE

The father has 113 days with his daughter. Mr. and Mrs. Hotel have one daughter, age eight. The mother was designated primary residential parent but shared decision-making authority over all major decisions. Here, there was a great deal of acrimony to say the least. The father claimed the mother had moved to Tennessee just to prevent parenting time but agreed to pay for all flight transportation of the child except for one flight per year because the mother was underemployed and father made a good living. In some high-conflict situations, the parents are not able to agree on many of the more important details on out-of-town travel. That is unfortunate but not unusual. This plan came out of a heated but ultimately successful mediation.

STATE OF TENNESSEE	COURT *(Must be completed)* CHANCERY	COUNTY*(Must be completed)* SHELBY
PERMANENT PARENTING PLAN ORDER ☐ **PROPOSED** x **AGREED** ☐ **ORDERED BY THE COURT**		**FILE No.** CH-03-ABCD-1 *(Must be completed)* **PART** I
PLAINTIFF *(Name: First, Middle, Last)* JANE ELLEN HOTEL x Mother ☐ Father	**DEFENDANT** *(Name: First, Middle, Last)* GRIFFIN HARDY HOTEL ☐ Mother x Father	

The mother and father will behave with each other and each child so as to provide a loving, stable, consistent and nurturing relationship with the child even though they are divorced. They will not speak badly of each other or the members of the family of the other parent. They will encourage each child to continue to love the other parent and be comfortable in both families.

This plan   ☐ is a new plan.

☐ modifies an existing Parenting Plan dated _____.

x modifies an existing Order dated July 17, 2006.

Child's Name	Date of Birth
Anna Elizabeth Hotel	June 16, 2004

I. RESIDENTIAL PARENTING SCHEDULE

A. RESIDENTIAL TIME WITH EACH PARENT

The Primary Residential Parent is Mother.

Under the schedule set forth below, each parent will spend the following number of days with the children:

Mother   252 days   Father   113 days

Note: In the event of a conflict between the number of parenting nights shown here and the parenting plan below, the parenting plan below shall control.

B. DAY-TO-DAY SCHEDULE

The x mother ☐ father shall have responsibility for the care of the child or children except at the following times when the other parent shall have responsibility:

From   Friday at 3:00 p.m.   to   Monday at 8:30 a.m.
      Day and Time   *Day and Time*

☐ every week   ☐ every other week   x other: one time per month except for months in which Father enjoys parenting time on Fall breaks and Spring breaks as described below.

The other parent shall also have responsibility for the care of the child or children at the additional parenting times specified below:

From _____ to _____
         Day and Time   Day and Time

☐ every week ☐ every other week x other: <u>as the parties agree.</u>

This parenting schedule begins ☐ _____ or x date of the Court's Order.
                                                 Day and Time

C.   HOLIDAY SCHEDULE AND OTHER SCHOOL FREE DAYS

Indicate if child or children will be with parent in ODD or EVEN numbered years or EVERY year:

	MOTHER	FATHER
New Year's Day	see Winter Vacation	see Winter Vacation
Martin Luther King Day	none	every
Presidents' Day	none	every
Easter Day (unless otherwise coinciding with Spring Vacation)	even*	odd*
Passover Day (unless otherwise coinciding with Spring Vacation)	N/A	N/A
Mother's Day	every	none
Memorial Day (if no school)	every	none
Father's Day	see Summer Vacation	see Summer Vacation
July 4th	see Summer Vacation	see Summer Vacation
Labor Day	odd	even
Halloween	every	none
Thanksgiving Day & Friday	odd	even
Child's Birthdays	see Summer Vacation	see Summer Vacation
Other School-Free Days	see below**	see below**
Mother's Birthday	every	none
Father's Birthday	none	every

<u>*Easter shall include all days the child is recessed from school for the Easter holiday.</u>
<u>**Father shall have school-free days if they fall on the day before or the day after Father's regularly-scheduled monthly parenting time or scheduled holiday parenting time.</u>

A holiday shall begin at 6:00 p.m. on the night preceding the holiday and end at 6:00 p.m. the night of the holiday, unless otherwise noted here: <u>day and time child is recessed from school to 6:00 p.m. the day before school resumes.</u>

D.   FALL VACATION (*If applicable*)

The day to day schedule shall apply except as follows: <u>Father shall have the child during Fall Break each year from the day and time the child is recessed from school to the day and time school resumes</u> beginning <u>2013.</u>

E.   WINTER (CHRISTMAS) VACATION

The ☐ mother x father shall have the child or children for the first period from the day and time school is dismissed until <u>December 26 at 1:00 p.m.</u> x in odd-numbered years ☐ in even-numbered years ☐ every year. The other parent will have the child or children for the second period from the day and time indicated above until 6:00 p.m. on the evening before school resumes. The parties shall alternate the first and second periods each year.

Other agreement of the parents: <u>The parties acknowledge that the child will be traveling by commercial airline and it may not be possible for the child to arrive by 1:00 p.m. The parties agree that the child shall take the earliest reasonable flight on December 26 each year.</u>

F.   SPRING VACATION (*If applicable*)

The day-to-day schedule shall apply except as follows: <u>Father shall have the child during Spring Break each year from the day and time the child is recessed from school to the day and time school resumes in 2014, 2015, 2017, 2018, 2020, and 2021. Mother will have parenting time in years 2016, 2019, and 2022.</u>

G.   SUMMER VACATION

The day-to-day schedule shall apply except as follows: <u>Father shall have the child beginning 7 days after school recesses for summer vacation until 12 days before school resumes for fall semester</u> beginning June 2014. For Summer 2013 only, child will travel to Father on June 2, return to Mother on June 10. Mother will return child to Father on June 17. Mother is paying all transportation expenses for the June 10 and June 17 exchanges via airlines. This counts as Mother's round trip expense for 2013. Father will return child to Mother on August 9. Also, on June 2, 2013, Mother will drive daughter to Nashville airport to fly daughter via Southwest for a flight around 12:20 p.m. to Raleigh.

Is written notice required?   ☐ Yes <u>x</u> No.   If so, _____ number of days.

H.   TRANSPORTATION ARRANGEMENTS

The place of meeting for the exchange of the child or children shall be: <u>The child shall travel to and from each parent by commercial airline unless otherwise agreed by the parties. Both parents shall arrange for the child to be accompanied at the airport when flying for scheduled flights. When the minor child is eligible under the airline regulations to fly unaccompanied or to fly non-direct, she shall be allowed to do so.</u>

Payment of long distance transportation costs *(if applicable):* ☐ mother   ☐ father ☐ both equally.
Other arrangements: <u>Mother shall pay for the child's round trip flight to Father in North Carolina one time per year. Father shall pay for all other flights.</u>

If a parent does not possess a valid driver's license, he or she must make reasonable transportation arrangements to protect the child or children while in the care of that parent.

I.   SUPERVISION OF PARENTING TIME (*If applicable*)
☐ **Check if applicable**

Supervised parenting time shall apply during the day-to-day schedule as follows:
☐ Place: _____.

☐ Person or organization supervising: _____.
☐ Responsibility for cost, if any: ☐ mother ☐ father ☐ both equally.

J.   OTHER

The following special provisions apply:

<u>The parties shall discuss discipline of their minor child and any corporal punishment shall only be administered by a parent, not stepparent, grandparent, paramour or other child care person.</u>

II.   DECISION-MAKING

A.   DAY-TO-DAY DECISIONS

Each parent shall make decisions regarding the day-to-day care of a child while the child is residing with that parent, including any emergency decisions affecting the health or safety of a child.

B.   MAJOR DECISIONS

Major decisions regarding each child shall be made as follows:

Educational decisions	☐ mother	☐ father	<u>x</u> joint
Non-emergency health care	☐ mother	☐ father	<u>x</u> joint
Religious upbringing	☐ mother	☐ father	<u>x</u> joint
Extracurricular activities	☐ mother	☐ father	<u>x</u> joint

III.   FINANCIAL SUPPORT

A.   CHILD SUPPORT

Father's gross monthly income is $ <u>6,161.00</u>
Mother's gross monthly income is $ <u>3,929.00</u>

1. The final child support order is as follows:
   a.   The   ☐ mother <u>x</u> father   shall pay to the other parent as regular child support the sum of $ <u>615.00</u> ☐ weekly <u>x</u> monthly ☐ twice per month ☐ every two weeks. **The Child Support Worksheet shall be attached to this Order as an Exhibit.***

   If this is a deviation from the Child Support Guidelines, explain why:
   _____

2. Retroactive Support: A judgment is hereby awarded in the amount of $_____ to ☐ mother ☐ father against the child support payor representing retroactive support required under Section 1240-2-4.06 of the D.H.S. Income Shares Child Support

Guidelines dating from _____ which shall be paid (including pre/post judgment interest) at the rate of $_____ per ☐ week ☐ month ☐ twice per month ☐ every two weeks until the judgment is paid in full.

    3. Payments shall begin on the _____ day of _____, 20___.

This support shall be paid:

☐ directly to the other parent.

x to the Central Child Support Receipting Unit, P. O. Box 305200, Nashville, Tennessee 37229, and sent from there to the other parent at: 123 Elm Street, Memphis, Tennessee 38111.

☐ A Wage Assignment Order is attached to this Parenting Plan.

☐ by direct deposit to the other parent at _____ Bank for deposit in account no. _____.

☐ income assignment not required; Explanation:_____.

☐ other:_____.

The parents acknowledge that court approval must be obtained before child support can be reduced or modified.

*Child Support Worksheet can be found on DHS website at http://www.state.tn.us/humanserv/is/isdocuments.html or at your local child support offices.

B.   FEDERAL INCOME TAX EXEMPTION[*]

The x mother ☐ father is the parent receiving child support.

The Mother shall claim the following children: _____

The Father shall claim the following children: _____

The x mother ☐ father may claim the exemptions for the child or children so long as child support payments are current by the claiming parent on January 15 of the year when the return is due. The exemptions may be claimed in: x alternate years starting _____ ☐ each year ☐ other.

The x mother ☐ father will furnish IRS Form 8332 to the parent entitled to the exemption by February 15 of the year the tax return is due.

C.   PROOF OF INCOME AND WORK-RELATED CHILD CARE EXPENSES

Each parent shall send proof of income to the other parent for the prior calendar year as follows:

- IRS Forms W-2 and 1099 shall be sent to the other parent on or before   February 15.
- A copy of his or her federal income tax return shall be sent to the other parent on or before April 15 or any later date when it is due because of an extension of time for filing.
- The completed form required by the Department of Human Services shall be sent to the Department on or before the date the federal income tax return is due by the

---

[*] NOTE: The child support schedule assumptions in the guidelines (1240-2-4-.03 (6)(b)) assume that the parent receiving the child support will get the tax exemptions for the child.

parent paying child support. *This requirement applies only if a parent is receiving benefits from the Department for a child.*

The parent paying work-related child care expenses shall send proof of expenses to the other parent for the prior calendar year and an estimate for the next calendar year, on or before February 15.

D.   HEALTH AND DENTAL INSURANCE

Reasonable health insurance on the child or children will be:

- ☐ maintained by the mother
- x   maintained by the father
- ☐ maintained by both

Proof of continuing coverage shall be furnished to the other parent annually or as coverage changes. The parent maintaining coverage shall authorize the other parent to consult with the insurance carrier regarding the coverage in effect.

Uncovered reasonable and necessary medical expenses, which may include but is not limited to, deductibles or co-payments, eyeglasses, contact lens, routine annual physicals, and counseling will be paid by ☐ mother ☐ father ☐ pro rata in accordance with their incomes x to be divided equally between the parties. After insurance has paid its portion, the parent receiving the bill will send it to the other parent within ten days. The other parent will pay his or her share within 30 days of receipt of the bill.

If available through work, the ☐ mother x father shall maintain dental, orthodontic, and optical insurance on the minor child or children.

E.   LIFE INSURANCE

If agreed upon by the parties, the ☐ mother ☐ father x both shall insure his/her own life in the minimum amount of $100,000.00 by whole life or term insurance.   Until the child support obligation has been completed, each policy shall name the child/children as sole irrevocable primary beneficiary, with the ☐ other parent x other each parent will choose their own trustee for the benefit of the child, to serve without bond or accounting.

IV. PRIMARY RESIDENTIAL PARENT (CUSTODIAN) FOR OTHER LEGAL PURPOSES

The child or children are scheduled to reside the majority of the time with the x mother ☐ father. This parent is designated as the primary residential parent also known as the custodian, **SOLELY** for purposes of any other applicable state and federal laws. If the parents are listed in Section II as joint decision-makers, then, for purposes of obtaining health or other insurance, they shall be considered to be joint custodians. THIS DESIGNATION DOES NOT AFFECT EITHER PARENT'S RIGHTS OR RESPONSIBILITIES UNDER THIS PARENTING PLAN.

V. DISAGREEMENTS OR MODIFICATION OF PLAN

Should the parents disagree about this Parenting Plan or wish to modify it, they must make a good faith effort to resolve the issue by the process selected below before returning to Court. *Except for financial support issues including child support, health and dental insurance, uncovered medical and dental expenses, and life insurance,* disputes must be submitted to:

- x   Mediation by a neutral party chosen by the parents or the Court.
- ☐   Arbitration by a neutral party selected by parents or the Court.

☐ The Court DUE TO ORDER OF PROTECTION OR RESTRICTIONS.

The costs of this process may be determined by the alternative dispute process or may be assessed by the Court based upon the incomes of the parents. It must be commenced by notifying the other parent and the Court by ☐ written request x̲ certified mail ☐ other: _____.

In the dispute resolution process:

   A. Preference shall be given to carrying out this Parenting Plan.
   B. The parents shall use the process to resolve disputes relating to implementation of the Plan.
   C. A written record shall be prepared of any agreement reached, and it shall be provided to each parent.
   D. If the Court finds that a parent willfully failed to appear without good reason, the Court, upon motion, may award attorney fees and financial sanctions to the prevailing parent.

VI. RIGHTS OF PARENTS

Under T.C.A. § 36-6-101 of Tennessee law, both parents are entitled to the following rights:

   (1) The right to unimpeded telephone conversations with the child at least twice a week at reasonable times and for reasonable durations;
   (2) The right to send mail to the child which the other parent shall not open or censor;
   (3) The right to receive notice and relevant information as soon as practicable but within twenty-four (24) hours of any event of hospitalization, major illness or death of the child;
   (4) The right to receive directly from the child's school any school records customarily made available to parents. (The school may require a written request which includes a current mailing address and upon payment of reasonable costs of duplicating.) These include copies of the child's report cards, attendance records, names of teachers, class schedules, and standardized test scores;
   (5) Unless otherwise provided by law, the right to receive copies of the child's medical health or other treatment records directly from the physician or health care provider who provided treatment or health care. (The keeper of the records may require a written request which contains a current mailing address and the payment of reasonable costs of duplication.) No person who receives the mailing address of a parent as a result of this requirement shall provide such address to the other parent or a third person;
   (6) The right to be free of unwarranted derogatory remarks made about the parent or his or her family by the other parent to the child or in the presence of the child;
   (7) The right to be given at least forty-eight (48) hours notice, whenever possible, of all extra-curricular activities, and the opportunity to participate or observe them. These include the following: school activities, athletic activities, church activities and other activities where parental participation or observation would be appropriate;
   (8) The right to receive from the other parent, in the event the other parent leaves the state with the minor child or children for more than two (2) days, an itinerary including telephone numbers for use in the event of an emergency;
   (9) The right to access and participation in education on the same basis that is provided to all parents. This includes the right of access to the child for lunch and

other activities. However participation or access must be reasonable and not interfere with day-to-day operations or with the child's educational performance.

VII.   NOTICE REGARDING PARENTAL RELOCATION

The Tennessee statute (T.C.A. § 36-6-108) which governs the notice to be given in connection with the relocation of a parent reads in pertinent part as follows:

If a parent who is spending intervals of time with a child desires to relocate outside the state or more than fifty (50) miles from the other parent within the state, the relocating parent shall send a notice to the other parent at the other parent's last known address by registered or certified mail. Unless excused by the court for exigent circumstances, the notice shall be mailed not later than sixty (60) days prior to the move. The notice shall contain the following:

(1) Statement of intent to move;

(2) Location of proposed new residence;

(3) Reasons for proposed relocation; and

(4) Statement that the other parent may file a petition in opposition to the move within thirty (30) days of receipt of the notice.

VIII.   PARENT EDUCATION CLASS

This requirement has been fulfilled by x both parents ☐ mother ☐ father ☐ neither. Failure to attend the parent education class within 60 days of this order is punishable by contempt.

Under penalty of perjury, we declare that this plan has been proposed in good faith and is in the best interest of each minor child and that the statements herein and on the attached child support worksheets are true and correct. *(A notary public is required if this is a proposed plan by one parent rather than one agreed by both parents.)*

_____   _____
Mother   Date and Place Signed

Sworn to and subscribed before me this _____ day of _____, 20_____.

My commission expires:_____   _____
                                                                             Notary Public

_____   _____
Father   Date and Place Signed

Sworn to and subscribed before me this _____ day of _____, 20_____.

My commission expires:_____   _____
                                                                             Notary Public

APPROVED FOR ENTRY:

_____   _____

ATTORNEY FOR MOTHER
NAME OF FIRM
Address
Address
Telephone
Supreme Court No.

ATTORNEY FOR FATHER
NAME OF FIRM
Address
Address
Telephone
Supreme Court No.

Note: The judge or chancellor may sign below or, instead, sign a Final Decree or a separate Order incorporating this plan.

COURT COSTS (If applicable)

Court costs, if any, are taxed as follows: <u>Father.</u>

It is so ORDERED this the _____ day of _____, _____.

_____
Chancellor

Chapter 58:

WHAT IS "STANDARD VISITATION"?

In Tennessee, there is no such thing as a "standard visitation" schedule in a Tennessee divorce or family law situation. Or is there? The first answer is no. In 2001, the Tennessee legislature removed the concepts of "custody" and "visitation." Instead, the terms were replaced with "parenting time" or "residential time" to be detailed in a parenting plan form.

The second answer is maybe. As a general descriptive term, "standard visitation" in Tennessee means a nonprimary residential parent enjoys parenting time every other weekend during the school year, two weeks in the summer, half of the holidays and winter, spring, and summer breaks. Sometimes, standard visitation can include an evening each week or every other week, say 5:00 p.m. until 8:00 p.m. Again, in general, this type of parenting schedule will result in the nonprimary residential parent enjoying roughly eighty days per year.

The third answer is yes. There is at least one place in Tennessee where parties can be awarded "standard visitation." That is in Shelby County's Juvenile Court. There may be others throughout the state. In fact, a few magistrates have their individual variations that can be ordered from the bench. A standardized form is there to help parents create a framework. In general, if the parents can agree to their own schedule, courts will allow it. Below is Chief Magistrate Dan Michael's "standard visitation" form order as of April 10, 2013. It is offered as a reference and also includes Tennessee statutory parental rights. Please note that this court ordered form can change over time.

1. That the noncustodial parent of said child(ren), _____, shall have visitation privileges with said child(ren) the first, third and fifth weekend of each month from 6:00 P.M. Friday until 6:00 P.M. Sunday, beginning _____; Thanksgiving Day from 3:00 P.M. until 6:00 P.M. the following day; December 24 from 9:00 A.M. until 6:00 P.M.; December 25 at 3:00 P.M. until December 27 at 6:00 P.M.; each summer from 6:00 P.M. June 1 until 6:00 P.M. June 15 and 6:00 P.M. July 1 until 6:00 P.M. July 15. There shall be no visitation from June 16 to June 30 and July 16 to July 30 annually.

2. That the noncustodial parent shall pick up and return the child(ren) to the home of the custodial parent.

3. That the parental rights of the parent/noncustodial parent when the child is in the other parent's home shall be as follows:

   i. The right to unimpeded telephone conversations with the child at least twice a week at reasonable times and for reasonable durations;

ii.   The right to send mail to the child which the custodial parent or guardian shall not open or censor;

iii.   The right to receive notice and relevant information as soon as practicable but within twenty-four (24) hours of any event of hospitalization, major illness or death of the child;

iv.   The right to receive directly from the child's school, (upon written request which includes a current mailing address and upon payment of reasonable cost of duplication), copies of the child's report cards, attendance records, names of teachers, class schedules, standardized test scores and any other records customarily made available to parents;

v.   The right to receive copies of the child's medical records directly from the child's doctor or other health care provider, (upon written request which includes a current mailing address and upon payment of reasonable cost of duplication); and

vi.   The right to be free of unwarranted derogatory remarks about the noncustodial, biological parent, or such parent's family,

vii.   The right to be given at least forty-eight (48) hours' notice, when possible, of all extra-curricular activities, and the opportunity to participate or observe, including but not limited to the following:

    1.   School activities;

    2.   Athletic activities;

    3.   Church activities; and

    4.   Other activities as to which parental participation or observation would be appropriate;

viii.   The right to receive from the other parent, in the event the other parent leaves the state with the minor child or children for more than two (2) days, an itinerary including telephone numbers for use in the event of an emergency; and

ix.   The right of access and participation in education, including the right of access to the minor child or children for lunch and other activities, on the same basis that is provided to all parents, provided the participation or access is reasonable and does not interfere with day-to-day operations or with the child's educational performance.

4. Parties have permission to change this visitation order without the participation of the Court, **if, and only if,**

    1. **BOTH** parents are in agreement **AND**
    2. The revised schedule is in **WRITING and SIGNED** by **BOTH** parents.

Chief Magistrate Michael also encourages parents to get two cheap calendars at a Walgreens and two highlighters, pink for the mother and blue for the father to mark up the calendar. The parents should make sure they are on the same page a full year in advance. While this may take some time, hashing out any misunderstandings in advance can pay serious dividends long-term.

Chapter 59:

ADAMS CHILD SUPPORT EXAMPLE

June and Ward Adams have two minor children. Wally is thirteen and Theodore is seven. Ward is the Primary Residential Parent and June is the Alternative Residential Parent. June has what is considered standard parenting time with the children of every other weekend, one half of the holidays, and two weeks in the summer, about eighty parenting days a year. In addition, June spends four hours every Thursday with the children, totaling 208 hours per year (4 x 52 = 208). This averages out to 17.33 twelve-hour periods. Thus, June has 97 parenting days (80 + 17.33 = 97.33) a year. See Part I of the following Child Support Worksheet, Identification.

Ward is a salesman for a printer supply company. Ward's adjusted gross income is $50,000 per year, $4,167 per month. June owns a home cleaning service business. June's adjusted gross income is $95,000 per year, $7,917 per month. The parties have a combined adjusted gross income of $12,084 per month. Ward has 34 percent of this, and June has 66 percent (see Part II of the following Child Support Worksheet, Adjusted Gross Income lines 1–3).

June's Basic Child Support Obligation (BCSO) is $1,717. However, June gets an adjustment for the additional parenting time she spends with the children that exceeds ninety-two days per year. The adjustment is a credit of about $37 per month. After the adjustment, June's BCSO is $1,096 per month (see Part III of the Child Support Worksheet, Parents' Share of BCSO lines 4–7).

Ward pays $1,200 per month for work-related child care expenses. Based on June's percentage share of income, she is responsible for 66 percent of the work-related child care expenses, or $792 per month. June pays $30 per month for the children's health insurance. Based on Ward's percentage share of income, he is responsible for 34 percent of the children's health insurance, or about $10 per month (see Part IV of the Child Support Worksheet, Additional Expenses lines 8a–11).

After the adjustments for work-related child care expenses and health insurance, June's child support obligation is $1,878 per month. This amount is the Presumptive Child Support Order. See Part V of the Child Support Worksheet, Presumptive Child Support Order (lines 12–13c).

The boys have additional expenses each month for activities that require a deviation from the Child Support Guidelines. Wally participates in competitive soccer at an average cost of $75 per month and takes piano lessons at $75 per month. Theodore has a math tutor at $100 per month, so Ward pays these monthly expenses. Based on June's income percentage, June is responsible for 66 percent of these expenses, $165 per month. After deviation adjustments, June's child support obligation is $2,043 per month. This is the Final Child Support Order (FCSO). See Part VI of the Child Support Worksheet, Deviations and FCSO lines 14–16.

Part I. Identification

Indicate the status of each parent or caretaker by placing an "X" in the appropriate column

		PRP	ARP	SPLIT
Name of Mother:	June Adams		X	
Name of Father:	Ward Adams	X		
Name of non-parent Caretaker:				
TCSES case #:				
Docket #:				
Court name:				

Name(s) of Child(ren)	Date of Birth	Days with Mother	Days with Father	Days with Caretaker
Wally Adams	3/13/2000	97	268	
Theodore Adams	4/5/2002	97	268	

Part II. Adjusted Gross Income

Use Credit Worksheet to calculate line items 1d - 1e

			Mother / Column A	Father / Column B	Nonparent Caretaker \ Column C
1		Monthly Gross Income	$ 7917.00	$ 4167.00	
	1a	Federal Benefit for child	+ 0.00	+ 0.00	
	1b	Self-employment tax paid	0.00	0.00	
	1c	Subtotal	$ 7917.00	$ 4167.00	
	1d	Credit for in-home children	0.00	0.00	
	1e	Credit for not-in-home children	0.00	0.00	
2		Adjusted Gross Income (AGI)	$ 7917.00	$ 4167.00	
2a		Combined Adjusted Gross Income	$ 12084.00		
3		Percentage Share of Income (PI)	66 %	34 %	

Part III. Parents' Share of BCSO

		Mother / Column A	Father / Column B	Nonparent Caretaker \ Column C
4	BCSO allotted to primary parent's household	$ 0.00	$ 1717.00	$ 0.00
4a	Share of BCSO owed to primary parent	$ 1133.22	$ 0.00	
5	Each parent's average parenting time	97	N/A	
6	Parenting time adjustment	$ -36.79	$ N/A	
7	Adjusted BCSO	$ 1096.43	$ 0.00	

Part IV. Additional Expenses

		Mother / Column A	Father / Column B	Nonparent Caretaker / Column C
8a	Children's portion of health insurance premium	$ 30.00	$ 0.00	$ 0.00
8b	Recurring uninsured medical expenses	$ 0.00	$ 0.00	$ 0.00
8c	Work-related childcare	$ 0.00	$ 1200.00	$ 0.00
9	Total additional expenses	$ 30.00	$ 1200.00	$ 0.00
10	Share of additional expenses owed	$ 792.00	$ 10.20	
11	Adjusted Support Obligation (ASO)	$ 1888.43	$ 10.20	

Part V. Presumptive Child Support Order

		OBLIGATION	
12	Presumptive Child Support Order (PCSO)	$ 1878.00	$ 0.00

* Enter the difference between the greater and smaller numbers from Line 11 except in non-parent caretaker situations.

Low Income?	N	(N=15% Y=7.5%)
Current Order Flat %?	N	(N/Y)

Modification of Current

Child Support Order

		OBLIGATION	
13a	Current child support order amount for the payor parent	$ 0.00	$ 0.00
13b	Amount required for significant variance to exist	$ 0.00	$ 0.00
13c	Actual variance between current and presumptive child support orders	$ 0.00	$ 0.00

Part VI. Deviations and FCSO

Deviations must be substantiated by written findings in the Child Support Order

14	Deviations (Specify):	$ 165.00	$ 85.00
	Piano, Soccer, Math		
15	Final Child Support Order (FCSO)	$ 2043.00	$ 85.00
16	FCSO adjusted for Federal benefit, Line 1a, Obligor's column	$ 2043.00	$ 85.00

State of Tennessee - Credit Worksheet

Part I. Identification

			PRP	ARP	SPLIT
Indicate the status	Name of Mother:	June Adams		X	
of each parent or	Name of Father:	Ward Adams	X		
caretaker by placing	Name of non-parent Caretaker:				
an "X" in the	TCSES case #:				
appropriate column	Docket #:				
	Court name:				

Part II. Additional Children

		Mother	Father
✓	If a parent is claiming more than five children on line 3 or line 7, use the Additional Credit sheet to list information for each child.		

Parent Income Information

1 Applicable gross income for credit worksheet $ 7917.00 $ 4167.00

In-Home Children 2 Below, list qualified children living in the parent's home (if none, skip to line 7):

Name(s) of Child(ren) for Mother	Date of Birth	Name(s) of Child(ren) for Father	Date of Birth

3 Number of qualified children living in the parent's home   # 0   # 0

4 Theoretical child support order (this parent's income on CS Schedule for number of children from line 3) $ 0.00 $ 0.00

5 75% of theoretical child support order from line 4 $ 0.00 $ 0.00

Not-In-Home-Children 6 Below, list qualified children not living in the parent's home:

Name(s) of Child(ren) for Mother	Date of Birth	Name(s) of Child(ren) for Father	Date of Birth

7 Number of qualified children not living in the parent's home   # 0   # 0

8 Average documented monetary support over last 12 months $ 0.00 $ 0.00

9 Theoretical child support order (this parent's income on CS Schedule for number of children from line 7) $ 0.00 $ 0.00

10a 75% of theoretical child support order from line 9 $ 0.00 $ 0.00

10b Allowable credit for not-in-home children $ 0.00 $ 0.00

Chapter 60:

BROWN CHILD SUPPORT EXAMPLE

Carol and Mike Brown have three minor children. Marcia is fifteen, Jan is twelve, and Cindy is seven. Carol is the Primary Residential Parent; Mike is the Alternative Residential Parent. Mike has what is considered standard parenting time with the children of every other weekend, one half of the holidays, and two weeks in the summer, which is about eighty parenting days a year. See Part I of the following Child Support Worksheet, Identification.

Mike is an architect. Mike's gross income is $70,000 per year, $5,833 per month. He receives an income adjustment for his support of a child outside the home. Mike has documented $750 per month in support. The theoretical child support order for this support (based on Mike's adjusted gross income and the number of children he supports outside of the home) is $888. The allowable credit for not in-home children is 75 percent of the theoretical child support order, or $666. This appears on page 1 of the Child Support Worksheet in Part II, Adjusted Gross Income (line 1e) but is calculated and brought forward from Page 3 of the Child Support Worksheet, titled Credit Worksheet, Part II, Additional Children (lines 6–10b).

After the income adjustment for Mikes' support of a child outside the home, his adjusted gross income is $5,167 per month.

Carol does not work. She is voluntarily unemployed. The Child Support Guidelines say that if she were working, she would be earning $29,300 yearly $2,412 per month. To learn more about voluntary underemployment and imputing income, see chapter 37, Voluntarily Underemployed or Unemployed.

The parties have a combined adjusted gross income of $7,607. Mike's percentage share of the combined adjusted gross income is 70 percent, while Carol's is 30 percent. See Part II of the Child Support Worksheet, Adjusted Gross Income (lines 1–3).

Mike's Basic Child Support Obligation is $1,005. See Part III of the Child Support Worksheet, Parents' Share of BCSO (lines 4–7).

Mike pays $38 per month for the children's health insurance. Carol pays for prescription medication for Marcia, $25 per month after insurance. This prescription is a recurring medical expense. Based on Mike's percentage share of income of 70 percent, his child support obligation is increased by $18 a month because of additional expenses. Based on Carol's percentage share of income of 30 percent, her child support need is reduced by $11 per month based on additional expenses. See Part IV of the Child Support Worksheet, Additional Expenses (lines 8a–11).

The additional expenses adjust Mike's child support obligation to $1,011, the Presumptive Child Support Order. See Part V of the Child Support Worksheet, Presumptive Child Support Order (lines 12–13 c).

The girls have additional expenses each month for activities that require a deviation from the Child Support Guidelines. Marcia is on a competitive cheerleading team at $100 per month. Cindy takes ballet lessons at $50 per month. Carol pays these expenses. In the Permanent Parenting Plan, Mike agreed to pay all of the children's extracurricular activities, including this $150, which increases Mike's child support obligation to $1,161 per month. This is the Final Child Support Order (FCSO). See Part VI of the Child Support Worksheet, Deviations and FCSO (lines 14–16).

State of Tennessee - Child Support Worksheet

Part I. Identification

			PRP	ARP	SPLIT
Indicate the status of each parent or caretaker by placing an "X" in the appropriate column	Name of Mother:	Carol Brown	X		
	Name of Father:	Mike Brown		X	
	Name of non-parent Caretaker:				
	TCSES case #:				
	Docket #:				
	Court name:				

Name(s) of Child(ren)	Date of Birth	Days with Mother	Days with Father	Days with Caretaker
Marcia Brown	3/16/1998	285	80	
Jan Brown	7/7/2001	285	80	
Cindy Brown	1/4/2007	285	80	

Part II. Adjusted Gross Income

				Mother / Column A	Father / Column B	Nonparent Caretaker \ Column C
	1	Monthly Gross Income		$ 2249.00	$ 5833.00	
	1a	Federal Benefit for child		+ 0.00	+ 0.00	
	1b	Self-employment tax paid		- 0.00	- 0.00	
Use Credit Worksheet to calculate line items 1d - 1e	1c	Subtotal		$ 2249.00	$ 5833.00	
	1d	Credit for in-home children		- 0.00	- 0.00	
	1e	Credit for not-in-home children		- 0.00	- 666.00	
	2	Adjusted Gross Income (AGI)		$ 2249.00	$ 5167.00	
	2a	Combined Adjusted Gross Income	$ 7416.00			
	3	Percentage Share of Income (PI)		30 %	70 %	

Part III. Parents' Share of BCSO

			Mother / Column A	Father / Column B	Nonparent Caretaker \ Column C
4	BCSO allotted to primary parent's household		$ 1436.00	$ 0.00	$ 0.00
4a	Share of BCSO owed to primary parent		$ 0.00	$ 1005.20	
5	Each parent's average parenting time		N/A	N/A	
6	Parenting time adjustment		$ N/A	$ N/A	
7	Adjusted BCSO		$ 0.00	$ 1005.20	

Part IV. Additional Expenses

		Mother / Column A	Father / Column B	Nonparent Caretaker / Column C
8a	Children's portion of health insurance premium	$ 0.00	$ 38.00	$ 0.00
8b	Recurring uninsured medical expenses	$ 25.00	$ 0.00	$ 0.00
8c	Work-related childcare	$ 0.00	$ 0.00	$ 0.00
9	Total additional expenses	$ 25.00	$ 38.00	$ 0.00
10	Share of additional expenses owed	$ 11.40	$ 17.50	
11	Adjusted Support Obligation (ASO)	$ 11.40	$ 1022.70	

Part V. Presumptive Child Support Order

		OBLIGATION	
12	Presumptive Child Support Order (PCSO)	$ 0.00	$ 1011.00

* Enter the difference between the greater and smaller numbers from Line 11 except in non-parent caretaker situations.

Low Income? **N** (N=15% Y=7.5%)

Current Order Flat %? **N** (N/Y)

Modification of Current Child Support Order

13a	Current child support order amount for the payor parent	$ 0.00	$ 0.00
13b	Amount required for significant variance to exist	$ 0.00	$ 0.00
13c	Actual variance between current and presumptive child support orders	$ 0.00	$ 0.00

Part VI. Deviations and FCSO

Deviations must be substantiated by written findings in the Child Support Order

14	Deviations (Specify):	$ 0.00	$ 150.00

Cheerleading, Ballet

15	Final Child Support Order (FCSO)	$ 0.00	$ 1161.00
16	FCSO adjusted for Federal benefit, Line 1a, Obligor's column	$ 0.00	$ 1161.00

State of Tennessee - Credit Worksheet

Part I. Identification

			PRP	ARP	SPLIT
Indicate the status	Name of Mother:	Carol Brown	X		
of each parent or	Name of Father:	Mike Brown		X	
caretaker by placing	Name of non-parent Caretaker:				
an "X" in the	TCSES case #:				
appropriate column	Docket #:				
	Court name:				

Part II. Additional Children

✓ If a parent is claiming more than five children on line 3 or line 7, use the Additional Credit sheet to list information for each child.

			Mother	Father

Parent Income Information

			Mother	Father
1	Applicable gross income for credit worksheet		$ 2249.00	$ 5833.00

In-Home Children 2 Below, list qualified children living in the parent's home (if none, skip to line 7):

Name(s) of Child(ren) for Mother	Date of Birth	Name(s) of Child(ren) for Father	Date of Birth

		Mother	Father
3	Number of qualified children living in the parent's home	# 0	# 0
4	Theoretical child support order (this parent's income on CS Schedule for number of children from line 3)	$ 0.00	$ 0.00
5	75% of theoretical child support order from line 4	$ 0.00	$ 0.00

Not-In-Home-Children 6 Below, list qualified children not living in the parent's home:

Name(s) of Child(ren) for Mother	Date of Birth	Name(s) of Child(ren) for Father	Date of Birth
		Peter Brown	1/2/1997

		Mother	Father
7	Number of qualified children not living in the parent's home	# 0	# 1
8	Average documented monetary support over last 12 months	$ 0.00	$ 750.00
9	Theoretical child support order (this parent's income on CS Schedule for number of children from line 7)	$ 0.00	$ 888.00
10a	75% of theoretical child support order from line 9	$ 0.00	$ 666.00
10b	Allowable credit for not-in-home children	$ 0.00	$ 666.00

BIBLIOGRAPHY

Ackerman, Marc J., and Colleen M. Drosdeck. *Should Your Infant Spend the Night?* Family Advocate (American Bar Association, Section of Family Law, 33(1), 12 Summer 2010).

Ash, Hon. Don R. *For the Children's Sake: How the New Parenting Plan Will Work.* 36 *Tennessee Bar Journal* 9 (September 2000).

Deutsch, Robin M. *When the Conflict Continues: The Right Parenting Plan Can Help Defuse Tensions. Family Advocate* (American Bar Association, Section of Family Law, 33(1), 40–45, Summer 2010).

Dwyer, Susan A. *How to Share Parenting So that "equal access" means "the best of both parents." Family Advocate* (American Bar Association, Section of Family Law, 33(1), 5–8 Summer 2010).

Gould, Jonathan. *One, Two, Buckle My Shoe. Family Advocate* (American Bar Association, Section of Family Law, 33(1), 8–11, Summer 2010).

Greenberg, Lyn R. *When Your Child Says "No, I Don't Want to Go!" Family Advocate* (American Bar Association, Section of Family Law, 33(1), 32–35, Summer 2010).

Hartson, John. *The Golden Rules of Coparenting: Fifteen Ways to Succeed. Family Advocate* (American Bar Association, Section of Family Law, 21(1), 46–48 Summer 1998).

Johnston, Janet R., Karen Breunig, Carla Garrity, and Mitchell A. Baris. *Through the Eyes of the Children: Healing Stories About Divorce. Family Advocate* (American Bar Association, Section of Family Law, 21(1), 17–19 Summer 1998).

Pruett, Marsha Kline. *All Parenting Plans Are Not Equal. Family Advocate* (American Bar Association, Section of Family Law, 33(1), 23–26 Summer 2010).

Rosen, Lee S. *Tools of the Trade: Technology for Parents. Family Advocate* (American Bar Association, Section of Family Law, 33(1), 2 Summer 2010).

Hon. Robert Schnider. *Who Knows Where the Time Goes? One judge's perspective on shared parenting.* *Family Advocate* (American Bar Association, Section of Family Law, 33(1), 36, 38–39 Summer 2010).

Siegal, Jeffrey C. and Michael C. Gottlieb. *Should Your Adolescent Have a Say? Family Advocate* (American Bar Association, Section of Family Law, 33(1), 16–19 Summer 2010).

Singer, Jacqueline. *Preparing your child for divorce. Family Advocate* (American Bar Association, Section of Family Law, 21(1), 10 Summer 1998).

_____. *Twenty-plus ways to talk with your kids about the divorce. Family Advocate* (American Bar Association, Section of Family Law, 21(1), 36 Summer 1998).

Stahl, P. *What to Do with Your Feelings, Coparenting After Divorce: A Handbook for Clients. Family Advocate* (American Bar Association, Section of Family Law, 21(1), Summer 1998).

ABOUT THE AUTHOR

Miles Mason, Sr. JD, CPA founded the Miles Mason Family Law Group, PLC, in Memphis, Tennessee, and serves clients in the area, including Germantown, Collierville, and counties throughout west Tennessee, including Tipton and Fayette, and eastern Arkansas. The firm also handles select cases in Davidson and Williamson counties, typically divorces including business valuations or forensic accounting investigations. For more information, see www.MemphisDivorce.com.

The firm handles family law matters exclusively—divorce, child custody, parental relocation, custody modification, parenting time modification, child support, child support modification, alimony modification, prenuptial agreement litigation, and complex divorces involving business owners, business valuations, and forensic accounting issues.

Miles Mason, Sr., has also authored *The Tennessee Divorce Client's Handbook: What Every Divorcing Spouse Needs to Know, Tennessee Patent Relocation Law* and *The Forensic Accounting Deskbook: A Practical Guide to Financial Investigation and Analysis for Family Lawyers*, published by the American Bar Association. All are available on Amazon.

Miles Mason, Sr., graduated from the University of Alabama in Tuscaloosa with a degree in accounting, became a CPA, practiced as an accountant, and returned to Memphis for law school. Along with Alan Crone, Miles cofounded Crone & Mason, PLC, and headed the firm's Family Law Practice Group for fifteen years. He formed the Miles Mason Family Law Group, PLC in 2010.

The firm's top priorities are leadership and service. Miles Mason, Sr., has served as chair of the Tennessee Bar Association Family Law Section and on the Tennessee Bar Journal's editorial board. He is an active member of the American Bar Association's Family Law Section, having served on its Continuing Legal Education Committee and currently serving as its liaison to the American Institute of Certified Public Accountants.

Rated 10 out of 10 for family lawyers by Avvo.com, Miles is often interviewed by television and print news media for comment on Tennessee family law and legal stories.

As an additional service to the bar, Miles frequently speaks at engagements to share what he has learned about complex financial matters in divorce, forensic accounting, and business valuation. His national conference speaking engagements include the American Bar Association Family Law Section conferences, American Institute of CPAs National Business Valuation Conference and National Forensic Accounting Conference, and the NACVA/IBA annual conferences. He also presents seminars for the Tennessee Bar Association, Tennessee Society of CPAs, Mississippi Society of CPAs, and other regional and local professional groups.

Miles Mason, Sr., has authored articles for publications by the ABA Family Law Section's Family Advocate, the Tennessee Bar Journal, and the Georgia Bar Association Family Law Section. A complete list of speaking and publications are listed in his professional biography at MemphisDivorce.com.

The Miles Mason Family Law Group team brings together very talented, dedicated, and compassionate attorneys and paralegals. Each professional focuses on what he or she does best. By working as a team and utilizing the latest technology to communicate, manage, and advance client matters, client interests are served more efficiently—and always with an eye to resolving matters as quickly as possible. With financial expertise second to none, the firm handles simple and agreed-upon family law matters as well as divorces involving complex estates with business valuations or requiring forensic accounting testimony.

Miles Mason, Sr. is also active in the community, having served several nonprofits, including as president of the Christian Brothers High School Alumni Association, on the board of directors of the Marguerite Piazza St. Jude Gala, and as cochair of the board of directors of the National Conference for Community and Justice (NCCJ).

He resides in Memphis, Tennessee with his wife, Sharon, and their three children. For fun, Miles enjoys Alabama football, cycling, writing, shooting, and travel.

MILES MASON,
FAMILY LAW GROUP, PLC

Clark Tower
5100 Poplar Ave. Suite 3200
Memphis, TN (USA) 38137

Phone: (901) 683-1850
Fax: (901) 683-1963

MemphisDivorce.com

WA

Made in the USA
Middletown, DE
16 February 2020